Begging to Be Black

Begging to Be Black

ANTJIE KROG

PENGUIN BOOKS

Published by Penguin Books
an imprint of Penguin Random House South Africa (Pty) Ltd
Reg. No. 1953/000441/07
The Estuaries No. 4, Oxbow Crescent, Century Avenue, Century City, 7441
PO Box 1144, Cape Town, 8000, South Africa

www.penguinbooks.co.za

First published 2009
Reprinted in 2010 (twice), 2014 and 2015

5 7 9 10 8 6

Set in 10.5 pt on 14 pt Minion

Printed and bound by Mega Digital
6 Koets Street, Tygerberg Business Park, Parow Industria

ISBN 978 1 77022 070 6 (print)
ISBN 978 1 77020 103 3 (ePub)
ISBN 978 1 77020 104 0 (PDF)

To Petrus

note

Begging to Be Black consists of the telling and retelling of old and new stories, known and lesser-known philosophies, as well as many conversations. I am indebted to a range of people and texts, but the (mis) interpretation and (mis)use of them is my own doing in my attempt to understand what we say and have said about ourselves and others in the long conversation between black and white in this country. My engagement is not with individuals, but with texts produced within specific cultures. Because everything is filtered through my own memory, culture and subjective interpretation, I often use fictitious names and places. I have avoided using footnotes, but quotations are acknowledged in the source list at the back of the book.

This is also not a biography of King Moshoeshoe I; I have focused on descriptions of parts of his life that contribute to the conversations I have tried to trace.

Parts of this text have appeared in a short Afrikaans novel *Relaas van 'n Moord* (translated into English by Karen Press), *Umama*, edited by Marion Keim, the yearbook of the Wissenschaftskolleg zu Berlin 2008, as well as a variety of local and international accredited academic journals.

acknowledgements

I would like to thank Kopano Ratele and Nosisi Mpolweni, who continued the destabilizing conversations that Sandile Dikeni started many years ago; as well as the sharp and challenging conversations and generous support of Ingrid de Kok and Tony Morphet. I have to acknowledge the patient engagement of philosopher Paul Patton during my stay in Berlin and his understanding of how the conversation texts would be used in this book, Yvette Christiansë who started it all, and Roz Morris who finished it with me. Thanks also to Nomfundo Walaza, Sipho Mbuqe and Hlonipha Mokoena for sharing their ability to formulate particular issues unforgettably succinctly; to David Ambrose of Lesotho, as well as Stephen Gill and his wonderful staff at the museum at Morija for their assistance; and finally to my remarkable companion in Lesotho, translator, inter-viewer and interviewee, Mannini Mokhothu.

I am greatly indebted to the University of the Western Cape, STIAS at Stellenbosch, and especially to the Wissenschaftskolleg zu Berlin, whose beneficent and supportive surroundings allowed me to engage more deeply with African philosophy, as well as giving me a space to 'test' some of my thinking against wonderful minds. A special word of thanks to the library at Wiko and all the fellows of 2007/08 who enriched my stay and thinking immensely. I have used material from some of the colloquiums by Randolph Nesse, Robert Pearlman and Raphael Rosenberg, while the conversations at our 'Third World table' sharpened my awareness of the dangers of essentialism and the possibilities of caring.

My sincerest thanks to Ivan Vladislavić and Tim Couzens for their careful readings and suggestions, and to Robert Plummer for his patience in editing the work of a non-mother-tongue-English-speaker. And, as always, a thank you to my husband John.

ANTJIE KROG
SEPTEMBER 2009

You, all of you, have to reconcile not with me, but with the meaning of me … The journey to your future goes through the dot of loving me, despite myself, on the world map that lays out journeys towards all kinds of human fulfilment.

– Njabulo Ndebele, *The Cry of Winnie Mandela*

PART ONE

The Long Conversation:
First Perceptions and
Un-Hearings

———

chapter one

A gunshot cracks. The man lunges forward, his hands groping towards a stationary taxi nearby.

Somebody yells.

Bystanders scramble in all directions. Waiting taxi drivers duck behind their steering wheels. Another shot and the man falls on the tar, his attaché case flung sideways. Blood streams from his shattered shoulder blade as he crawls towards the vehicle. He would reach it, but a figure wearing a balaclava closes in on him. Light-footed, as if with sprung ankles, his pursuer stands astride him as he comes to a stop.

The wounded man turns on his side to look up.

From the planted stance of the heels, the perfect balance of the pelvis, the way the arms in red sleeves reach down, with strange grace, to point the pistol at his forehead, the wounded man knows: this is the end.

A final shot. But because the wounded man moves his head at the last moment, the bullet that kills him does not leave his body: it penetrates the frontal skull bone two centimetres above the eye and exits four centimetres behind the left ear, where it is caught between the skull and the black skin in a small swelling.

Quickly, the killer pulls off the balaclava, rolls the pistol in it and, with elated energy, runs off – accompanied by another man – away from the body and towards the station, sidestepping taxis and terrified spectators.

~

It is 25 February 1992 – quarter past six in Kroonstad.

Of what has just happened, we know nothing. Serene from deep-breathing exercises, J. and I roll up our yoga mats and call our youngest child, who is playing with other kids in the garden outside the house where we have our weekly classes. We drive to the local café for milk and bread. I greet the woman working at the bread-cutting machine, but instead of her usual banter, she lowers her eyes and disappears among the shelves. Later, at the till, I pick up her voice in heightened conversation at the back, where fresh milk is being carried in.

I don't make anything of it, knowing too well that trying to live across racial lines in a rural town is not always easy – for black or white. J. puts the groceries on the back seat and flips Willem a packet of wine gums.

We drive home and we seem what we are: a reasonably comfortable middle-class family in a small rural town. During the height of apartheid we consciously decided to live among poor people and bought a house near the railway line. When our daughter went off to a birthday party one Saturday and came home distraught, after being pushed into the street towards a bakkie draped in AWB flags and called the child of a terrorist, we sent our children away to boarding schools in Bloemfontein.

It is not always easy to work out how to *live* a righteous life. That apartheid is wrong is relatively obvious, but how to live *against* apartheid is the harder question, because even the smallest decision has complicated consequences. Moving in and out of townships, without permission, for rallies, meetings and workshops causes tension at home. Sometimes J. calls me The Great Moral Denouncer, who judges every decision taken by the family as white-privileged, exploitative, unfair. Shall we go and see the *Lohengrin* production in Pretoria? Of course not: the money paid to the soprano flown in from South America would keep our local township in electricity for a year! Even the choice of black or white coffee acquires political undertones in our house, J. says. Sometimes he turns the argument around: because *he* is working hard, and is civilized to rich clients, his wife can *afford* to put his cars, fax machine, phone, house and life at the disposal of the oppressed.

So let me try again to describe this moment. A very precise moment in which the terrible has already happened but has not yet reached you, and it's only looking back that you realize how protected, fortunate and naive you were at that moment, in the car along the familiar streets in which you grew up. (But, as always when I start this story, I feel I am sinking – as if my brain loses its capacity to maintain a physical integrity, a coherent skin around the story, as if my being becomes dispersed in the telling. I also know that when I reach the end of this tale, completely worn out, I will still be asking: What would have been the right thing to do? – and the terror, the real terror of moral bewilderment, is lost among the words.)

So: We're coming back from yoga. With milk and bread, we stop in our garage. When we get out, Reggie is peering down from the stoep above the driveway. This is a surprise, because I didn't see his car in front of the house. I laugh: 'Are you now so high up in the political structures that you are being dropped by helicopter?'

We walk towards the front stoep, where Reggie and three other men are standing.

'We need a lift,' he says. He doesn't introduce the others – which isn't unusual, because he is often accompanied by chance passengers or political figures who need to remain incognito.

'Don't you want coffee or something cold to drink?' J. offers.

'No, thank you,' says Reggie. 'We're in a hurry.'

Seeing it's already dark, J. says he'll quickly take them.

'No,' Reggie stops him. 'I have to discuss something with your wife.'

I get into the car, with Reggie in front and the other men in the back. I start reversing and, just before I'm all the way out of the garage, Reggie says cursorily, 'Get rid of this for me.' And he hands me a red T-shirt.

I open the window and throw it into a box of old clothes that people come and drop off at our place. I drive and turn into Voortrekker Road. Reggie tells me that Regina, his wife, is not doing well and asks whether

I can recommend a 'right' psychologist in Welkom: 'You know what the doctors in Kroonstad are like!' After being in solitary confinement for four months in '76, Regina had a nervous breakdown and is still battling with the consequences.

I talk about their eldest daughter, Winnie, who is in Standard 9 at Brentpark High, where I teach. She was recently made hockey captain. 'No other centre forward breaks through like her,' I say. 'Takes after her father …'

Reggie laughs, pleased at the compliment.

At the crossroads he says, 'Rather take us to Maokeng.' I turn right to the black township instead of left to Brentpark, the coloured area. We drive. The men in the back start talking in Sesotho. They sound angry. Reggie says something, also in Sesotho, which calms them down.

Suddenly police cars come racing past us – it looks as if everyone inside has a walkie-talkie against his mouth. 'God,' I say, 'the police can sometimes look hysterical when they want to.'

Reggie placates the men in the back. 'It's a free country,' he says, speaking Afrikaans now. 'We can say what we like; we can drive where we like.'

I stop at Tau's shop. Everyone gets out, and I see my passengers for the first time. Later, however, I will remember only the tall black man with the paper bag and the short one with the long hair and yellow-green eyes.

I drive back. At home J. is busy making toast. I go outside to cut some roses: Porcelain, Duet and the big ochre Just Joey. J. finds me in the passage, holds up my hand with the bunch of roses, and dances with me to his new *Harvest Moon* tape:

When we were strangers
I watched you from afar
When we were lovers
I loved you with all my heart

He kisses my neck and our hands are clasped together around the roses and the scent of jasmine. From somewhere a phrase drifts up in me:

'*'n haag van bloed*' – a hedge of blood. I go and write it down, the beginning of a poem. Our youngest is sitting at the table doing his homework. The phone rings. 'Where's Reggie?' a voice asks. 'The Wheetie is dead and the police are looking for Reggie.' I say I don't know and hang up.

'There's something bloody funny going on,' I say to J. and fetch the T-shirt from the garage. 'Let's burn this.'

'You don't do anything,' says J., 'until you know what's going on.'

I do not argue. J. is irritated enough. We have a couple of especially difficult months behind us. At the office people started asking what architectural work he thought the firm would be getting if a partner's wife collaborated with those endangering the lives of the people who used architects in the first place. Some weeks before, there were photographs in the local newspaper of me and Reggie attending ANC rallies, with reports of how we incited innocent children to take part in life-threatening marches.

Last week Thursday, after I put my bags in the boot, something on the car's roof caught my eye. Leaves, was my first thought. Then, in a panic: The car is peeling to bare *blik*! J. will be furious. He often complains that I don't look after his old car properly. Then, simultaneously, the acrid smell of acid hit my nose as I saw black paint spelling *AWB* on the door.

At the police station they ignored me. After some minutes I tried to address a policeman who was just sitting there staring at me. '*Haai meneer?*'

Without taking his eyes off me, he shouted to the back, 'She's here.' To which somebody replied, 'Hope she's not looking for police protection!' Sniggering all around. And later, again to the back: 'I was told it was a fucked-up Mazda, now I hear it's an Alfa,' and they laughed.

'Sorry, *mevroutjie*,' he said cheerfully, 'we can't do anything – there was an AWB meeting in Kroonstad last night.'

We used to accept this kind of harassment, because it fitted within a particular security police logic *before* 1990, but what we can't understand is why it has actually *intensified* after the release of Mandela and the unbanning of the ANC. What on earth is going on in this miserable little town?

The ANC is *not* illegal, I often argue with J.; the current government is negotiating with the ANC and recognizes the things that it stands for. F.W. de Klerk is talking peace and elections. But I have no explanation for why there seems to be a structural break between what the government is saying and what its agents in rural areas are doing.

On the other hand, for the township comrades it is as clear as daylight: this is how the Boere are. 'They will never change.'

'You are wrong,' I reply to Reggie. 'The Boere must have been talking to the ANC for a long time before you and I heard of it. They are not stupid; they know that this political repression is no longer defensible. What we experience in Kroonstad is simply isolated, unchecked, local racism!'

And now here I stand, holding the red T-shirt lightly between my fingers. 'If we burn it, we don't have it, and nobody can accuse us of anything.'

'And what will you do when four people, after being roughed up by the police, say that the T-shirt was given to you?'

'If only I knew what happened to the Wheetie!'

The Wheetie is the leader of the Three Million Gang, which rules with a reign of open terror in Kroonstad. Anything happening anywhere in the township will always end with somebody mumbling: Three Million. A year ago they moved from hearsay into fact for me when an ANC organizer in the Free State turned up late one night at our house: Terror Lekota had asked that I please type up a handwritten list of names and charges – people who'd suffered at the hands of this gang. I typed more than two hundred names, with a charge next to each one. The organizer gave us the fax number of the Minister of Justice and asked J. to send the list the following day, together with a letter signed by Lekota. Within a couple of weeks the Wheetie was charged on various counts, of which a large number were postponed, others dismissed because documents had disappeared, and others fell away, because most people were too scared to testify against him.

Around the same time, I was shown a pamphlet in which it was announced that an Inkatha branch would be established in the black township the following Sunday.

'But surely there aren't any Zulu-speakers around here!'

. 'That's just the point,' said Denzil Hendricks, my deputy head at Brentpark High. 'We hear that the Three Million's people have joined, and the Wheetie is now the leader – everything nicely organized by the police.'

'Now why would they do that?' I asked.

'All clashes between the Three Million and the ANC suddenly become political clashes, and have nothing to do with revenge and gangsterism any more.'

I put the T-shirt back in the box, and go to the kitchen to make a salad, while J. helps Willem with his homework. Both of us are unusually silent, as if our thoughts don't even want to begin to probe the possible scenarios. My husband is a level-headed man, but as he rolls restlessly around during the night, I know that I am, we are, in a bigger mess than I probably imagine.

The next morning I drop the youngest one off at nursery school and drive towards Brentpark High. At the main crossroads I read a headline poster: 'White woman in jail for gang murder.' My foot freezes on the accelerator. I drive to school in a daze. Everyone is standing in little groups, and classes have been suspended. I look for the deputy head.

'Where is Denzil?'

'Don't you know,' someone says, 'he was caught last night because he helped Reggie with the Wheetie's murder.'

Bit by bit I am told different and clashing versions of the event. One says that Reggie arranged for his cousin, an eighteen-year-old MK guy, to shoot the Wheetie. Denzil drove them to Selborne Square, next to the taxi rank. Once they'd stopped, Reggie opened the back door and three men rushed out. One charged after the smartly dressed Wheetie, who was on his way to the taxi rank after his umpteenth court appearance. The first shot missed. The second hit him in the back. When he fell, the MK man stood over him and shot him in the head twice at close range. The gunman was masked and wore a red T-shirt, which he pulled off after the shooting and threw into the crowd. The Wheetie's brother held his head while blood foamed from his mouth. Then the gunman disappeared among the people.

Others say, no, Denzil and the rest had been following the Wheetie for three days, but just couldn't get close enough to shoot. The MK guy started getting impatient. Others say the three men, some say two, others only the one with the red shirt, went back to the car where Reggie and Denzil were waiting, as if nothing had happened. They climbed in, and Denzil drove them away in full view of hundreds of taxi passengers. The police came to get Denzil and are still looking for the others.

And now nobody's going to school, because the police are messing around with the ANC again.

The word blazing through all the detail is 'red'.

'And the white woman?' I can barely get the words through my lips.

Her name is Cecily Shahim, somebody informs me, and she's been arrested for supplying Reggie and the others with guns and for fetching the MK guy from Johannesburg.

My head is swirling. I listen to something here, then overhear something there, but it's as if I've shrivelled up completely inside my body. My brain tries to fathom exactly what I am involved in. I go to the bathroom and throw up. I walk to the café and buy cigarettes and a *vetkoek* – but I can't eat a thing. I smoke. I sit alone in my classroom for a while, trying to think what is happening at this very moment. When the school choir uses the interruption to practise, I accompany them on the piano. I look at my fingers as if I'm seeing them for the first time.

The bell rings. I drive home. I go and sit on the globe chair in the passage. I sit like that for hours until J. comes home from work. I don't think I've been thinking about anything. I'm not afraid. I just sit, like someone waiting.

~

I met Reggie Baartman in 1985. It was a bad year for activists – for architects too. J. was struggling to keep his head above water. Because the three older children were already at school, we put little Willem in day care and I started teaching at a training college for black teachers in Kroonstad. My first project was to take the students to a production of Shakespeare's *Julius Caesar* at a secondary school in the township. Before the performance, a student nudged me gently: 'That's comrade Reggie Baartman sitting there in front.'

While I looked at the profile of his face, the student filled in the details: Reggie was a member of a well-known coloured family in the northern Free State. His father, Oom Simon Baartman, owned a café in Brentpark. The police had been harassing them, the student said, ever since the day Oom Simon painted on the glass door of his café: *Thou shalt love thy neighbour as thyself.* Reggie ran a few taxis in Brentpark. I couldn't, however, deduce anything from the cap pulled down over his eyes, the torn T-shirt with 'We Believe in Unity' on the back. He seemed a man like any other.

I wondered what he made of this performance in the baking hot gravel quad of the black school in Maokeng with a cast costumed in various cast-offs from the white suburbs. The boy in the candlewick dressing gown delivered the famous words:

> I was born free as Caesar, so were you;
> We both have fed as well, and we can both
> Endure the winter's cold as well as he.
> ...
> And this man
> Is now become a god, and Cassius is
> A wretched creature, and must bend his body
> If Caesar carelessly but nod on him.

Behind the speaker the crowd huddled, identified in our prescribed texts as Citizens, Guards and Attendants, dressed up in sheets, evening gowns, confirmation and bridesmaids' dresses from various periods of white affluence. The Conspirators wore sun-filter curtains from the sixties, tied with ropes, with plastic Wimpy takeaway knives strapped to their sides.

To one side, on a school bench, Calpurnia was waiting her turn in a navy crimplene suit. The only scenery was a small Formica table, on which stood a jug of Oros, polystyrene cups and a plate full of bananas. Every monologue saw the deliverer diving for a reward from this table.

During her prophecy, Portia stood with her fist raised in the air.

Blood and destruction shall be so in use,
And dreadful objects so familiar,
That mothers shall but smile when they behold
Their infants quarter'd with the hands of war.

~

Finally J. comes home. He makes coffee while I tell him what I heard about the murder of the Wheetie at school.

'You must go to the police and hand over the T-shirt,' he says. 'Silence gives consent.'

'I can't do that. I'd be working together with the very people who have always been the enemy to activists here, the people who've harassed us the most.'

'Don't be stupid. Of course they already *know* that you took Reggie and company to Maokeng and that you've got the shirt. Who do you want to be a heroine for?'

'It's got nothing to do with heroism; it's about what's right. Is it justified to turn against your comrades in the struggle and work with the police?'

'My dear wife, you've got no choice. They've left you absolutely no choice. If you don't go to the police yourself, you'll go to jail. And, in the name of God, just don't come to me with some glamorous notion of jail or do a goddamned Breyten on me.'

'It's *you* who are not understanding. It's got nothing to do with whether I think jail is glamorous or whether I'm frightened of going to jail. It's whether I'm prepared to go to jail for this. And I haven't a clue what this "this" is. What are we talking about here?'

'We're talking about murder. If you don't go to the police you're an accessory to a murder. It's that simple.'

The word suddenly lies between us. Not as metaphor or idiomatic expression, but as killing, violently, and as fact.

'You forget I supported the ANC's armed struggle,' I say.

'Man, it looks to me as if you and your comrades are as backward as this town itself,' J. replies. 'It's after 1990 now! Even the ANC has abandoned violence.'

'Maybe, but I think the issue is whether the Wheetie's murder was political. He is now an Inkatha member, remember?'

'You know as well as I do where this all started.'

'That doesn't matter!'

'Of course it does. You told me yourself that the Wheetie caught Mishack with his wife that time. It's sex, not politics! Or do you want me to believe that I commit a political act every time I make love to my ANC-supporting wife?' He grabs me by the arm. 'Jirre, sweetheart, you haven't got time to talk rubbish ... You need to deal with this!'

'What do you think I am trying to do! If it was a revenge murder, I can't support it; but who says the police themselves aren't behind it? This single action could conveniently immobilize all the troublesome ANC members as suspects in a murder.'

'Whatever you decide, all of us, and that includes me, and each of your children, will have to be able to live with it.'

'Thank you. That's precisely the point I'm trying to make. It's a moral decision, but the thing is, to what extent can you make a moral decision within an immoral context?'

J. rolls his eyes heavenwards. 'Stop talking kak. There's no moral decision here; you've broken the law of the land and you can be hanged as an accessory.'

'And what if you say the laws of the land have no legitimacy for you? Do you then make your own, no doubt unimportant, but individual decision in terms of a bigger moral framework?'

'Djeezus! What are you talking about! Listen to yourself: a bigger moral framework.' He covers his face with his hands, muttering, '*Here God, help ons!*'

I'm suddenly filled with anger. 'I know nothing, nothing about this murder; all I know is that I was misused, misled and exploited in terms of every single basic struggle principle. A, the murder of the Wheetie has no anti-apartheid effect; in fact, it only confirms that blacks think nothing of killing other blacks. B, I wasn't consulted; C, I was simply ordered; D, not the slightest gesture has been made to explain the so-called politics of all of this to me; E, I'm in the deepest shit for an amateur plan in which a bunch of men wanted to prove in front of hundreds of commuters which one of them was the most powerful. And this is just half of it. My freedom has been undermined, my worth as a human being has been disregarded, my intelligence and family have been trampled on for "the cause" – but, hey, what other use is there for a pampered, sentimental white family.'

J. lights a cigarette. 'Good, you're beginning to think straight.'

'Oh, shut up! I don't want anything to do with this whole thing. It's got nothing, absolutely nothing, to do with me. I'm the moer in, and no one will tell me what I should or shouldn't do – including you!'

J. shakes his head. 'I'm not forcing you to take any specific decision. All I'm saying is that I'm the one who'll stand by you in the end; I'm the one who sat up with you last night after the call looking for Reggie came; it's me who's going to take every twist and turn with you during the coming months – and don't kid yourself, the newspapers are going to love it! All I'm doing is telling you what I think your options are. And a wife in jail for a pathetic, look-who's-the-strongest-black-among-the-blacks – hey, man, that's going to be very difficult for me. Don't shift the target of your anger – it's not me, it's your own so-called comrades who've left you no choice.'

Memories crowd my brain. Once some national ANC bigwig came to address a rally in Kroonstad. The comrades asked me to help the women prepare a lunch that would be held afterwards. They needed tablecloths, glasses, flowers, etc. This meant I had to miss the rally, in order to take care of things at the home where the man would eat. I protested, but it was pointed out that only the best was good enough for the leaders – and I had proper glasses and roses in my garden. When the men arrived by car in clouds of dust, we dished up, poured cooldrinks, cleared away, refilled plates, washed up – in our places, we little women.

I also remember how I came to know how the enmity between the Wheetie and the ANC started, three years ago. I met Mishack when the Maokeng Youth Congress was founded in April 1989, in the Roman Catholic church hall in Seeisoville. I was asked to come to the hall, 'so that the police don't just take action'. The venue was full of youth, dirt poor and unemployed, among them quite a few who would under any other circumstances qualify as seasoned tsotsis. Anyone who wanted to climbed onto the stage and delivered a speech. There was translation back and forth between Sesotho and English, which initially I thought was for me as the only non-Sesotho-speaking person present, but then I became aware how the comrades were actually practising the rhetoric of their own English. The first furious pronunciations of 'cuppatalisssssma' eventually became more or less 'capitalism' and one after the other, in deep voices that reminded me of oral poet and activist Mzwakhe Mbuli, roared: 'Why therefore buy time …', and everyone cried in unison, 'when the crocodiles are against you?'

Soon people were on their feet and someone shouted, 'Down with P.W. Botha!' Everyone jumped up and stamped their feet on the wooden floor. 'Down! Down! Down!' they thundered. Outside, the police circled the hall.

Another young man shouted, 'We are tired of pap and meat; we want good food. We want Calvin Klein jeans. We want what is there!' – and everyone pointed to the white town. 'We want what is there! There! There!'

Everyone sang, 'Six feet under the ground', and then the melody went soft like a dirge while the names of those killed in the political violence in Kroonstad were called out. Later they sang, 'America, we hate you and despise you, for what you have done to us.'

'It's time you understand your local politics,' Mishack enlightened me. We were smoking outside while others 'redistributed' the rest of our cigarettes. 'The ANC here is divided into the Young Lions – that's us: the youth, with Reggie Baartman as our leader – and the other side is the old AFs, from the defunct African Foundation. We, the Young Lions, initiate revolution, call for boycotts, organize the marches.' He snorted derisively. 'But these white bastards here don't want us to march – they tell Reggie: "Here we still know how to keep a kaffir a kaffir." We instigated the consumer boycott, the school boycott, the non-payment for services, and so on. The AFs, on the other hand, are the so-called respectables. They were already ANC members years ago – they are educated people with good careers, good reputations, and they actually don't want anything to do with the way we conduct the struggle. Mostly they work against us, and more than once they've stabbed us in the back.'

Some weeks after this, Mishack pitched up at my front door, disguised in a raincoat, sunglasses and a very tattered, very old pith helmet. It took me a few seconds to recognize him through the obvious disguise. He wanted a lift out of town and fifty rand.

'A pith helmet – for God's sake, Mishack ... everybody can see you coming miles away!'

'That's why they won't think it's me,' he answered, unruffled.

'Can I drop you at the taxi rank?'

'No ... the taxi I'm taking doesn't go through the town.'

'But all taxis go through Kroonstad.'

'Not this one. It comes from Steynsrus and turns off for Rooiwal and Koppies.'

I suspected he was lying, but I was busy working out how to explain satisfactorily to J. that I was going out in the night to drop somebody off on the abandoned Koppies road.

'You know him?' J. asked.

'Yes, he's a COSAW member like me.'

'*Gots vrou.*' My husband shook his head as he gave me fifty rand.

On the way in the car, Mishack told me that he was on the run. The Wheetie wanted to kill him. The Wheetie, he explained after seeing that I (at that stage) had no clue who he was talking about, was the formidable leader of a gang called the Three Million, operating in the black township.

'So why does the Wheetie want to kill you?'

He laughed softly in the darkness. 'The Wheetie caught me with his wife. I lay low for a couple of days, but Reggie feels I should get away, because the Wheetie is swearing revenge against the ANC Young Lions. He's already threatening Reggie.'

'And you make me drive around at night for this kind of crap?' I was suddenly furious.

'I'm asking you for help as a friend, not as a comrade.'

chapter two

'There is Moshesh,' said Krotz to me.

With these words, recorded after that snowy morning on 28 June 1833, the king of the Basotho stepped into written Western history.

> The chief bent upon me a look at once majestic and benevolent. His profile, much more aquiline than that of the generality of his subjects, his well-developed forehead, the fulness and regularity of his features, his eyes, a little weary, as it seemed, but full of intelligence and softness, made a deep impression on me. I felt at once that I had to do with a superior man, trained to think, to command others, and above all himself.

Moshoeshoe could not have known, and nor could Eugène Casalis, the twenty-year-old French missionary with a flair for writing, have known, that in time most of the texts about the king by historians would include this description of their first meeting.

In places, Casalis' portrayal reads like a love poem:

> He appeared to be about forty-five years of age. The upper part of his body, entirely naked, was perfectly modelled, sufficiently fleshy,

but without obesity. I admired the graceful lines of the shoulders
and the fineness of his hand. He had allowed to fall carelessly round
him, from his middle, a large mantle of panther skins as lissom as
the finest cloth, and the folds of which covered his knees and his feet.
For sole ornament he had bound round his forehead a string of glass
beads, to which was fastened a tuft of feathers, which floated behind
the neck. He wore on his right arm a bracelet of ivory – an emblem
of power, – and some copper rings on his wrists.

I have been under the spell of this paragraph since I read it so many
years ago, captured by the rustling 'f's' in 'fastened a tuft of feathers,
which floated'. The solid majesty of beads, panther skin, ivory and copper,
body and knees, made vulnerable by the delicate movement of floating
feathers in the neck. And I suppose it is partly this fearless admission of
a shimmering softness that has kept me glued to the life of Moshoeshoe
ever since.

Casalis' account also exemplifies a dilemma particular to colonial representation: how to present admirable, worthy, even enviable qualities
observed in black people in a way that did not diminish their readiness
and urgent need for conversion and civilization?

The first step was to portray the king as an exception: he might look
noble, majestic and benevolent, as in the case of Moshoeshoe, but his
people certainly did not. Compared to 'the generality of his subjects', he
was 'a superior man'. Thomas Arbousset, the missionary who accompanied Casalis, wrote that Moshoeshoe had 'a deeper yearning for complete
knowledge' than his followers, and that, 'unlike them', he was interested
in exploring his country, the origin of rivers and hidden plateaus. To
divorce an exceptional man from the culture and society that produced
him was often the first attempt at appropriation.

Underlying Casalis' well-known passage were also the different ways
in which these two forces, an African king and a European missionary,
prepared and presented themselves for their first meeting. Moshoeshoe
didn't sit on a throne or a stone, or in a hut; he didn't stand, or demand to
be carried, but waited cross-legged on a mat in the open, with his people

standing in a half-circle behind him. Being well informed, Moshoeshoe knew exactly what he was doing: sitting cross-legged on a mat – how much more unkingly could he make himself for Westerners? It is difficult to make an impression sitting on a mat while everyone else is standing. What did he expect would follow? Did he want Casalis to kneel, or to come and sit opposite him on the ground, or join him on the mat, or crawl on his stomach towards him, as visitors to Shaka had to do? There was a moment when they were both looking at each other, making their own assessments of how the other planned this meeting, before the 'long conversation' could begin.

Casalis, too, prepared the first impression he wanted to make on the Basotho king: he arrived without presents. Several similar encounters had occurred since the arrival of whites in southern Africa, in which mirrors, beads and a variety of mostly worthless trinkets would be used to try to lure the king or chief into allowing an establishment in the area.

But the meeting between Moshoeshoe and Casalis had already started on a different footing: the king had made the first move by asking the missionaries to join his kingdom, so *he* would determine the codes and rules as he saw fit.

~

The young Casalis, highly intelligent and exceptional in his devotion, came from a background in which the church provided the only opportunity for education and upward mobility. In those days, becoming a missionary was a way for bright young men to escape impoverished surroundings and class entrapments without prospect. After years of studying, praying and responding to diverse callings, he found himself, together with the equally youthful Thomas Arbousset as his fellow missionary, on a ship to southern Africa in the service of the Paris Evangelical Missionary Society (PEMS). With them was the older Constant Gosselin, as a kind of handyman missionary. The year was 1832.

When they arrived in Cape Town, they heard from their host, the well-known Dr John Philip, controversial for his public and effective defence of the rights of 'Hottentots', Bushmen and slaves, that the mission station initially targeted for their assistance had been destroyed by raids from hostile neighbours. After awkwardly waiting in Philip's house for some months, they decided to move into the interior, trusting that God would use them as part of His plan for salvation.

It is astounding to think how these three men, without any fixed agreement with any mission station, took a ship to the Eastern Cape, found an ox wagon and a driver, and simply trekked up north, not only believing they were part of God's plan, but that He would provide until His plan for them was revealed.

They trekked for many months, and one senses from Casalis' account of the journey that after some time, having just crossed the Orange River, a degree of desperation set in. What if God didn't respond? What if they were misreading His will? How long should they trek before giving up? So by the time a Griqua leader named Adam Krotz came to tell them that a king was actually *asking* for missionaries, they were overjoyed. God had spoken, as of course He would!

Seeing Moshoeshoe was therefore not only seeing an African king, but seeing the face of God's plan. In the famous description of Moshoeshoe, Casalis on the one hand celebrated this particular face by emphasizing the beauty of the king's physique, his obvious intellectual power, his striking aristocracy and his moving simplicity, but on the other he had to portray him as a naked pagan in animal skin who was in need of God and conversion – the worthy noble savage.

And because Moshoeshoe had chosen them, providing a purpose to their young, feverish lives, it was obvious that to convert him, the king, would be tantamount to adding the most valuable diamond to God's crown. Up until the day he died, Moshoeshoe's soul was regarded by all the denominations working in Lesotho as the ultimate trophy. The missionary who could convert thousands of Basotho would not matter half as much as the missionary who could convert this beautiful king.

~

Peter Seboni, whose thesis on Moshoeshoe draws from a long list of oral sources he found in Lesotho, opens his account with a troubling story about the young Moshoeshoe's all-consuming ambition: 'He entertained this notion in his early life. He wished to be acknowledged as a man of high status and be obeyed without being questioned.' This ambition took a terrible form: 'At one stage while being a young boy he is reported to have killed five young boys who infuriated him by not obeying his command. He wanted to command respect and be revered.'

This is an uncomfortable story. How does one reconcile a delinquent murderer with a heroic founder king? Whether it was five boys or three, whether they were boys or young men, what does not change in all the different versions based on oral sources is Moshoeshoe's uncontrolled ambition to be obeyed and revered – all products of a strong individual with a drive that can best be described as arrogant, combative and megalomanic.

Moshoeshoe, called Lepoqo (Dispute) at birth, was the eldest son of Mokhachane, the rather weak and irascible head of the small, unimportant Bamokotedi clan, who lived in what is today northern Lesotho. Moshoeshoe's grandfather, called Peete because he spoke Sesotho with a Xhosa accent and therefore sounded like a stutterer ('peetepeetepeete'), was particularly perturbed about how to raise an obsessively ambitious young boy within a community where survival depended on interconnectedness and cooperation. Raising such a belligerent child could lead to revenge attacks within the clan, which would be the end of the child as well as the clan itself.

Nearby, as head of a very important and much more powerful clan, the king and sage Mohlomi lived. Having travelled widely in Africa, he was a phenomenon in his own lifetime, known for his wisdom in political, diplomatic and philosophical matters, and his powers of rain-making and healing, based on a scientific approach to illnesses and a stern rejection of some claims about the power of witchcraft. Peete decided to take the young boy to Mohlomi, and this, according to several scholars, had a calming effect on him. It was Moshoeshoe's first visit of several.

Initially, all was well. From his various names, one can see how Lepoqo's character evolved from Tlaputle (Energetic-One) and Lekhema (Hasty-One) to the reconciliatory Letlama (Together-Binder), the name given to him in his initiation praises. One day, so it is still being told in school books in Lesotho, Letlama was fixing the roof of his mother's hut. As he looked up he saw beautiful cattle grazing at a nearby village of chief Ramonaheng. He quickly called his age-mate, Makonyane, later to become his army general, and they executed a cattle-raid so quick, neat and unnoticed, that a self-praise song had to be composed, with rustling *sh*-sounds indicating the fast, swishing, snappy, snipping way in which the raid had been carried out:

Ke'na Moshoeshoe Moshoashoaila oa ha Kali
Lebeola le beotseng Ramonaheng litelu.

I am the sharp shearer, the shaver of Kali (Monaheng)
The barber's blade that shaved the beard of Ramonaheng.

From that day Lepoqo's name became Moshoeshoe (Sharp-Shearer), pronounced Mo-shwe-shwe, of which Moshesh became a Western distortion.

Moshoeshoe married, had children, and lived under his father, Chief Mokhachane, but eventually his ambition flared up once more with even greater urgency. Seboni writes: 'His anxiety for megalomania made him appear as though he was mentally deranged. According to Peete and Mokhachane he was to be cured of this "madness".' Moshoeshoe was sent to Mohlomi again, and both his father and Peete expected the old sage to give him medical treatment and a talisman. Scholar L.B.J. Machobane attributes a more deliberate desire to Moshoeshoe to obtain guidance on leadership and cites sources indicating that at Mohlomi's place he underwent an intensive training programme on leadership, stretching over a much longer period than the cursory meeting generally suggested by historians. They all agree, however, that being a student of government under Mohlomi radically changed Moshoeshoe. The younger man came to understand very clearly that in order to become a great leader, his attitude had to change: *Motse ha o na sehlare; sehlare ke pelo* (Power is not acquired through medicine; the medicine is the heart).

After the training, which would have included celebrations and payment with cattle, Mohlomi rubbed his forehead against Moshoeshoe in a gesture of blessing that symbolized the passing of wisdom from the elder man into the younger.

What was it that Mohlomi told Moshoeshoe that fundamentally changed his personality and the way he perceived leadership? According to one account, Mohlomi said that if a chief's rule was not based upon peace, justice and '*botho*' (humaneness), the chieftainship would not stand the difficulties of governing; and, even if it did hold, it would never bring benefit to anyone. 'If you drive people away from you by inspiring people with fear for you and by killing some, whom then are you going to rule? Experience I have gained as a chief … has brought me a clear realisation of the fact that a chief becomes and remains a chief only by the people's will, recognition and support.'

After the visit, says Seboni, Moshoeshoe 'put [it] into practice with his own remarkable intelligence and growing wisdom'.

The first test to Moshoeshoe's newly acquired wisdom came from his own father. Mokhachane, still the chief of the Bamokotedi, refused to protect a group that had just raided another chief's cattle and were now urgently seeking asylum. Mokhachane had the men tied up, and his clan demanded that they be killed and their spoils distributed among everybody. This was the moment that Moshoeshoe chose to enter the meeting place: he pointed out that the chief of these raiders had valuable skills as a rainmaker, herbalist and warrior. Mokhachane should rather set him and his men free and restore their cattle, on condition that they settle among the Bamokotedi as subjects and so strengthen and enrich the clan. This suggestion was accepted 'with a roar of approval'.

It was clearly time for Moshoeshoe to become a ruler in his own right. He left the place of his father, and moved to Butha-Buthe, a well-scarped hill, where the turmoil created by Shaka in Natal soon spilled over and trapped him on the Highveld. The feared warrior woman Manthatise and her army, formed in violent response to migrating groups fleeing Shaka, swept the Caledon River area around 1821, destroying everything in their path. Moshoeshoe took shelter with his people and cattle in a large cavern, where they thought they would be safe. After the first attack by Manthatise, which they barely survived, they moved higher up on one of the mountains. Another attack took place, which Thomas Arbousset would later describe, after being told the story by the king: 'Moshoeshoe … took charge of the battle, giving advice, inspiring his soldiers and encouraging them by his cries and by the brandishing of his assegai. All the while, he was carrying his son Molapo on his shoulders. 'Mamohato, the queen, carried Masopha at her breast, and one of the officers of the King led the princess, Tsoamathe, by the hand.' After narrowly escaping defeat, Moshoeshoe realized that he would have to find a secure place for himself and the large number of people he had already accumulated around him.

He chose a place which over the years came to represent his extra-ordinary ability to perceive the essence of a problem and to solve it in an unexpected way. He again chose a mountain, but an unassuming one that looked like nothing much from afar. It rose a hundred metres from the surrounding valley, with a belt of perpendicular cliffs some twelve metres high that gave access via only six passes. The top provided ten square kilometres of good grazing and at least eight good springs. Strategically it was an excellent choice, enabling him to provide safety and sustenance to his growing number of followers without reverting to war and attack. Up to three thousand people lived on the mountain, and over the years several villages sprang up at the foot of it. Thaba-Bosiu, the Mountain of the Night, has a reputation that it grows higher during the night. It is also believed that no dust ever sits on one's clothes or feet when one walks there, because everything on it is held as part of Moshoeshoe.

In the coming years, Thaba-Bosiu was often attacked, but not even the most serious attempts by Matiwane (1828), the Korana (1831), Mzilikazi (1831), Sir George Cathcart (1852) or Boshof of the Free State Republic (1858) managed to conquer the mountain. 'This mountain is my mother,' Moshoeshoe would say to the missionaries: 'had it not been for her, you would have found this country entirely without inhabitants.'

~

The move from Butha-Buthe to the mountain fortress took place by night. While Moshoeshoe and his people were wading through long grass, dongas and at least five river courses to reach Thaba-Bosiu, the unthinkable happened. The upheavals of the Lifaqane had driven some people to cannibalism. A group of cannibals, who lived in the area, grabbed the king's grandfather Peete, killed him and ate him.

One can hardly imagine the terror this incident must have caused among the people trudging through the dark in dispersed groups. When Moshoeshoe's followers tracked down the leader of the cannibals, Rakotsoane, and those who ate Peete, everybody expected the king to order their killing – especially in light of the decisive role the old man had played in his grandson's development. But Moshoeshoe did something unexpected and extraordinary. He pointed out that the bodies of the cannibals now contained the body of his grandfather, and that to kill them would be to dishonour Peete's grave. He therefore requested that the traditional funeral and grave rites be performed on them, which involved the contents of cattle intestines being smeared on their bodies. He then gave them cattle, ordered them to stop eating people, and allowed them to live near the royal household.

This was unheard of. What was especially disarming was the logic behind Moshoeshoe's decision: killing them would simply make him part of the larger killing sprees of Shaka, Manthatise and Mzilikazi that were devastating the area. Emphasizing the cannibals' digestive interconnectedness to Peete and, through the grandfather, to himself as king, he opened up the possibility of change. Through rituals, cattle and a safeguarded home, the cannibals could change their habits and earn their place back in the realm of humanity from which their behaviour of devouring fellow humans had expelled them.

This incident, more than anything else, made the foundation of Moshoeshoe's strategy clear: he was not kind and caring out of weakness, but out of a strengthening belief that safety, care and trust unlocked powerful energies to the benefit of a community. No wonder that conquered, impoverished, hunted and haunted people from everywhere, fleeing Shaka or other aggressors, singly or in small groups, turned up at the foot of the Mountain of the Night to experience the benevolence they had heard about, making the Basotho a richly diverse group.

Adapting the description of Napoleon as a 'son of the revolution', Seboni calls Moshoeshoe 'a son of the Difaqane'. The idea that cannibalism forms part of one's history is just as uncomfortable as the story that Moshoeshoe murdered the young boys, but, again, to dismiss it is to narrow the scale of possibilities that confronted him and undervalue the full meaning of his growth in wisdom.

During an expedition to find the source of the Orange River many years later, Moshoeshoe, travelling with his entourage and the young Arbousset, insisted on spending a night in a cave among people known as 'reformed' cannibals. Writing about this encounter, Arbousset, his imagination clearly heightened, described the leader, Ramantsoatsane, as a 'thin, slender, pale, horrible man' who told them how people took to cannibalism: slow, doddering and famished people were easily caught by wild animals that often didn't devour them completely. The leftovers were then cooked and offered as dassie meat to those among them who were most ill. 'Once they have tasted it,' Ramantsoatsane said, 'they found that it was excellent.' Walking alone in the veld, desperately looking for bulbs or leaves to eat, one would see a person, overwhelm him, and soon his limbs would be 'boiling away in pots ... It is now, especially, that I feel ashamed of myself. I look at my limbs and I shiver. What! I tell myself, it was us eating ourselves!'

Although Moshoeshoe praised them for having abandoned cannibalism, reaffirming his promise that they would never go hungry while he was king, Arbousset found sleeping among them most distressing. He had nightmares about the French Revolution; he remembered how slowly one of the former cannibals licked his finger and then cleaned Arbousset's grill pan with it, how another lifted his frying pan to his mouth, exclaiming what a beautiful 'vase' it was, and how a third 'sunk his teeth into a fat sheep's tail as if it were a piece of bread. All this proves that they have not completely lost their past tastes.'

Yet Moshoeshoe's decision to embrace these cannibals sent out such important signals of change and acceptance that, according to Daniel

Kunene, they later found their way into some of the praise poems about the king:

> Lepoqo is a Charmer, for he charms,
> He charmed the grave of his grandfather.
>
> (*Lepoqo ke Thapisi, oa thapisa,*
> *O thapisitse bitla la rr'ae-moholo.*)
>
> Letlama is a Tight-sitter, he encircled tightly with his legs,
> He tightly drew his legs around a young untamed bovine.
>
> (*Letlama ke Makgwape, oa kgwapela,*
> *O kgwapetse kgongwana e le mohatelo.*)

Kunene says the words *ho thapisa* mean 'to charm, to tame the wild nature of', conveying an image of the king sitting tightly on and taming the wild bull of the turbulent forming years of the Basotho. Part of this 'wildness' was the cannibals. The word *charm*, with its meanings of attracting and winning over, sums up the technique Moshoeshoe used: no force or violence, but convincing people with gentle but firm domestication.

True to Mohlomi's advice, Moshoeshoe also tried to put a stop to certain destructive practices stemming from witchcraft, particularly the claim by witches that they could 'sniff out' people. (Some biographers erroneously state that the king was against witchcraft, but it would be more correct to say that he was against certain aspects of it, because right through his life he was surrounded by and regularly consulted traditional healers and diviners.) When his followers stoned to death a woman accused of being a witch, a very upset king called them together and reprimanded them: 'In my infancy I received the name Lepoqo (dispute) because I was born at the moment when they were fighting in my father's village about a person accused of witchcraft ... I have never killed people except on the battle-field. This is the first time that the vultures have eaten anyone at my home ... Hear me well today! Let no one ever have the audacity to come and tell me: "I have been bewitched!" May that word never again be pronounced in my presence!'

Moshoeshoe established practical formulae for living in peace with neighbouring chiefs, and many of them volunteered to give up their chieftainships, enabling him to knit together a new nation that continued to grow steadily. He extended a hand of friendship to all who reached him.

Very soon, however, he came to realize that it was not enough simply to gather people and care for them. He needed new strategies to create and maintain a safe space in which people could become a community without violating the values that bound them. He set out to build what Seboni calls an 'ethical foundation and eternal values' to unite people in a sustainable and prosperous way. Whether imbued with wisdom from the sage Mohlomi or practically realizing what was already known to people, Moshoeshoe started to secure space for his community to live its daily life within a creative stream of events that would allow everyone to 'build' themselves in relation to others. With cattle, land, labour and marriage, a network of larger and smaller relationships was woven.

The heart of Moshoeshoe's achievement, Seboni argues in his thesis, was the impressive range of measures he introduced to create a humane space for people to live their lives. These measures, all aimed at achieving lasting peace and prosperity, rested on three basic principles: to uplift the poor, to stabilize the area through diplomacy, and to involve everybody in decisions affecting their lives.

The first structure was a kind of Marshall plan to improve the lives of the poor and destitute who came to Thaba-Bosiu. Moshoeshoe instituted the *mafisa* system, in which he would 'lend' cattle to the poor. This not only saved many people from starvation (or cannibalism) but created a strong, reliable, loyal gratefulness which led people to return cattle to the king, once they were on their feet, so that he could help others. In addition, Moshoeshoe gave *bohadi* cattle to young men who were not able to raise cattle for marriage. The children born of such a relationship, according to custom, would be Moshoeshoe's, because he provided the cattle. Being linked to the king but able to live sustainable lives within peaceful surroundings created a strong sense of interconnectedness and coherence, especially from the new arrivals. The cattle exchanged for marital purposes guaranteed a lifelong relationship between Moshoeshoe and a large number of families.

It is important to understand the role of cattle in matters of marriage, fines, sacrifices and cattle raids. In this part of the world cattle were called *Modimo o nkô e metsi* (God-with-the-wet-nose). Cattle were believed to have souls and to be a personal extension of the self. Exchanging, raiding, paying with and sacrificing cattle built one's personhood, made one a human being. One became irremovably woven, through these exchanges, into the herds and therefore personhoods of others. There was an idiom that a fool with an ox is no longer a fool. Through cattle people became intimately related to one another, and there are several stories in Basotho culture about the important life-saving role played by particular famous cows or bulls.

The second structure Moshoeshoe created involved diplomacy and used personal marital and public relations (with chiefs and agents) as strategies. Moshoeshoe, following Mohlomi's advice, married daughters of other chiefs, thereby fostering diplomatic alliances with other areas around him. These daughters often remained with their families and had children with a man of their choice, but, again, because Moshoeshoe had paid the marriage cattle, the children were regarded as his, and a certain political loyalty was expected from the family. In 1865, when Moshoeshoe was nearly eighty years old, the Catholic Sisters of the Holy Family estimated that he had a hundred and fifty wives. According to another source, the king's friend Nchakala reckoned they numbered about two hundred.

Moshoeshoe also introduced a broader kind of diplomacy by forming links with other chiefs. When the young, keen Batuang chief Moletsane, who had survived the last part of the chaotic Lifaqane, came to ask to serve under him, instead of incorporating his chiefdom, Moshoeshoe settled him at Maquatling to stave off any attacks that might come through the Caledon River valley. He also installed another chief, Moorosi, in the south of Lesotho in order to prevent the influx of lawless groups and dissidents fleeing from the Cape government.

Envisioning a semicircle of allied African states as far back as 1830,

Moshoeshoe entered into a treaty with Bapedi chief Sekwati, who had repulsed Zulu and Swazi attacks. Sources indicate that official treaties between black groups were unheard of when Moshoeshoe and Sekwati set out with two large entourages to meet at the Vaal River, where they established lasting diplomatic relations.

One of the sons of the wise Mohlomi, Letele, destitute after raids and attacks, asked sanctuary from Moshoeshoe. The king made him a senior councillor and provided him with *bohadi* cattle for a wife. A diviner named Tsapi left Moshoeshoe's enemy Sekonyela, and came to live on Thaba-Bosiu. Other chiefs were co-opted to form part of the trade routes for horses and firearms.

The largest diplomatic structure, however, was Moshoeshoe's network of messengers and information-gatherers at the courts of friendly chiefs. These messengers used routes known only to themselves in order to improve the speed of delivery and to avoid recognition. This was Moshoeshoe's unique innovation and created the belief among his followers that his messengers were 'flying' to their destinations, because no sooner was a decision taken at Thaba-Bosiu than people far away would know about it. It must have made Moshoeshoe the best-informed ruler in southern Africa.

Moshoeshoe used three types of messengers: *lititimi, lihloela* and *maqosa. Lititimi,* their name denoting the speed and efficiency with which messages were transmitted, delivered oral messages to the king's allies in the Caledon River valley. They were chosen on the basis of reliable, retentive memories proven during initiation. The *lihloela* were a kind of intelligence corps who gathered information and secrets in and outside of the Caledon River valley pertaining to the security of the state. Lastly, there were the messenger-ambassadors, called *maqosa,* whom Moshoeshoe used for all external communication and who operated with diplomatic immunity. Invoking a Basotho saying, *Legosa la morena ha le na molato, molato ke oa khaloli* (The king's envoy is not to blame, only the sender is responsible), these envoys requested safe conduct wherever they went. Their duty was to keep contact with chiefs in areas beyond the Caledon River valley, and to build up intimate knowledge of the cultures and languages of the people they dealt with. For example, a member of the Amavundle clan was asked to be a *maqosa* to all the Xhosa chiefs in the Cape, as he could speak several Xhosa dialects.

As a form of conflict prevention, Moshoeshoe allowed groups with different cultures, such as the Amahlapo from Natal and the Amavundle from the Eastern Cape, to keep their language and to practise their culture. He gave strict orders to his headmen to see that nobody interfered in their affairs. Even today, there are groups of Xhosa-speakers living in Lesotho.

In addition to accommodating people and setting up diplomatic relationships, a third structure introduced a form of democratic participation. Urgent matters would be discussed at a meeting of *matona*, senior councillors who specialized in particular fields such as warfare or custom. The next tier consisted of village headmen and territorial chiefs, who could consult their own councillors before responding to Moshoeshoe. The third tier was the large council known as *lekhotla la mahosana* (council of princes), which would discuss international affairs. Finally there was the *pitso*, to which all male followers were invited in advance by the *Morena e Moholo* (Great Chief or King) and which they were supposed to attend fully armed. Here an issue would be introduced, concerns identified, and the matter discussed with frankness. It was said that Moshoeshoe believed that suppressing people's freedom to express their opinion would only lead to discontent, and he therefore put considerable pressure on people to formulate in public whatever might be brewing under the surface. At the end of the meeting he would sum up what had been said (incorporating the unpopular in a way that both legitimized it and defused it), put everything within a specific historical context (it is a Basotho belief that every event is always the son of another event), and then he would make his ruling.

The only piece missing in this impressive bulwark-in-progress of participation, accommodation and diplomacy was a link to the white people who had begun to appear in the region. Moshoeshoe saw white farmers crossing the Orange River and was, through his information-gathering, well informed about their modus operandi. Instead of asking one of the passing trekkers or a civil servant from the colony to become part of his diplomatic corps, Moshoeshoe decided that a missionary would be the most beneficial. He contacted the Korana chief and hunter Adam Krotz, gave him some cattle, and asked him to bring a missionary to Thaba-Bosiu.

It was to this man, who was busy putting such a sophisticated system in place, that the twenty-year-old Eugène Casalis was riding with ardent eyes and a feverish heart.

chapter three

The coffee is finished. J. and I do not know a single lawyer who would be on our side with whom we could discuss the matter. For more than an hour we argue the whole dilemma to tatters. My hand is heavy as it dials the home number of Jonty Saunders of the security police. Jonty went to school with us. 'Can I come and see you?'

'Of course,' he says, in what sounds to me like a studied neutral tone.

J. asks a neighbour to stay with Willem for a short while, because we just want to drop something off. We drive to Jonty's house, which is in the best suburb. Among the impeccable lawns, white Greek goddesses and spouting fountains, his house is nondescript. 'As the house of a security policeman ought to be,' my husband the architect mutters. As I reach down for the plastic bag with the T-shirt, I see J. opening his door. I pull him back: 'I'll do this alone.'

'No, it involves us both.'

'This whole mess is my making. Let me take the responsibility.'

'But I am with you in this.'

'I know, and as you rightly said, you will have to carry it with me, but let me physically be the person they have to deal with; it is better than taking us both.'

J. slowly closes his door.

As I walk up the paved path from the front gate, the door opens and

Jonty steps out quietly. He has been watching. We meet on the steps of his stoep. I try to find something in his face that will guide me in how to approach him, how to extricate myself from this predicament I find myself in. He is a few years younger than me and has kept the young sportsman looks he had at school. But there is not even a trace of vanity or flirtation in him that I can exploit, nor any judgement in his eyes to at least make me angry.

'Hello, Jonty,' I smile, as friendly as possible as I hold out the plastic bag. He greets me but doesn't take the bag.

'What is this?' he says.

For a moment I'm confused. Maybe they don't know! But just the mere thought of rethinking this once more pushes me into replying. 'It's a red T-shirt. I am bringing it to you because I want to have nothing more to do with this whole thing.' Clumsy, I know, but afraid of compromising myself even further, I put the bag down in front of him and turn to walk back to the car.

'Yes, well, it won't be that simple.' He chuckles slightly as he looks at his watch. 'We had orders, if you didn't come out by yourself, to come and pick you up at seven this evening. So now that you've confessed, I'm afraid we have to take a statement.'

'I refuse,' I say. 'I'll do it later, when I've spoken to an attorney or someone.'

'I'm afraid that won't be possible.' His voice is suddenly official. 'You're a key witness, and there's a good chance that you'll be murdered, either by the Wheetie's followers, who've sworn revenge – they saw how you dropped Reggie and the others off at Tau's shop like guests of honour – or by Reggie's ANC followers who want to silence you.'

'But I'm *not* a key witness – I know nothing about what happened, not even who organized the murder.'

'But you've got the red T-shirt. We're also looking for the balaclava and the gun. A couple of men are already on their way to search your garden.'

As J. and I drive back in the dark, I relate the conversation to him.

'This is going to turn into something terrible,' he says slowly.

Back home we hurry the babysitter out with a bottle of wine and put Willem to bed. We tidy the house. We wait.

'What do I tell them?'

'The truth.' After a slight pause he adds, 'The truth about that day.'

They arrive in two cars and seem jolly, as if they're on an outing. Some of them are in uniform, others in plain clothes. I notice that Jonty Saunders is not among them. They walk in through the open front door without knocking. Some are already snooping and lolling on the steps and stoep, as if the house no longer belongs to us. One of them announces himself as the sergeant heading the investigation, another one is introduced as the feared Captain Potter, and J. leads them into the sitting room.

'You don't mind my men taking a look around,' the sergeant says rather than asks. J. and I are sitting on the couch. It feels strange: one upholds a civility which is being deliberately trampled on by an attitude that says, We have seen through your façade – you are nothing but common murderers.

'I have to clarify something first,' the sergeant says. 'Why did you go to Lieutenant Saunders?'

As I start saying, 'Because I want nothing to do with this whole mess,' J. says: 'Because we know Saunders. The two of us went to school with him.'

The sergeant eyes us suspiciously. 'Take him to the dining room.' He points at J., who is escorted out by a group led by Potter to have his statement taken down separately.

'You see, mevrou, it is a problem for us. Why did you go to the security police and not the ordinary police. Why?'

'Because I know Saunders.'

'Yes, but do you think it's a matter for the security police or is it police business? Is it political or is it criminal?'

'I believe it's criminal, but I went to Saunders because I know him.'

After some discussion among themselves, they decide that the police will take the statement, but the security police will sit in. Through the open door I hear my husband's voice and see a policeman casually browsing through our CDs.

I begin, as I have begun in my own head many times: On Tuesday evening at a quarter past six we were on our way home from yoga. We stopped to buy milk and bread.

'Yes,' nods the sergeant, 'our surveillance man said that you looked very relaxed at the café.'

I look at the man in front of me, the coarse nose below the eyes that are too close together. This is the face of a force that over the years has invaded my life and sullied its most normal moments. And it jumps up at me, something I have forgotten, deliberately forgotten: the day my daughter phoned from boarding school in Bloemfontein – it was a few months after I had been told that our phone was tapped. She sounded as I had not heard her sound before. 'I have started to menstruate.' She spoke with the thrill of threshold, with the shock that comes from seeing blood spill from your body, not from harm or hurt, but from becoming closer to what you are. I went ice cold. The knowledge of the hairy police ear eavesdropping into this most private of all moments between a mother and her daughter immobilized me into stone. I cannot remember what I said, only that I have been haunted for the rest of my life by my inadequacy to break through their malice in order to embrace my child.

Tonight, the sergeant no longer needs a secret device: he can ask me directly, and his men can snoop anywhere. I recount the whole event in short, simple, easily spelt sentences, so that the policeman next to him can write everything down on his clipboard. No opportunity for a Moral Manifesto here. Slowly: subject ... verb ... object, sentence by active sentence, we progress.

While I am talking I hear our garden gate's peculiar little squeak. Oh God no, if anyone comes now, what will I say, how will I explain? Every hour that can pass without the newspapers or the town knowing is an hour of mercy.

'Excuse me a moment,' I say. I turn up the volume of the radio for them and slip out the side door before the visitor has even knocked. On the dark stair outside I am astonished to see Denzil Hendricks.

'My God, Denzil, what the hell are you doing here?' I whisper. 'I thought you were in jail!'

'They released me earlier this evening, but the MKs contacted me to come and fetch the pistol and bullets from your stoep.'

Hysteria wells up inside me. 'Don't you see the cars? My whole bloody house is full of police. Do what you have to do, but leave me out of this! For God's sake, I know nothing, nothing about this!' Helpless fury shoots through me like a jet of water from a loose fire-hose.

I return to the sitting room and fumble for a cigarette. It gives me a reason to avoid looking them in the eye. Can they see that my hands are shaking? Do they know what has just happened? I light the cigarette and resume my account. Just behind my chair is a small round window, half-open onto the stoep. While I squeeze out one sentence after the other, now including even punctuation marks, I hear dry leaves rustling as Denzil carefully digs in the pot plants, looking for the pistol.

My mind is only half on what I am saying now. The other half is wondering: What are the police who're supposed to be searching the garden doing? Aren't they watching him anyway? But a more devastating thought bites me in the heel: If I'm sitting with the police because I think murder is wrong, why don't I tell them right now that the recently released Denzil Hendricks is busy outside looking for the gun that those bastards hid on my stoep?

But, my thoughts plead, if he takes the gun with him, then maybe all of this will go away. That's a dishonest and inconsistent argument, I answer back. The original decision to go to the police was based on something that was either right or wrong. Now you yourself are changing the rules: it is right to hand over the red shirt, but you turn a blind eye to Denzil on your stoep. I try to silence this internal debate by blowing my nose.

'Yes,' the policeman says, 'and then you brought the T-shirt because you were scared.'

'I wasn't scared.' This I say in a clear, unambiguous voice, remembering that J. once said he thought I was the bravest person he knew, until he married me: then he realized I do these 'brave' things out of naivety.

'No,' he says, 'I mean frightened and nervous.'

'Listen carefully, meneer.' The hairs on my neck are now standing upright. 'I wasn't frightened. I'm sitting here because I was dragged into something I know nothing about and want nothing to do with. If I look frightened to you, it is because I'm upset that you and the politicians have made sure that an honourable position is no longer possible for an ordinary person in this country. Why don't you write that down?'

He stares at me, open-mouthed.

It's after one in the morning when they leave.

~

J. and I sit and smoke outside in the garden. I tell him about Denzil's appearance. He shakes his head.

'You know what's the worst for me? We are in the hands not of the mean, but of the inherently stupid. During my statement when I said I had asked Reggie that day, "Wouldn't you like coffee or something cold to drink?" the constable sitting next to Potter *sommer* answered, "Ag, no thank you, sir."'

We laugh a little. We go to bed. The inadequacy of my statement goes round and round in my head. We sleep badly.

At school the next day I go to Denzil's office. He closes the door and takes an envelope out of his bag. He is shaking. A pistol, bullets and a balaclava slide across the table. We stare at them. It's the first time in my life that I've seen a pistol in reality.

'Denzil, you have to take it to the police. If they find it on you, you're in big trouble. It looks to me anyway as if they know everything. Ten to one they saw you last night and they're giving you until eleven o'clock or something. Phone Saunders and say you have it; you've just gone to fetch it on my stoep. In heaven's name *please* don't say you were there last night ...'

And these lies? Telling others to lie to cover up my own lie? I feel like someone drowning.

Denzil goes back home to phone Saunders and to wait. I teach my classes like a zombie. Some hours later he is back, standing breathlessly at my door. We go around the corner, behind one of the outer classrooms where no one can hear us, and speak in whispers.

'Man, things aren't right,' Denzil says. 'I phoned Saunders and he said he'd come at once. The moment he got to my house, suddenly the police and Potter with them came racing up, and you could see Saunders didn't expect him at all.'

'For God's sake, are they bugging each other's telephones?' We laugh in desperation.

As he was getting out of the car, Potter was already asking Denzil where he'd got the gun. On our stoep, Denzil told him. 'Yes, hell,' Potter said, 'I've been telling you all along that she's the one behind it all. And now I won't let myself be stopped – I'm going to pick her up right there at the school.' Then Saunders grabbed Potter by the arm and pulled him aside, and talked to him for a long time – but Denzil couldn't hear what they were saying. Potter was really fed up when he left.

'Did Saunders take the gun?'

'No, the most bizarre thing is still coming! Saunders said I couldn't give him the weapon then: people would say I was splitting on the comrades. He said I must go and put the pistol and the balaclava back at your house, drive once around the block and then go and fetch them again. Then they would catch me red-handed – and I would have no choice but to hand everything over to the police. So that's what we did.'

Denzil and I look at each other in silence. Things are going from strange to bizarre. A moral morass.

'But what the hell happened the day before yesterday?' I ask him.

He tells me the story, all the time wiping sweat from his face. For three days they'd been tailing the Wheetie in town, Denzil driving the others in his car. That afternoon, at Selborne Square, Reggie Baartman suddenly ordered him to stop, and then the whole thing happened.

'There was such a commotion on the square that my own doctor, can you believe it, my own doctor came out of his consulting room and saw these guys with guns jumping into my car.'

When they were all back in the car, Reggie told Denzil to take them to Johannesburg. No, Denzil said, surprised, he couldn't go to Jo'burg then; he collected his wife every day at five from work, and anyway he didn't have enough petrol. They considered the situation. All right, then they must take a taxi to Johannesburg. Fine, but no one had money. Money? Reggie ordered Denzil to take them to Cecily Shahim – she would have money. He dropped them there, went to fetch his wife, and was arrested by the police that night.

Denzil had been told that the Wheetie's corpse lay on Selborne Square for hours and hours while taxi after taxi offloaded passengers who wanted to come and see for themselves that the much-feared gangster was dead. They say the people in Maokeng partied until late that night with joy.

'So why is Cecily in jail?' I ask.

'Last night one of the cops told me she's innocent. She took Reggie and them to your house, but when the police went to question her she refused to give a statement. She refused to talk to people who can't prove anything against her.'

The dusty dry wind of the township blows bits of rubbish towards us in scampering waves. I cover my face with my hands, but inwardly I fight against the word 'ashamed', which is pushing its way to the centre of my brain. And the word 'blind'. Cecily had immediately seen it as a purely legal issue and not a moral one. But why drop them all off at my house?

Cecily comes from a well-off Lebanese family in Kroonstad. She was deeply involved with feeding schemes, and had a good relationship with the comrades, but she was so severely harassed by the police that she seldom attended rallies, marches and other 'incidents of unrest'. 'I don't have the security blanket of fame,' she once pointedly said to me.

We return to our classes. I walk, but it feels as if I am walking on heaps of old mattresses. My classroom is empty, except for Reggie's sister, Thulie, waiting, looking so agitated that I close the door behind me.

'They have been arrested!' she bursts out. 'All of them! It's that bloody Denzil! They say he sang like a canary. He gave away everything. The fucking swine! But he always was a real coward.'

I try to placate her. 'You have to remember, Thulie, Denzil hasn't got taxis or a shop; he's a teacher. If he's found guilty in a criminal case he'll lose his job and then he'll have nothing.' Am I pleading for myself?

But Thulie is adamant. 'No-no! I am sorry. One stands by the comrades. In the end we'll all share in the liberation.'

'My God, Thulie, what does murdering another murderer have to do with liberation?'

She looks at me – shocked, as if there is something elementary that I don't understand. 'The Wheetie destroyed the community. We stand by our own people.'

As I drive home through the miserable dry February wind, I find myself thinking about the words of my eccentric uncle, who said, 'I fear neither God nor man, lion nor snake, shark or rat, but, by God, I fear the month of February.' No one asked him why. We all knew that in order to prove to my aunt that he was not an alcoholic, he would stop drinking for a month – February, the shortest. What did Saunders tell Potter that made him not arrest me?

J. comes home. He says the town is humming with gossip: that Reggie and I are lovers; that I fell to my knees and cried when the police threatened to arrest me and just told them everything; that for me politics was just for kicks because, when it came to principles, I abandoned them. The police say it was terrible to see how I split on my comrades. J. and I look at each other. He stretches his hand across the kitchen table. I kiss his knuckles and we sit like that for a long time – in a way, conquered.

~

'We have to tell the children, before it gets into the newspapers,' J. says the following day. We fetch Willem early from school on Friday and drive to Bloemfontein. The other three are neat and sparkling in their school uniforms when we pick them up, their faces radiant with unguarded joy to see us. In the Spur they are full of stories and jokes, and both J. and I do our best to act normal. As we are finishing our meals, I am just about to begin with There is something that I have to tell you, when Willem speaks in a clear voice that makes the people from the nearby tables look up.

'Juffrou Botha prayed for Mom in class today! Yes!' He nods his head several times as he sees the disbelief on our faces. 'E*specially* for Mom.' He emphasizes the word by spreading his hands in the kind of gesture that can only come from Juffrou Botha. All my children went through Juffrou Botha's hands in Sub A and they loved her, not at all concerned by her complaints that they disrupted her class by wanting to know where the dinosaurs fitted into the scheme of Adam and Eve.

'And why should everybody pray *especially* for me?' I ask with a freezing voice, as J. kicks me lightly under the table.

'Juffrou says we should all pray for our parents but today especially for Mom.'

'That is very good,' says J. 'In fact something did happen that we have come to tell you before you hear it from other people.' In precise unemotional sentences he sets out the incident and I see our children's faces change as words like *shoot, blood, pistol, murder* and *proof* fall like small unexploded hand grenades in the friendly space among us, finally part of our family's reality. Everybody is quiet.

Willem speaks again after a sip of milkshake. 'Was that oom who was there the other day who had Mom hiding in the bathroom; was he a murderer?'

(Willem was referring to his mother's 'normal' reaction when a policeman came to the house on an unrelated matter.)

J. closes his eyes as if to draw strength from somewhere. 'No, he was an ordinary man, a good man, in fact – your mother just forgot to pay a speeding fine.'

'Shadap, Willem. Gaan Ma tronk toe?' It's the third one: practically working out the worst scenario.

'No,' says J.

'Nico en Hans-Werner se pa werk by die tronk,' says Willem.

We break into a bit of laughter.

'Why doesn't Ma say anything?' asks my daughter.

'I just want you to know what has happened, so that if anybody asks you, you can just say: Aag, I know about it, it's nothing.'

'But did you do anything wrong?' asks my eldest. His face is serious, and I think of how the school principal phoned the year before last to tell me that he had been spotted entering the ANC offices in Bloemfontein, a few weeks after it had opened, to sign up as a member. Despite the unbanning, the negotiations, it was still the time of the watchers and the watched.

'No.' I sound more convinced than I really am. 'Or let me put it this way: I haven't done anything wrong, but whether I did the right thing is difficult for me to work out.'

Having paid the bill, I lag a bit behind on the way back to the car. In front of me my family walks spread out. All of a sudden they look so frail to me: rearing against the wind, inclining towards each other yet walking so apart, as if the wind against them has become the only thing they know. They are all I have, I think, and I will see this through.

~

Other families also find it difficult to cope. As my initial anger abates, it becomes more and more difficult to face Reggie's eldest daughter. I can see in Winnie's eyes that she is more confused every day. When I accompany the choir and she sings the descant with a perfect, pure pitch, I look up and see she's watching me. Bewildered. And what can I say to her? How can I explain this whole mess that I don't understand myself?

Then the story hits the newspaper. Front page. Photos. Quotes from the police. According to reports, the court case has been postponed. At every mention there are photos and details of how the murder weapon was hidden in my house, of how nervous I was. This is obviously not a court case that will pass unnoticed. We also learn the names of the other accused: Jantjie Petrus, Hankan Petrus and Dudu Mofokeng. We live in a daze. We hardly discuss it. We do our daily chores with endless care and concentration. Apart from work, we go nowhere, but the rumours keep coming.

We hear that Cecily was released after a week and went straight to Johannesburg, where her family has instituted legal proceedings against the Minister of Police.

We hear that after the three MKs, Jantjie, Hankan and Dudu, were caught, they confessed everything and, together with Reggie, were released on bail.

Denzil lets me know that the ANC head office is sending an investigative team to find out exactly what happened. We, two ANC members, are not contacted, and neither the Northern Free State nor the Free State ANC branch communicates a word to us as explanation, denunciation, advice or warning.

Two days after the release of the MK operatives, I arrive at the school to find everybody standing outside again. The students refuse to go into their classes because Hankan, one of the three accused, was shot dead the previous evening in Brentpark. It happened after a soccer match. As the crowds of people were leaving, amidst the usual confusion of excited voices, dust and car lights, a shot was heard. People ran in all directions and came closer to see who it was only when the ambulance arrived.

'Cool cats,' says J. when I phone him. 'Now they can pin everything on the dead one!'

The murder of Hankan Petrus has serious repercussions in our school. One of our students maintains that in the chaos of running away he saw the maths teacher, who plays in a soccer team funded by the Wheetie's Three Million Gang, bent over the dead body before he too ran away. The student body says pupils will only take classes after all staff members who play soccer with the Three Million have left the school grounds. The principal tries to sit it out by doing nothing, but they start to burn papers and tyres. Denzil is ill and I don't have the gall to sit with the other teachers drinking tea, so I lock myself in my classroom.

The next day the students become openly aggressive. They start throwing stones and breaking windows. 'Down with Three Million supporters, down, down, down!' While shards of glass scatter sighingly across the floor, I hide under my classroom table. 'Is that me?' I think, crouching under the table. Somebody tries to break open my door, but all I can think is that I am dying for a cigarette. As I carefully pick up the pieces of glass under the table and put them in the small rubbish bin, I find myself wondering how the students argue in favour of one murderer over the other. Is there such a thing as a bad murderer and a good murderer?

What am I missing? Why does my choice not give me any moral satisfaction, but make me feel as if I am standing on sand?

A declaration that killing is wrong comes from an unexpected source. We are all called for an assembly. As head of the school committee, Reggie leads a protest against the teacher who allegedly ran away from the murdered body of the accused Hankan Petrus. In the meeting he declares that the teacher must be fired immediately, because he, Reggie, does not want murderers, people without respect for the lives of others, to be teaching his children. I sit there, too astonished to utter a word.

For the umpteenth night I sit rigid in the bed with questions whirling in my head. To what extent is my position not moral at all, but simply privileged middle class? Am I against murder because I can afford to be? I'm white; I'm barricaded by money against anything that threatens my life. If I get a death threat, I go to the police. I even choose a policeman to suit my needs, because I was at school with them. Reggie can't. He has to defend himself within a hostile context where comrade and cousin, murder and protection have no separate meanings any more. But, again, it is post 1990. In what way is Reggie, with his extended house, his upholstered furniture and his BMW not middle class – perhaps not in education, but certainly in aspiration? Is Reggie not also better connected to powerful institutions than I am? Is it then the access to things like power and class that determines whether something is moral?

But isn't respect for life something basic? Isn't it the oldest principle, the first major decision that a society takes? But, because of our fractured past, we as South Africans have never formed a coherent enough whole to decide what kind of principles we agree on. It was okay to kill blacks, but not whites. It was okay to steal from whites, but not from blacks. How do we change that into: It is wrong to kill or steal?

Did I go to the police out of rage that I wasn't consulted or because I'm against murder? Is rage a principle? One's view on murder certainly is. But if I'm against murder, if I respect life, why did I have two abortions years ago without any qualms?

'I have always believed that the oppressed should decide for themselves exactly what they need from me,' I say out loud to escape the vicious circle of my thoughts. 'I hoped it would be insight or skills or even poetry, but it seems to be my fax machine and my car.'

'*My* fax machine and *my* car, you mean,' J. mumbles, turning over on his side of the bed to switch off the light. 'And have you ever asked yourself to what extent you yourself are to blame for Reggie's perception that you'll do anything he orders, just like his own wife does?'

Oh my husband, I think in the dark, so secure in finding the weak spot. It is true. Suppose Reggie had told me straight out that day that he had just shot the Wheetie and asked me to take them to Maokeng; would I have said, But that's terribly wrong and I condemn it and he should realize this and sort out his own transport and get the hell out of my house? Or would I have given them a lift out of loyalty and then afterwards shifted the whole moral issue from respecting life to supporting the oppressed?

~

It's weekend and early morning. The heat arrives with blue clarity. I take out the bottle with the family 'plant' to bake some *beskuit*, remembering how I first came to understand the importance of this family recipe. One morning I overheard my mother saying to my father, 'My plant is dead. I'm going to Ta'Maria in Parys to get another one.' Plant? Ta'Maria? Who on earth was still being called Ta'Maria?

The 'plant' appeared to be my mother's bread-yeast plant that she got from her mother, who got it in turn from her mother, and so forth, back to the Anglo-Boer War – that was the origin of this plant. One bakes bread and *boerbeskuit* from this plant with nothing more than one spoon of sugar, one spoon of salt, six spoons of fat and ten double hands of flour.

I went with my mother to Ta'Maria. She waited on a *bankie* next to the kitchen door of a small, roughly plastered house, with two long, limpid grey braids and a fruit jar on her lap. My mother handed over a bundle of notes and I remember noticing that Ta'Maria's feet looked like two roughly plucked chickens.

The jar was quarter full of plant. From that very same plant comes the one in my own and my sister's fruit jars. Yes, although it is the twenty-first century, with the biggest variety of breads and *beskuit* available in human history, I bake *boerbeskuit*.

The steps to bake this *beskuit* are usually as follows: I notice that the *beskuit* is finished. I think I will go and buy some. I stand in the *tuis-nywerheid* or in front of Ouma's Rusks at the supermarket and remember my mother saying: '*Jong*, a woman who does not even bake her own *beskuit* ...' The silence completing the sentence conveys possibilities ranging from treason to fratricide to rotting fingernails. Then I sigh, and go back home. I take the plant from the shelf, as I do now, add sugar, salt and lukewarm water. I clean the pans, and wait for the yeast to rise up to make a second, bigger, morass-like batch with fat, lukewarm milk and flour. I start to wonder why I am going to all this trouble. But this time, with my head filled with thoughts of murder and betrayal, the baking keeps me busy with safe, familiar rhythms.

The main characteristic of *boerbeskuit* is that it is quite hard and unsoakable. 'You mean hardish,' my mother would sniff. 'But it had to withstand all kinds of weather in a leather *saalsak* while on commando. Your ancestors fought the whole war on this.'

And finally it is time to knead. Knead? 'How can a woman negotiate her own life if she can't knead properly?' my mother would ask. Yes, not pummelling against a hump of dough with skinny red fists, no, but bringing the fists down, slow and purposeful, right from the armpit down into the dough as if to measure the real extent of one's power. I feel how my fists become broad, placing themselves with buttery strategy, and how the texture of the dough generously changes under my knuckles. As I knead I feel how the heat rises blissfully towards my elbows.

I put a lid on the bowl and cover it with the bread blanket. 'People don't have bread blankets any more,' my mother would sigh, 'because nothing grows old in their houses – everything is either new or rubbish.'

By early midday the dough has risen smoothly like a maiden's buttock from the bowl. I roll arms of dough, cut them with a knife, pack double layers in the bread pans and put them into the oven. After half an hour the smell starts to fill the kitchen. It drifts into the neighbourhood. It teaches people the word 'reeling'. It enables them to spell 'salivary glands'. My children, who are home for the weekend, appear from their rooms and games and books and homework to stand in the doorway. I boil water for coffee.

When I turn the batch with its light-brown bursting crests out onto the table, everyone is ready with plates and butter, knives, apricot jam and Marmite. I grate some cheese. Thick soft pieces disappear with burning fingers. 'People don't cook properly any more,' my mother would say. 'In these white kitchens, they only seem to mix cocktails or chop vegetables for the TV.'

What is left goes into the oven to be dried overnight.

I know what will happen next time. I'll think: This really takes too long. I'll choose a five-star recipe with a brick of margarine, two cups of sugar, a house-payment of seeds and fruit, yoghurt and vitamins. And everyone will become sick of it, sick! And then, next time ... the fruit jar will come off the shelf ...

~

'This book must go back to the library, but I want to keep this quote. Please read for me so I can type it?'

J. reads: 'Quotation mark capital letter I have chosen justice dot dot dot so as to keep faith with the earth full stop close quotation. Capital letter by refusing a command at a certain moment one upholds not only one's own human worth comma but that of all subjects full stop. Capital letter refusal sets a boundary around authority in the name of all people full stop. Capital letter human value is the basis for solidarity and for rebellion full stop. I rebel comma therefore I exist full stop.

'New paragraph. Quotation. Capital letter the rebel demands undoubtedly a certain degree of freedom for himself semicolon but in no case comma if he is consistent comma does he demand the right to destroy the existence and the freedom of others full stop. Capital letter he humiliates no one full stop. Capital letter the freedom he claims comma he claims for all semicolon the freedom he refuses comma he forbids everyone to enjoy full stop. He is not only slave against the master comma but man against the world of master and slave full stop.'

'This all sounds so right,' I say, 'but it doesn't really help in practice.'

chapter four

For Moshoeshoe, the meeting with Casalis was only one component of the extensive plan that he was putting in place to secure a safe and prosperous future for his kingdom. Before he took Casalis' outstretched hand on that day, he had already established himself on Thaba-Bosiu, worked out diplomatic relations with Shaka, beaten off Manthatise's ferocious army and dealt with her vengeful son; he had made contact with the Bapedi chiefs Sekwati and Sekhukhuni, was in conversation with King Sobhuza I about the pros and cons of missionaries, had been approached by Moroka for land at Thaba 'Nchu, had determined his position on cannibals and witchcraft under his reign, had made himself mobile and armed by using horses and guns, and, above all, was successfully combating the poverty of his people. Added to this was the intelligence he had gathered from the leaders of indigenous and coloured groups who moved in the margins between white and black – all of which gave him an intellectual grasp of southern Africa shared by few other political leaders of his time. In his efforts to stabilize the borders of the land belonging to him and his people, Moshoeshoe must have been acutely aware of the encroachment of white people in their wagons: initially only one or two at a time, and always moving on. Then came more, who stayed longer and in bigger groups, provoking bloodier confrontations to enforce their frameworks of ownership. Moshoeshoe

would have realized very quickly that he did not yet have the right negotiating tools to deal with them when they finally turned their eyes to the
luscious red-grass plains stretching north from the Maluti Mountains.

Despite briefings from his fellow missionaries, Casalis could not have
known much about what lay behind this man sitting on the mat, 'bending'
a certain look upon him. Yet, the young missionary was filled with good-
will that stemmed from his youth. As he would later write in *My Life in
Basutoland*, even as a nine-year-old child in France 'there began to show
itself in me … [a] love for the coloured races that seemed almost innate.
When I saw a negro or a mulatto, which, indeed, rarely happened, I felt
towards him a lively sympathy. I wanted to stop him, to get him to seat
himself by me and tell me his history. This taste seemed the more remarkable as these people, at that time so little known in our small provincial
towns, were the objects there of a special repugnance.'

From a very young age, and under the spiritual guidance of a dynamic
pastor, Casalis decided to become a missionary. He was admitted to the
Mission House in Paris, where he studied theology 'from morning till
night … We were living in an atmosphere of enthusiasm. Our fathers, at
first roused by the great ideas and terrible experiences of the Revolution,
then dazzled by the glories of the Empire, had bequeathed to us a spirit
militant and full of ardour.' The young men hoped for a 'pacific renaissance' to which they could all contribute. As if to confirm his conviction,
Casalis experienced a 'miracle' in Paris. A cholera epidemic had swept
across Europe and had reached the city. Casalis was praying at a church,
asking God to protect them from the plague and prepare them for death.
'I had not even finished,' he writes, 'when I saw a man totter in the midst
of the congregation. I descended precipitately from the pulpit, and held
him in my arms. His vomitings covered my clothes. We carried him away.'
Within hours, the man was dead, 'and the next day, when I conducted
his funeral, his coffin was laid in the midst of twenty others'. Although
thousands of Parisians died of cholera during the following weeks,
Casalis was spared.

Initially, the PEMS decided to send Casalis and his colleague Thomas
Arbousset to Algiers, soon after it had been colonized by the French

in 1830. Not particularly troubled by the morality behind this war, they started to learn Arabic and the rudiments of Islam, and attended lectures at the Sorbonne on philosophy, Egyptian hieroglyphs and anthropology, as well as a special series of lectures by the famous scientist and discoverer Georges Cuvier.

Unexpectedly, however, they were told that they were needed instead at a mission station that 'penetrated' the interior of southern Africa, Robert Moffat's mission at Kuruman, and that they had to leave for the Cape of Good Hope. At first they were upset. It was far from Europe and their families, but after intense praying and reflection, they dutifully changed their courses from Arabic to Dutch, Egyptian hieroglyphs to primary health care, and read everything they could about the indigenous peoples of southern Africa.

As one of two sons, it was difficult for Casalis to leave his family. Although his parents accepted his wish to become a missionary, the idea that they might never see one another again was hard to bear for both the young missionary and his family:

The horses were brought before the door of our house at four o'clock in the morning. After a prayer mingled with sobs, there began a scene which I can only compare to that of the supreme separation in the moment of death. My father, my brother, my sisters were overwhelmed. My mother alone had power to speak. Seeing I was overcome, she cried, 'Courage, my son, it is for your God; go without regret; commit yourself to Him … I know that He will take care of you.'

A moment after we were in the saddle, and had gone some steps, when I heard my father calling me back. 'Descend,' said he; 'I must embrace you once more.' – 'No, I beseech you. We shall lose what little strength we still have left.' – 'I command you!' I threw myself again into his arms, and he clasped me to his breast in a convulsive embrace, gasping in a broken voice, which went to my heart, 'I shall never see you again here below!'

Two hours afterwards we reached our first halt, and it was then only I could stop my sobs ... I did not regain entire possession of myself till four days afterwards, on my arrival in Paris.

In Paris Casalis and Arbousset were ordained, before setting off for the ship. As the coach drove out of the court of the despatch office, Casalis looked back and saw his mentor of many years leaning against a column, 'wafting me a kiss with one hand and with the other pointing to the skies'. The young missionaries were joined by Constant Gosselin, a thirty-year-old mason with practical experience and 'muscular strength'.

On the ship, Casalis had a dream: a man was standing near his bed. He immediately recognized him and saluted him as 'Daniel'. Daniel took Casalis in his arms and ascended rapidly to 'the celestial regions', where they passed large clusters of stars. They kept rising and rising. At last they arrived at the gates of a palace 'whose extent appeared immeasurable, and whose splendour was greater than that of a thousand suns'. Surrounded by heavenly sounds and choirs, Casalis wanted to enter the gate: 'this then is the abode of my Saviour! Let us enter; I too would see Him, adore Him, and for ever sing His praise.' But Daniel replied, '*Not yet*.' The prophet took him from gate to gate and kept saying, 'Not yet.' Then they descended 'lightning-like ... towards the abodes of labour and sorrow. Soon I saw in a savage country a peaceful cottage, in which I could discern my own form, a church where hundreds of eager natives were assembled, and schools where a great number of children were being taught to sing the praises of God. "*That first*," then said the prophet to me: "then, I will return for you, for a place is reserved for you in the palace of your Redeemer, on condition that you are faithful to Him."'

It is interesting to compare Casalis' dream with that of another man who forms part of Moshoeshoe's story, his mentor Mohlomi. It was from this dream that Mohlomi learnt the insights that in turn influenced Moshoeshoe. Details about it have come via oral sources from Mohlomi's wife, 'Maliepollo, who described events while Mohlomi was undergoing initiation. 'One night when all were asleep in this village of boys, Mohlomi also asleep, had a dream; he beheld the top of their hut open.' After a great twirling ball of light descended, there arrived a 'bird like an eagle, it took him, put him on top of its wings and flew with him, until it put him on top of some tall mountain. On top of this mountain he found a lot of people who had long died … Then after some time one of the men stood up and said Mtanami [my child] you should not be afraid because here where you are is a place of your ancestors. After some time you will be a king; you should rule our people well [with peace] and study medicines, so that they may not be troubled by illness while you are still around.' Thereafter they promised to protect Mohlomi if he became such a ruler.

The two dreams reveal striking parallels and equally notable differences. Mohlomi had his vision while in the *mophato* or initiation hut, during his transition from boyhood into manhood; Casalis was on a ship travelling from Europe to Africa when his dream occurred, when he was moving from student to practising missionary.

Mohlomi saw a hurricane from which a great ball of light emerged and descended to the hut. The roof opened and an eagle settled next to him. Casalis saw a man standing next to his bed and recognized him as the prophet Daniel.

The eagle put Mohlomi on the 'top of its wings' and ascended to the highest mountain peak, where he was left among his ancestors. Daniel took Casalis in his arms and ascended with him past the stars into heaven, where he saw the splendour of God's 'abode'.

Mohlomi was instructed by the ancestors in how to be a good ruler through bestowing care on his people. If he followed their instructions, the ancestors would reward him by protecting him on earth. Casalis was told that if he could get the eager natives of a savage country to sing the praises of his God, a place would be reserved for him in heaven: the work was on earth, the reward in heaven.

Casalis' dream can be read against three idealized worlds that are identified by Jean and John Comaroff as lying close to the heart of European missionaries: a capitalist age where he (intelligent but coming from a poor background) was free to aspire to greater heights; an idyllic countryside where peasants under his tutorship would work hard but happily; and a sovereign empire where the divine authority of God was his only instructor.

Mohlomi's dream, on the other hand, presented three idealized concepts close to the heart of African philosophy: a communal system based on the 'wholeness of life', signalled in rituals; an idyllic cosmos where hurricanes, comets and birds are interconnected in one another's beingness; and an unbroken connection with the realm of the living dead, through which the ancestors sent clear instructions.

These two dreams express two profoundly different approaches to living a worthy life on earth. For Casalis, this involved freeing people from their bondage of sin through the self-discipline and sacrifice found in church, school and serving God. The reward would be in heaven. For Mohlomi, it was achieved by creating a better life for others by caring for them, especially children, the elderly and the weak. The reward was on earth.

~

Casalis, Arbousset and Gosselin set foot in Cape Town and were overwhelmed by the 'stern and savage grandeur' of Table Mountain, with its 'frowning wall'. Many travellers arriving at the Cape by sea have described the mountain in ecstatic terms, but Casalis recalls that they had 'sinking hearts as we pondered on what awaited us behind that sinister rampart'.

While staying in Cape Town with the London Missionary Society's Dr Philip, they learnt that Moffat's mission stations, which were their destination and the express reason why they had been sent to Africa, had been destroyed by Mzilikazi. This was devastating news. Nevertheless, after a while, perhaps feeling that they could not make use of Dr Philip's hospitality indefinitely, they decided to venture into the interior after all and let God use them as He saw fit. And so they journeyed to Port Elizabeth by ship and started their trek north by ox wagon.

By this time, Casalis had developed into a talented diarist, and his literary flair, as well as the translation of his books from French into English, led to his writings about Lesotho becoming better known than those of Arbousset.

In his memoir Casalis paints vivid cameos. For example, he records that one morning, two-thirds of the way to the Orange River, his spectacles broke. His eyes were so weak that, at a distance of three steps, he could not distinguish his two friends and the driver from one another. But he was not worried; he had foreseen that something like this might happen and had had three pairs of glasses specially packed for him by a Paris optometrist. When he opened the parcel, however, every single lens was shattered.

By pure luck a coach appeared, going in the opposite direction, and Casalis travelled with it back to Graaff-Reinet. But, on arrival in the town, he found to his horror that there were no glasses for his kind of myopic eyes. All he could do was order some from the Cape, which would take three or four months to reach him, wherever God's plan would have taken him by then. In the meantime he was provided with blue spectacles with concave lenses, which improved his eyesight somewhat.

Now how to get back? As fate would have it, he was offered a one-eyed pony on which he, half-blind, with blue glasses and long swinging legs, trotted northwards through the Karoo, without knowing exactly where he was. Overwhelmed by the enormous silence around him, he started seeing things. A dog came running towards him and passed. At one stage he saw an enormous lion coming for him. What should he do? He had no gun. Would turning around help? Could he outrun a lion, on a pony – and a one-eyed one at that? But it was already too late! The lion was upon him, so he decided simply to close his unseeing eyes and wait for the predator's teeth to sink into him. Preparing to die there on the road, he confessed later, did produce 'a little mist in the eyes'. But nothing happened. When he turned around, he saw the lion continuing down the road, away from him.

A few hours later, towards sunset, he observed more lions coming towards him, six of them. This was surely the end! But praise the Lord, the pony, either through mercy or impaired eyesight or both, was not frightened by their scent and simply trotted on. The lions did not attack. Still in shock, Casalis suddenly recognized a familiar silhouette and found himself among his colleagues, who had set up camp for the night. He told them about God's special protection against these lions, and one can assume that their prayers that night were filled with thanksgiving.

The following day Casalis saw another lion and shouted out in terror as he pointed at it, but everyone burst into laughter: it was no lion; it was a gnu, a wildebeest.

The men trekked for many days through the 'wild', until they reached a mission station called Philippolis, after Dr Philip. 'Without knowing it, we had reached the place and the hour where God was about to reveal the field of labour He had destined for us.' Providence then spoke to them in the voice of Adam Krotz, the Griqua hunter sent by Moshoeshoe to tell them they were wanted by a king.

From this moment in his narrative, Casalis' crisp, anecdotal writing style changes: beautiful lyrical passages, mingled with descriptions of the devastation of the Lifaqane, depict the landscape as they approach Moshoeshoe. The tone of writing evolves from mere lively curiosity to a sense of accepting, almost claiming, the landscape that is to become their 'field of labour'. As they leave Thaba 'Nchu he notes: 'Almost everywhere were human bones. In some places their number indicated battle-fields.' The Basothos they meet make a 'most favourable impression upon us ... Their features and their colour were in no way disagreeable ... Their skin was soft, bronze rather than black in colour, their limbs robust and well modelled ... We were struck by the dignity of their bearing, the grace of their movements, and the deference and cordiality which characterised their manner of address. The mantles, made of the skins of animals, with which they covered their shoulders, the huts in which they lived, and the pleasure they took in anointing their limbs with oil, seemed the only things that assimilated them to the savage.' The word 'savage' implies, of course, that the Basotho were in need of salvation.

They soon realized that Krotz, whom Casalis describes as 'a very intelligent hunter', was using the journey to Thaba-Bosiu as an excuse for an extensive game hunt, turning a three-day journey into ten days. Resigned to this, Casalis relished in describing the quaggas on the ridge one morning just as the sun rose: in a straight line they stood, nostrils dilated, flanks 'curried' by the pollen of the mimosa blooms. He wrote of eland, hyenas, lions sitting on the driver's seat of the ox wagon, every incident described in a way that allowed journey and dream to run together through the wild, untamed yet holy beauty that led to the king who wanted them.

At last they crossed the Caledon River, near to Thaba-Bosiu, and again Casalis' tone changes: now they were making history by travelling 'where Europeans were for the first time leaving the imprint of their footsteps'. The landscape had transformed from endless veld to something resembling a garden, from wilderness to paradise. 'The two banks were shaded with willows whose roots buried themselves in the water. These trees were all alive with scarlet chaffinches and small ringdoves.' The bottom of the river was of 'smooth basalt blocks, lilies and flowers grew on both sides', and in between were 'crystals of great transparency'.

Early the next morning a 'noisy cavalcade' exploded onto the camp. It was the two eldest sons of Moshoeshoe, Letsie and Molapo, sent by their father to welcome the guests. Although this was meant in good spirit, the missionaries were filled with misgivings: to be welcomed by jolly bareback riders, dressed in old leopard skins, naked legs dangling over steaming horses, did not seem appropriate to the importance of the occasion. A nearby chief then arrived with fresh milk and cooked mielie cobs to welcome the 'Foreigners of Moshesh', after which Casalis was delegated to make a courtesy visit to the king, with Krotz as translator.

Thaba-Bosiu looks completely inaccessible from afar, with huge perpendicular rocks, but, as they drew nearer, Casalis saw a line 'winding serpent-like round it from the top to the bottom. This ... was, in fact, a path, or rather a ravine serving as a path. I can compare it to nothing better than to the longitudinal furrow we sometimes see in the rind of an over-ripe pomegranate. To make the resemblance perfect, it would be only necessary to take the blocks of basalt which formed the stairway for the pomegranate seeds.'

As they slowly climbed the steep pass, they noticed people peeping down curiously. Close to the top, they stopped, dusted their clothes, tidied themselves, took the horses by the bridle and climbed the last stretch to the plateau, where they were welcomed with a gun salute. A praise singer with feathers and strange growls led them to a semicircle of people standing behind a man sitting on a mat.

'There is Moshesh,' said Krotz.

Moshoeshoe stood up. Having initiated the meeting by summoning the missionaries, he did not let the control slip: '*Lumèla lekhoa,*' he said, 'Welcome, white person.' A simple action, standing up, but it could imply many things: I stand up because I respect you; I stand up because I want to change the physical relationship between us, so that you are looking up at me, not looking down.

Even more intriguing are Moshoeshoe's first words: Casalis was addressed not as *moruti* (preacher) or *ntate* (sir), but as *lekhoa* (white) – a deliberate choice of focus. Casalis had not been called to Thaba-Bosiu because he was a missionary or a sir, but because he was white, and, as such, particular things would be expected from him. Moshoeshoe was more interested in what his colour could produce than his preaching.

The term for white people in Sesotho is interesting: *lekhoa* (plural *makhoa*). The prefix *le-* is that of a Class 7 noun, which is used for people of debased status: *leshahe* (albino) and *legodu* (thief). The word *khoa* as a noun refers to a kind of lice found on the hindquarters of domestic animals, but as a verb it could mean 'to fight' or 'to shout', or 'to lack decorum, to be rude, to cause embarrassment, to be disrespectful, to have no regard for other people'. Whatever interpretation one chooses, *lekhoa* indicates a disrespectful person, someone who is part of a class of people who lack respect for other human beings. When a white person behaves humanely and contrary to the white stereotype, it would be said that '*Ga se lekgoa, ke motho*' ('He/she is not white, he/she is a human being').

Moshoeshoe was using a word already invented in the Sesotho language by that time. Under closer scrutiny it seems as if the word does not necessarily identify white people as a contrasting group, or The Other, but indicates a group that itself regards the rest of humanity as The Other. He was therefore not contrasting blackness to whiteness, but accommodating a new kind of relationship that was closing in on the Basotho.

This was indeed a unique moment for the two men: each of them was looking at the other through his own, still reasonably intact world view.

One saw a person without regard for other people, the other saw a savage soul worthy of salvation. Neither of them knew that a day would come in which Moshoeshoe, his kingdom almost destroyed by this very whiteness, would say: 'O Casalis ... *You are a true MoSotho.*' (Or that, after nearly two centuries, Casalis' name on the internet would be found only in connection to Moshoeshoe.)

But it is 1833. One can imagine the small mists coming from people's mouths on this cold June morning. Moshoeshoe stands up on his mat. Casalis approaches and stretches out his hand. The king takes it without hesitation. With Casalis at his side, Moshoeshoe walks to his main residence, where Queen 'Mamohato serves them food. As young as he was, Casalis was struck by the civility between the king and his wife, by the way they did small favours for each other, by the kind tones of their voices when they addressed each other, by the way Moshoeshoe had his young four-year-old son stand between his knees and carefully fed him while the conversation flowed.

As I worked through material about Moshoeshoe, I came across several suggestions that this kind of behaviour was spread more widely among the Basotho. An early visitor travelling through the country remarked on the complete safety he experienced. Moshoeshoe had, he wrote, 'by his example and interference, imparted to the Tribe a character of humanity and gentleness of manners, very remarkable. Robberies and murders are almost unheard of. Foreigners are everywhere respected and well received. Capital punishments have been done away with.'

This traveller also confirmed Casalis' observation that Moshoeshoe was a superior spirit who exercised a marked influence on those with whom he had direct dealings: 'He has an active mind, and always appears to be thinking; his eyes, when there is anything to rouse him, flash with intelligence ... In conversation he delights, and discovers great versatility of mind, can suddenly adapt himself to those whom he addresses, and turn from one subject to another with a facility that is seldom seen, except in those who have been accustomed to move in good society.'

~

After that first meeting between Moshoeshoe and Casalis, the king came down from Thaba-Bosiu to meet the other missionaries at their camping place. Casalis was upset that, because all their crockery was still in the wagon in Philippolis, they had to serve the king's food on the lid of a pot.

After dinner the missionaries explained to him, through Krotz as translator, that they were sad that his people were suffering so severely at the hands of their enemies (which is what Krotz had told them), but that they had brought a remedy for the Basotho. All misfortunes of men, they explained, proceeded from their evil passions and ignorance. But they, the missionaries, were messengers of a God of Peace, and this God would protect the Basotho if they so wished. If they wanted to put themselves under the care and direction of this God, the incursions of their enemies would cease. A new order of tranquillity and abundance would begin. To show the honesty of their intentions they would stay in the midst of the Basotho and share their lot, whatever it might be. They wanted nothing in return. They would look after themselves, needing only a piece of land near wood and water.

It is of course impossible to know how Moshoeshoe understood this astonishing promise and whether he suspected that these two mere boys could only be referring to a spiritual state rather than to a day-to-day reality.

'My heart is white with joy,' said Krotz in Dutch, translating Moshoeshoe's Sesotho. These words were diarized into French by Casalis, and translated years later into English, from which these paragraphs are now being typed. One can imagine Casalis sitting in his study somewhere in Europe, writing his memoir based on this original diary. It remains surprising that, despite the hindsight of a lifetime, he allows no space for possible ambiguities from Moshoeshoe. According to him, the king wholeheartedly accepted what these youngsters had to say: '[Y]our words are great and good. It is enough for me to see your clothing, your arms, and the rolling houses in which you travel, to understand how much intelligence and strength you have. You see our desolation. This country was full of inhabitants. Wars have devastated it. Multitudes have perished;

others are refugees in foreign lands. I remain almost alone on this rock. I have been told that you can help us. You promise to do it. That is enough ... Remain with us. You shall instruct us. We will do all you wish.'

'My heart is white with joy' has become another often-quoted phrase, because it signifies for some a keen and immediate acceptance of the missionaries and everything white. Unfortunately, the original word Moshoeshoe used has not been preserved, but it was probably a Sesotho idiom such as 'O pelo e tšoeu' or 'Pelo eaka e tletse bohloeki', which means the heart is happy or filled with purity. Neither of these idioms refers to the whiteness of whites.

Moshoeshoe might have meant that his heart had become young and youthful with the arrival of the missionaries – he had enough reason to, because the last piece of his diplomatic strategy had just slipped into place. He could at last look forward to a time in which his kingdom could prosper in peace.

The missionaries stayed for three days at their wagon near Thaba-Bosiu before setting off to find a place for a mission station. During this time several women and children squatted on the ground some distance away to watch them, with a mixture of curiosity and fear, speaking in low voices and wondering if they were 'really men' or if they were ghosts. The missionaries 'encouraged the bolder spirits to make an examination of our persons, and thus reassure themselves. It was then discovered that our hair, [in] spite of its resemblance to that of baboons, was real hair, that our boots and stockings covered our toes, and that my spectacles did not form a part of my physical structure ... They learned with pleasure that we had fathers and mothers.'

Moshoeshoe allowed the missionaries to decide where they wanted to settle. They found a place that was close to water and wood, called Makhoarane, which they named Morija. 'After a prolonged search, we fixed upon a spot which seemed to offer every desirable advantage, water in abundance, a fertile soil, firewood, timber, and a picturesque situation ... Delivered of [the] vociferations [of lions], we were able to enjoy in peace the murmur of a brook which tumbled over a cataract into a basin carpeted with watercress. This murmur mingled with the cooing of an infinitude of turtle-doves … showing us how gracefully and daintily they could mark the impression of their little red feet on the sand. A few paces away we flushed a covey of noisy guinea-fowl, which fled bewildered into the brushwood.'

Their chosen place might have been perfect, but the indifference of nature was immense. Two or three days after their arrival, they found themselves 'in a solitude almost absolute … Some shrubs, which the winter had not despoiled of their foliage, sheltered our little tent from the wind. The wagon served as a sleeping-place. Thousands of antelopes roamed around us, without appearing to trouble themselves about our presence. At first, far from cheering us, the spectacle made us sad.' Here they erected a rough wooden cabin as a temporary shelter while a proper house was built.

However vast the difference in background and expectations between Moshoeshoe and Casalis might have been, a strong bond began to develop between them. The gentle Casalis, with his sharp intellect and excellent education, must in many ways have been the older man's ideal son: one who, like Moshoeshoe, worked hard at trying to do the right thing, the good thing. Instead of keeping his sons away from Casalis, he sent them to live with the missionaries and later even sent some of his younger sons to distant Cape Town to study at Zonnebloem College.

(Years later, in 1857, while Moshoeshoe was pleading through letters for the survival of his people, his son at the college, Tsekelo Moshoeshoe, was writing letters to the famous linguist and recorder of /Xam language and culture, Wilhelm Bleek. 'Sir, I beg to inform you that I told you I would write Basuto words on the paper you were so good as to give me. And when I brought the paper to Mr. Arbou[sset?] he said he had no time to write the English or French though promised to do so, and therefore I must return to you the paper as it is.')

Moshoeshoe, gentle and sharp, but with far-reaching royal powers, might have been the closest Casalis, with his humble background, could come to a kingly father on earth: materially successful, powerfully protective, wise and open to any kind of discussion.

Indeed, not long after the missionaries had settled in, crying was

heard from the cabin, because a letter had brought the news that Casalis'
father had died. 'People ran from all sides: a deputation from Moshesh
speedily arrived … a lively sympathy painted itself on their features as
they saw me weep,' wrote Casalis. Having already a few Sesotho words at
his command, Casalis said: '"God has done it." *Ntaté o magolimong.* "My
father is in heaven."' The discovery that white people were also mortal,
Casalis wrote, made a deep impression on the Basotho. One might
wonder, however, whether their reaction was not due to the open display
of grief by one of these sturdy, upright, emotionless people. It didn't
dawn on Casalis that the Basotho might also be wondering why he
was crying when his father was with the almighty God so loved by the
missionaries.

Moshoeshoe visited the missionaries regularly, often bringing presents
of eggs, berries or meat sent by 'Mamohato. Several descriptions survive
of his dynamic participation in conversations – how his mind was always
searching for the 'philosophy of the subject', how he would strike his
thigh with his right hand when he thought of a counter-argument, how
he would throw himself back on a sofa when he hit upon a new idea and
then expressed himself 'with feelings bordering on extacy'. From the time
that he came down to inspect the missionaries' tent and tasted sugar,
coffee and salt for the first time, they were struck by his curiosity. They
were also impressed by his physical prowess – the precision and power
with which he threw his assegai to bring game down, which he often
brought for them to eat.

Amidst the excitement as they came to know one another, a sceptical
voice emerged: that of Moshoeshoe's father. Mokhachane had settled with
his son on Thaba-Bosiu, where he enjoyed a lifelong privileged place; he
was allowed to speak his mind, and more and more he would criticize
his son. 'Very good,' he said, after being introduced to the missionaries;
'you have now the direction of affairs; I have seen your white men; do
with them what you judge best.' Casalis describes him as a 'dry old man,
with a cynical look, and abrupt and brief of speech … Suspicious and
mocking, a thorough egotist, he despised men.' It fascinated Casalis that
Mokhachane refused to kill anybody with his own hand, but directed

others to do it for him. Several sources mention how, after their first meeting, the old man derived great pleasure in scorning and ridiculing the missionaries, keeping resistance to this new influence alive.

For their part, the missionaries planned not only to convert people, but to instil in them their own social values of self-discipline and self-sacrifice. They also hoped that the station would become such a haven of prosperity and prestige that the king himself would move there.

Gosselin taught the young missionaries, who knew nothing about 'sawyering', how to work with a saw and an axe. They took turns to cook, and had to deal with the absence of salt and bread (terrible 'for French stomachs'), the presence of 'serpents' and lions circling the camp, and the inconvenience that any request or letter took ten to twelve months to reach them from Europe. Casalis confesses in his memoir that a longing for his family led to a depression that made him contemplate suicide. Arbousset, who quickly perceived this 'sadness', said to him: 'Family affection is no longer a benediction when it unmans the heart ... You, so young, and yet to be thinking of ending.' Casalis writes: 'These words restored me to myself. I saw clearly enough where I was going, and blushed at the revelation.'

Within a few years of the missionaries' arrival, the whole of Basotho-land would be in grave danger. After the clash between the trekkers and Dingane in Natal, which culminated in the Battle of Blood River, white settlers streamed into the Highveld. None of the indigenous groups were strong enough to offer resistance to this encroachment, and Moshoeshoe, with his loyal following of thousands of Basotho and two white missionaries, became the only one who could.

chapter five

The ANC has sent a team of attorneys and advocates for Reggie. Nelson Mandela visits Kroonstad, and we hear that during a closed meeting he refers to the way the Three Million have abused the ANC and says we must stand by our people.

The fight between the ANC Young Lions and the Three Million has spilt over into the school. The community of Brentpark is clearly torn between ANC politics and Three Million activities. And then there are those supporting the old 'respectable' ANC group, the AFs.

I am engulfed in violence. When I come out of my classroom, one boy has another pinned against the wall, a knife stuck in just above his balls. I see a bloodstain spreading. One child stabs another in front of the woodwork class. Quick, deft movements of the hand with what looks like a dagger. Is a chest so penetrable? How does a hand become so adept at stabbing? During athletics a gang fight breaks out that wrecks the whole pavilion. From the bus, from bags, from clothes, knives, pangas, clubs, chains and what look like hessian bag needles are pulled out. What I assumed was a ramshackle old bus is actually a weapon carrier. A pupil storms past me, a member of my long-jump team, chopper in hand, his eyes glittering ecstatically.

I dwell on the edges of chaos. No one talks to me. During breaks I go and sit with Denzil. He is just as distraught. He is being hunted with death threats. The court case is on its way and he has been acquitted as an accessory, because he, like me, is a state witness. The two of us are coming a long and humbling way.

Sometimes we reminisce about our experiences. 'Do you remember the day the demonstration was cancelled and the children marched alone?' he asks.

I do. Maokeng, the black township, was supposed to march with Brentpark into the white town. They were to meet at the edge of Kroonstad, but the Maokeng youth were distracted by municipal officers, so the demonstration was cancelled.

Denzil and I went to warn the children and found about eighty of them already marching in the streets under a single tattered poster of Mandela. On the other side of the stop street a Casspir and two yellow vans pulled up. The police climbed out with a rattling sound as they loaded the magazines of their huge guns. When the dogs jumped out, the children ran away, down the street.

'Sjoe,' I said to Denzil. 'This nearly turned bad.' Just as we were turning around to go back to the school, we heard the children further down the street. They were singing 'Senzenina', slowly and with a determination that made us stop in our tracks. They came into our line of vision. I recognized Celestine Wilson from my Standard 9B class, who had just got eight out of ten for her essay. The clever Johannes Vemminck. Out of the corner of my eye I saw the police cock their guns and take aim, while over the megaphone a warning was issued that if the children crossed the stop street, shots would be fired.

Standing at the opposite corner we were too late for any kind of intervention.

'Do you think we were really too late to stop them, or were we scared?' I ask Denzil.

'Ag, *jong*, the way I remember it, the two of us were just taking orders, and the order was that the march was cancelled.'

My memories of that day are more anguished. It felt as if the students were already sealed off in a collective purpose. I remember my heart ransacking my paralysed body as I saw their feet in their weather-beaten shoes hesitate for a fraction of a second just before the line of the stop street, I heard the song; my eyeballs pulsed as a gun clicked; my throat went dry.

I grabbed Denzil by the arm. He was streaming with sweat. The children didn't look at anyone; they gazed into the distance in front of them, towards the black township there on the hill.

Then they simply stepped across. Those feet simply crossed the line. They walked, fearless; they walked past the police, a mere three steps away from them, contemptuous of all power, contemptuous of death.

Denzil and I sank to our haunches, trembling, he swearing in a variety of tongues beside me. The whole day I was in shock – dumbfounded by the intensely contrasting emotions I'd felt during the incident: the fear and anxiety, and in spite of that the hope, the all-defying hope that said, 'Go on, please step over that line, yes, do it', knowing full well that if they were shot I would have to live with my cowardice.

'I often think back on that day, Denzil. Doesn't it feel to you that by simply standing there and watching, we destroyed our own authority and integrity? That those children, Celestine and Winnie and them, crossed a boundary that we would never be able to cross? I mean, how could we ever say to them afterwards: Work hard so you don't fail liberation?'

'That is your question. My question is what do I teach children who are not scared of death?'

~

One morning, as I'm putting money on the counter at the café for cigarettes, an arm reaches across me to take a straw from the box. I look up, straight into the eyes of Jantjie Petrus, the MK man who shot the Wheetie. I look down again at his young hand here beside my white hand and think that this smooth brown hand actually pulled a trigger to kill someone and that my life has reached a point where I stand in a shopping queue with murderers. Ashamed, I think that I could perhaps just as easily have been standing next to someone in the white church or at the school bazaar who takes his children out in the afternoons to have fun watching him torture black people. It is rumoured that one of Willem's friend's mothers is making torture bags for the police on her sewing machine.

Something like revulsion rises in me. I yearn to be elsewhere, within another ethos, another life, unpolluted by human.

~

'Do you think there's such a thing as black morality and white morality?'

'Of course,' J. says, while changing the bulb in the bedside lamp. 'A white life has meaning only for whites, while a black life means nothing for both white and black.'

Ignoring his sarcasm, I press on. 'Maybe there's something important that I'm missing here. Maybe there is a way to look at this murder that would turn it into an understandable moral act.'

'There's now two murders,' J. remarks dryly.

Through the apartheid years I maintained that whites should never say: Here is where I draw the line. We have lived in this country on our terms; now we should be prepared to spend three hundred years living on other people's terms. I was even proud of the fact that I could keep going precisely because I didn't draw any line. And now suddenly I have drawn one. I can't exist in a space where certain things don't count, old-fashioned things like respect for life, respect for each other as human beings, honesty and something that perhaps I'll call beauty, or, more specifically, something uncontaminated by people – like trees, grass, birds.

Sometimes, during the long periods of school boycotts, I climb through the hole in the fence of the school and walk down to the nearby river where it smells of thorn trees, willows and river water – but then I see a beer bottle or a turd or a shoe or some plastic and I get so sick of the way the land has been defiled by humanity, how you never ever get away from human breath and human shit any more.

~

Once, while I was teaching at the black teachers' training college in Kroonstad, a student was killed over the weekend. The following Monday there were no classes. The students congregated in the hall and talked angrily for hours. Around midday they came out, the men forming a kind of battalion, armed with knives and pangas and what have you, pouring into the street and running in step towards the home of the person who had allegedly killed the fellow student. I was in my classroom on the third floor, compiling an exam paper. Standing up, I was able to see the group moving like a black arrow along the dirt roads of the township, and I thought: these are students, they've finished school, they are studying maths and science and literature, they sing and pray in the mornings, and there they are, breaking into the famous ox-horn movement, enclosing the backyard room where this person is supposedly hiding.

Before I could finish my exam paper, I heard shouts and ululations. The women students were waiting at the gates as the men toyi-toyied back, welcoming them with cooldrinks and chips from the tuck shop. The man in front held a T-shirt and a cap triumphantly in the air. The offender had been 'dealt with'. Nobody would say by whom exactly, but the song they were singing indicated that the students had done what they had to do. The community was now clean.

It was during this time, in the mid-eighties, that rumours surfaced of a group of white men armed with guns and sjamboks who patrolled the smallholdings and farm roads on the lookout for white men who picked up black women. They would be beaten up and, if they were 'trapped' a second time, their registration number would be given to the newspapers that were prowling for a story of sexual activity across the colour bar, a second Excelsior. This meant that domestic workers couldn't be taken to the station or taxi rank inside a white person's car. If they were taken by bakkie they had to sit on the back. I remember seeing a black woman sitting in the boot of a car holding the hatch open. One evening this group of *uitroeiers* came across an old barn that was used once a month for a get-together of gay people in the area. The barn was stalked so that nobody could escape. Those who were not beaten were marked with knives. The floor, it was said, looked like a red stoep the following morning. On Sundays the leader of this group was baptizing people in his swimming pool.

~

I stand in our garage putting ice cubes into buckets. Behind a makeshift bar counter J. is pouring drinks for guests. After the second postponement of the court case, we have decided to throw a party for my fortieth birthday and have invited people we've befriended from the coloured area, the township and the white town.

'Dinge gaan taai,' whispers J. as he fetches another big bottle of Coke from the fridge. Apart from a few people, white and black, who left immediately when some of the cars in the street suggested 'other races', people are friendly and civilized, although they aren't really mixing. It is only at the bar, in a deluge of brandy and Coke, that things are slowly thawing. I hear the doorbell ring, but as the front door is already open I assume people will let themselves in. After a second ring Willem comes to say that there is a man who wants to talk to me. As I walk to the front door, past guests sitting and standing, I am struck by a stunned silence. All eyes stare at the figure at the door. The first thing I see is a T-shirt with the words 'Die Wit Wolf' and a photograph of Barend Strydom, who shot eight black people on Strijdom Square in Pretoria just four years ago. I stop and meet the eyes of the young man with closely cropped hair, standing on my threshold. One of his hands is behind his back. He has a gun, my mind tells me, but my legs take me right up to him.

'Can I help?'

'I collect money for the Wit Wolwe,' he says jauntily.

'Jammer, meneer, but I don't give money to them.'

He stands there for a few seconds. We measure each other up, but he is really just out of his teens, and the combination of my older presence and smart-looking guests wins the moment. He turns around and runs down the steps. Before I close the front door I hear him shout, 'She says she does not give money to the White Wolves' – to a lot of laughing and backslapping in the street. A car pulls off, its tyres screeching.

The sound in the house has become more animated. One couple leaves, but others begin turning to those they have previously only acknowledged with a nod. Time for food. I call the men at the braai to bring the meat that is done and I peel the wrapping off the salad bowls.

6

'Come outside,' J. says. Little Jôhnnie is standing next to the roses and is vomiting his heart out. I take a cloth and some water. 'Are you ill, Jôhnnie?'

'We were playing; he ran a lot,' offers Willem.

'No,' Little Jôhnnie gasps, 'it's not the running, it's the food. It tastes like … it's the food.'

'He has been eating meat since we started to braai,' says J.

Things are picking up. 'Jirre, maar die Boere drink vir jou,' says one of my colleagues from the school as he puts the meat down, 'and it doesn't seem as if they get drunk.' There is a slow mixing as people converge at the food table. There is laughter at the bar and sounds of children playing in the garden. I dim the lights and light candles, and the teacher who conducts our school choir starts to play the piano. His wife joins him, along with others as they sing old forties' songs: 'Love Me with All of Your Heart', 'Some Enchanted Evening', 'Smoke Gets in Your Eyes'.

I am emptying another ice tray into a bucket when I hear a loud crash and splintering wood. As I swing around I see people bursting in through the garage door and the side door. 'The lights! Switch on the lights!' somebody shouts as frightening figures move around in the flickering candlelight.

J. switches on the light and we see it is the police, armed with batons and sjamboks. Things happen all at once. One of the biggest farmers grabs a young policeman by the shirt, saying, 'Fokken los ons uit, Bennie, ons party hier.' The police commander stops in his tracks and lowers his baton as he stares at one of my guests. 'Jirre, Dok, wat maak *jy* hier?'

Between 'Doc' and his patient, the farmer and his nephew, things are sorted out: this is not an illegal gathering of terrorists making a lot of noise, as the neighbours have complained (It's not even eleven o'clock, manne!), but an ordinary private social gathering. The police leave and now the party is in full swing. Our guests bond with energized speed. There is admiration for the brave way in which some of them confronted the police, and a sudden vivid understanding of black people's vulnerability in the face of such raids.

It is long after midnight when J. and I get into bed after what must have been the very first party in Kroonstad where all races were present as social equals.

'I shudder to think what would have happened if we'd only invited black people,' says J., 'and I have to say I'm quite proud of the way the whites behaved. Aren't you?'

'I am, but something else stays with me. When I came back from the braaiplek with the lid of one of the meat containers, I was looking at the house from the outside. And it was filled not only with soft light, but with a sound – a right sound is what I want to call it – with all that singing and laughing, the children and different languages and accents.'

'Some would call it a politically correct sound.'

'I guess I'm trying to say that this house has never sounded like that before, like it's a complete place, a whole place, a fully lived space, if you understand what I mean.'

~

After one of the postponements, *Die Volksblad* reports that Reggie's lawyer, Mr Patel, has successfully demanded that a senior advocate with knowledge of 'criminal matters that have a political colour' should be appointed. His case will be split from the other two accused, and, as George Bizos is not available, Dennis Kuny will be representing him.

We read in the paper that the judge was irritated by the prospect of a further postponement and berated Mr Patel for not securing 'silk'. In the court case transcript, which I read more than a decade later, one can see how the power relations were established even before the case started properly. Patel was asked to explain whether dereliction of duty was 'abnormal' or 'normal' for him.

COURT: So what you are saying is that although the matter of the possibility of senior counsel was raised with you, whether briefly or not ... I mean one's brain registers that in a split second, surely, in spite of that you did not give the matter any further thought?

MR PATEL: Yes, m'lord, that is my honest answer. I did not give ...
(*Intervenes*)
COURT: Well you must agree with me, Mr Patel, that that is rather
strange, not so?
MR PATEL: M'lord ... (*Intervenes*)
COURT: Or is that normal for you?
MR PATEL: No, it is not normal. One sometimes inadvertently do [*sic*]
not think about many things.
COURT: No, is it abnormal for you to act in such an irresponsible way?
Is it not irresponsible?
MR PATEL: M'lord I should have applied myself to it.
COURT: Yes, and it was irresponsible of you not to do so. Now that is
abnormal, not so?
MR PATEL: Yes, m'lord.
COURT: Unless it is normal.
MR PATEL: No, it is not normal.

Postponement was also requested on behalf of Jantjie Petrus and Dudu
Mofokeng, because they 'were not in a position to place the attorney in
funds for the purpose of the trial'. Jantjie's father promised to put his
house up for sale in order to raise the money.

~

At last the final summons arrives: the case is due to begin in Bloemfontein. I am suddenly nervous. What do I answer, for example, if they
ask me why I didn't tell the police that Denzil was looking for the pistol
on my stoep?

Late on the Friday night before the case Denzil phones. I must meet
him on the main road. From a dark corner he appears and slithers into
the car. 'Drive,' he says nervously. He tells me that Reggie's family came
to order him to change his testimony – to say that Reggie wasn't in the
car at all.

'I told them I couldn't do that; I'm a state witness and I was warned
that if I wavered in my evidence the judge would immediately make a
case against me as an accessory. Then they said I shouldn't worry, the

ANC are sending their best advocates, and in any case everyone is going to get off free in the end on amnesty.'

Amnesty? Where does that word come from all of a sudden and how would the family know what's going to happen? As things are now, we will not even get a new government! We sit like that – each of us as confused as the other.

I wake up early on the Sunday and I know straight away what to do. I put on pantihose, a jacket and a scarf and drive out to the coloured township. At the Mission Church I slip in through the back door and onto the nearest pew. Although we left the white church in the mid-eighties for this one, since the murder I haven't really felt like coming.

In front of the church, as always, stands Liesbeth our *voorsinger*, with her small leather cushion, beating it in the palm of her hand to keep time. We sing 'God is liefde'; we sing 'Our Father, mme re tsamaya ka pelo tse ntle re hlwekileng'. From the pulpit Dominee Jubelius speaks, as if by appointment, about two kinds of betrayal: the betrayal of Judas Iscariot – committed out of arrogance and avarice – and the betrayal of Peter – committed out of fear.

I slump forward in the pew – fear: will the word stay with me for the rest of my life? Does it want to force me to acknowledge that, yes, I am terrified to find that the moral framework that has served me so adequately all my life is suddenly inadequate to assist me in distinguishing what is right and wrong? Yes, I fear the fact that the more I think I am doing the right thing, the more I feel unhappy about it. I fear how kindly people, who do not understand why I went to the police, assume that I did it out of fear.

We all stand with closed eyes and sing 'Sy naam is soos wasem vir my'. Dominee Jubelius says, 'While we stand and sing like this, all the children here, go and hug your mothers; it's Mother's Day today.' We sing – I close my eyes and long for my children, so far away, waging their own separate battles.

Someone is beside me. It's Winnie. She puts her ice-cold hand on mine. I look up into the mixed emotions on her face. 'Winnie,' I manage to say. I open my arms and hold her tight against me – her thin body, her fine-spun plaits, her lively nostrils. We stand like that, as if drowning, and after a while I become aware that we're surrounded by the singing congregation. They have their arms on us, embracing us, swaying, all of us singing in Sesotho, '*E ne e le selemo – dipalesa di le teng dithupeng*' (It is spring – the blossoms are on the small branches).

And in a way this congregation has over the years become my and my family's only community, the people we feel ourselves closest to, the place where our lives and the world make sense. But as we all stand there, holding onto one another in the simple, haphazard church, the emotional bewilderment is visible on all our faces. What is going on in this town? We have all been battered in our efforts to live in the way we think is right.

chapter six

Only men turned up to hear the first service on Thaba-Bosiu. When Moshoeshoe, sitting in what was to become his regular place at the services, became aware of this, he stopped proceedings and insisted that the women be called. 'They came at last,' Casalis writes, 'a dazed expression on their faces, but advanced no nearer than the entrance of the enclosure, where they squatted down, squeezed together like a flock of sheep, and taking care to turn their backs to the assembly. *Ba téng*, "they are here," said Moshoeshoe to us, "Begin."'

Every week either Casalis or Arbousset would hold a service on the mountain. The moment they arrived, a town-crier would summon the people. Moshoeshoe would always be the first to take his place. Any visitor to Thaba-Bosiu was amicably obliged by the king to attend.

At first, the missionaries used an interpreter, Sepeami, for the services, but they soon noticed that he spoke in a tone and with a facial expression that suggested 'I do not believe a word of what I am translating'. It took all of their youthful authority to force him to put on a jacket and take the pipe out of his mouth while interpreting during the service. And he sometimes made mistakes. The Dutch word *zaligmaaker* (saviour) was translated as *zadelmaaker* (saddle maker). One can imagine how many bareback horse-riders came to the following sermon to meet this almighty saddle maker. The missionaries realized that mastering Sesotho should

77

be their first priority. Of this Moshoeshoe strongly approved: 'Now ...
you will be indeed my missionaries ... Every time you come to teach us,
I shall be there to get my people together.'

After their services the missionaries would eat with the royal household. While Moshoeshoe cut and distributed the meat, and 'Mamohato
the other food, they would discuss the sermon.

Moshoeshoe found many similarities between the knowledge and
beliefs of the Europeans and those of the Basotho, but, he lamented,
'because the Basotho didn't have a book', these were difficult to prove.
His opinion on the Ten Commandments was that the same law was
'written in all our hearts. We did not know the God you announce to
us, and we had no idea of the Sabbath; but in all the rest of your law
we find nothing new. We knew it was very wicked to be ungrateful and
disobedient to parents, to rob, to kill, to commit adultery, to covet the
property of another, and to bear false witness.'

'Black or white,' said the king, 'we laugh or cry in the same manner
and from the same causes; what gives pleasure or pain to the one race,
causes equally pleasure or pain to the other.' He also observed that whites
were clever, but not clever enough to have made up the Bible.

On another occasion, Casalis recalls, 'he discovered, to his great
surprise, that our teaching was based on facts, or real history, and was
not, as he had thought at first, composed of myths and allegories. "You
believe, then," said he to me one evening, pointing me to the stars, "that
in the midst of and beyond all these, there is an all-powerful Master,
who has created all, and who is our Father? Our ancestors used, in
fact, to speak of a Lord of heaven, and we still call these great shining
spots (the Milky Way) you see up above, "the way of the gods;" but it
seemed to us that the world must have existed for ever, except, however,
men and animals, who, according to us, have had a beginning, – animals
having come first, and men afterwards. But we did not know who gave
them existence."'

Casalis replied: 'You were in darkness, and we have brought you
the light.'

One needs, of course, to examine Moshoeshoe's words, as quoted by the missionaries, with care. To what extent have his words and their meaning survived? How accurate could the renderings be, when they were translated from a language that the missionaries were only beginning to understand, filtered through inadequate knowledge of the world of the Basotho, and written into books many decades later in Europe, with hindsight, based on the diaries that they had kept in Africa? Moshoeshoe's words were understood and recorded from the perspective that the Basotho were a special people who were in darkness and needed salvation from those who had light.

~

Moshoeshoe enjoyed talking to Casalis, and, as his fluency in Sesotho improved, their discussions became more and more complex. Casalis records that, on one of his weekly visits to the palace, Moshoeshoe pointed to a nearby hut and ordered him to wait there, as he still had to oversee some business. Inside the hut two mats were already rolled out. Two hours later, Moshoeshoe slipped in. He wanted them to talk and had formulated particular topics. 'Our conversation was in full flow when a dark body presented itself at the entrance,' Casalis recalls. '"Keep quiet," said the chief; "pretend to be asleep."' The man, however, continued to beg Moshoeshoe to give a decision in his case, because he had been waiting at the palace for three days already. Moshoeshoe ordered him to go and get a leg of mutton from one of the houses of his wives and then continued the conversation.

Moshoeshoe arranged for both missionaries to engage in regular discussions with the *Bagolous*, the society of old men at Thaba-Bosiu, where various topics were debated and a variety of questions asked. Arbousset recorded a conversation with a Mosotho who found himself overwhelmed by 'sorrowful' questions such as: Who has touched the stars with his hands? On what pillars do they rest? Why do the waters never weary flowing night and day? Where do they stop? Who made them flow like this? Where do the clouds come from and why do they burst into rain? 'I cannot see the wind,' the man said, 'but what is it? Who brings it, makes it blow, and roar and terrify us?'

Moshoeshoe was fascinated by the different stories in the Bible and regularly confronted the missionaries with inconsistencies. They said that Jesus had come to bring peace, he pointed out, and yet white people were making wars. The missionaries were against polygamy, and yet Abraham and Isaac and Jacob all had more than one wife, not to mention Solomon and the other kings. Moshoeshoe sometimes spoke on behalf of the missionaries when his own people questioned them. On one occasion Casalis told a group of people that God was the father of them all. A member of the audience asked: 'You are white; we are black: how could we come from the same father?' Moshoeshoe answered him: 'In my herds are white, red, and spotted cattle; are they not all cattle? do they not all come from the same stock, and belong to the same master?' Whenever he heard a story, whether it was from Greek, Roman, French, Hebrew or Sesotho origin, the king would pinpoint the universal human element as an example that people everywhere, of whatever colour or culture, were related.

Casalis recorded Moshoeshoe's repugnance to the shedding of blood, even to his own detriment. 'He was not wanting in personal courage, but on almost all occasions when he had taken arms to resist the invader, he drew upon himself the blame of his subjects by the extreme facility with which he gave up the results of a definite success as soon as the enemy sued for peace.'

In the cases he presided over, Moshoeshoe almost never asked for capital punishment, even for murderers: killing them would not bring back the victim, and instead of one death, there would now be two. This position, long before the death penalty was abandoned in most European countries, drew the following commentary from Casalis: 'At the same time it was impossible not to admire (especially when one compared him with other African chiefs) his good nature and his inexhaustible patience. I have seen him endure from some of the most scoundrelly of his subjects invectives and affronts which it would have been very difficult for me to digest. "Let them alone," he would say, smiling, "they are mere children." And his dignity lost nothing by this, for never was [a] chief more respected or more loved.'

In a praise poem about Moshoeshoe, the conditions for a prosperous society are set out: one can build nothing with violence or arrogance.

Put down the knobkierie, son of Mokhachane,
Leave it on the ground:
A village cannot be built by a knobkierie,
'What can you do to me!' does not build a village.
The one who builds a village, is the Binder-together, Thesele,
He is a cave of refuge for the poor and for kings,
This grandchild of Peete, the Strong One.

(*Beha molamu, mor'a Mokhachane, / U lule fatše: / Motse oa molamu ha o hahe, / 'U ka nketsang?' ha e hahe motse; / Motse ho haha oa morapeli, Thesele, / Lehaha la mafutsana le marena, / Setloholo sa Peete, sekoankoetla.*)

Moshoeshoe's standing among his people was visible in their reactions to him when he travelled through his territory. 'Everywhere on the way,' Arbousset wrote during one such expedition, 'people flocked from numerous villages towards Moshesh, to hail him and present him with sacred reeds. Others, the better to celebrate his passage, brought him cattle as presents. In everything, this African prince showed a tact that I greatly admire. His affability did not flag for an instant. Warmth, gaiety, nothing is lacking. He talks to everyone without distinction of age or rank. He even amuses himself with children as if he were one himself; and, still more astonishing, his memory is so good he seems to know the name and the history of each of his subjects.'

This testifies to the personal journey of Moshoeshoe from a belligerent child who, as legend has it, killed five boys, to a king who allowed his subjects to insult him without it affecting his stature. One might well ask why neither Casalis nor Arbousset ever questioned how this feat could be possible outside the ambit of Christianity.

For Moshoeshoe, evil was simply the result of incurable weakness: 'To do good ... is like rolling a rock to the top of a mountain; as to the evil, it comes about by itself: the rock rolls without effort to the bottom.'

When he asked Casalis how nations that recognized Jesus could still fight wars, Moshoeshoe said, 'It was excusable in us … who had no other models than wild beasts, but you who profess to be the children of Him who said, "Love your enemies," for you to take pleasure in fighting!' Casalis, who was becoming increasingly aware of the gulf between belief and actions, tried to point out that they might fight wars, but they fought differently: Christianity made people care for the wounded, as there was no personal hatred in the hearts of soldiers. Moshoeshoe responded with sarcasm: 'Then you work this evil without anger, mixing wisdom with it!'

In his book on the Basotho, Casalis gives his view on their morality:

> The heart is deeply corrupt [here] … They will endure acute suffering without a groan or a murmur. Hunger, thirst, fatigue, when they are inevitable, do not alter their serenity … *Morality among these people depends so entirely upon social order, that all political disorganisation is immediately followed by a state of degeneracy, which the re-establishment of order alone can rectify* [my italics] … The sudden and premature introduction of new laws and customs, and the imposition of a strange authority, are, for the same reason, equally fatal to their moral character … The external appearances of moderation and decency constitute in the eyes of the natives what they call *botu*, the *title* or *dignity of man*.

For the Basotho, Casalis writes, moral evil is '*ugliness … odious* in itself', because it destroys and spoils and is caused by man's weakness.

> Among all the virtues, that which the natives most appreciate is *kindness*. They had words to express *liberality, gratitude, courage, prudence, veracity, patience*; but their vocabulary offered but very vague terms to express the ideas of self-denial, temperance, and humility.

As I read this, I can feel Casalis breathing next to me. He is being confronted with a moral framework rooted in a communal life, which questions the idea of individual responsibility and conversion. Does it mean that a person has to be turned into a sealed-off individual before he or she can be converted?

In his less formal memoirs it is clear that Casalis' interaction with Moshoeshoe constitutes a real conversation, a real exchange of ideas, with one thought stimulating the formation of another within a more or less equal power relationship – at least at the beginning. Casalis noted that the king dominated the discussions with an insatiable curiosity and relished a worthy interlocutor.

The oral sources quoted in Seboni's thesis indicate that Moshoeshoe had several interesting conversation partners. Mention is made of his un-adulterated joy whenever he engaged with the younger Moorosi, whom he installed in the south of the country, in creatively planning and, with precision, executing successful cattle raids. Moshoeshoe also tested his decisions and ideas on his lifelong friend and initiation mate, Makonyane. Makonyane was one of the first to be converted, and one can imagine many discussions between them, dealing with Moshoeshoe's belief that Christianity was good for one's followers, but not for the king.

~

The missionaries' perseverance with the Basotho eventually bore fruit: after nearly four years of weekly preaching and living exemplary lives, they had their first real success. On the evening of 9 January 1836 they heard a young man spontaneously offering a fervent prayer a distance from their house. The three of them slipped out and silently approached him in the dark. 'It was really so!' Casalis wrote. 'Astonished, moved beyond expression, we fell on our knees and burst into tears.' Baptized by Arbousset, Sekhesa became their first convert.

Casalis and Arbousset assumed that Moshoeshoe would move down from Thaba-Bosiu to live with them. As time passed, they realized that, while seemingly allowing them to make their plans, he arranged very carefully that they should establish themselves at Morija with his sons and subordinates, in the hope that some of the people living on the mountain would move back to the plains. The idea was that he would keep some thousand people and a few principal councillors up there to protect the fortress if new troubles should break out.

Most people preferred to stay on Thaba-Bosiu, however. Frustrated by Moshoeshoe's unwillingness to convert, and not understanding why he wanted his sons to live with them while he himself chose not to, the missionaries decided to set up a second station at the foot of the mountain. Casalis volunteered to run this post, and Moshoeshoe encouraged him to move there without delay. It seemed that resistance to the missionaries' teachings had emerged and was growing, so that if they waited longer, Moshoeshoe might have to go against the will of his people to allow a new establishment. According to Casalis, Moshoeshoe was concerned about an 'approaching struggle' in which he would need Casalis' presence and help.

It goes without saying that converting Moshoeshoe was the main target of the move. As Casalis euphemistically suggested, 'The man who had brought us into the country had the first right to our instruction.' They visited him often, and he received them with much pleasure and 'revealed himself more and more to us as a superior man, well meriting the title of *Mothou oa litaba*, "man of wisdom"'. In one of their praise songs, the Basotho describe Moshoeshoe as follows:

When you sing of heroes, do not leave out Thesele, the Binder-together of Mokhachane; the one we refer to as Moshoeshoe-Moshaila, the cloud who moved from the east, who made a shooting line and was seen in the west by Thaba-Bosiu, where the councillors sat. All the nations heard him, they know of Moshoeshoe, the one who sweeps away the dead grass, so that people walk freely. Moshoeshoe-Moshaila from Rakali, the Beard-shearer.

When you sing of heroes, do not leave out the grandchild of Peete, Moshoeshoe-Moshaila, the one who is a cave of refuge for the poor and for kings; the one who broke Shaka's assegai, binding it to others; the one who is loved when the shields are being held; the one who is loved when the knobkieries of the young men are being lifted. Would ever such wisdom grace us, like that of Thesele, the

Bringer-back-of-cattle who saved the nation? He is the curd of the tawny cow of MaMui who fed us, the tall-long-jumper up to the fountain, Moshoeshoe-Moshaila, the beloved that surpasses all others.

But Moshoeshoe had no interest in converting. Seboni asserts that he was keenly aware of an encroaching civilization and decided to accommodate it rather than ignore or fight it. The king used the missionaries as political tools. Through them he gathered intelligence; they expanded his knowledge about a wide variety of matters. But becoming a Christian would mean submitting his power to theirs. With an open mind, he used the white men to introduce his people to the ways of this approaching civilization in the hope that they would not be engulfed by it, but empowered to survive it. Moshoeshoe also deliberately allowed other religious groups to open missions, thus preventing any one group from obtaining too dominant a hold, and demonstrating a healthy scepticism towards a single foreign claim to truth.

When the missionaries arrived, Moshoeshoe seemed to have a belief system that dealt adequately and fairly with the good and the bad in his African society. What he did lack was a framework through which to understand those who said it was wrong to steal, but stole; who said one should care, but didn't care. Casalis, on the other hand, intelligent, sensitive and deeply fond of Moshoeshoe as he was, seemed unable to grant Moshoeshoe a position of integrity if it was not founded in Christianity.

~

With the prospect of a new mission post, and finding himself falling into depression and melancholy regularly, Casalis set out for Cape Town to find a wife. His approach to this task was the same as his approach to finding Moshoeshoe: Providence would speak. On his arrival at the house of Dr Philip, one of the 'mulatto sons of Dr Read' took him to a shop to replace his tattered clothing. Behind the counter was a young lady, Sarah Dyke, whom Casalis married on 13 April 1836 and whom he called his 'second self'.

The fact that he now had a wife greatly pleased the Basotho, and Moshoeshoe in particular. 'You are a man now ... a man much better able to understand and to aid us ... [W]hen you rallied us about our polygamy we used to ask ourselves if it was not a little out of envy.'

Polygamy was one of the first issues about which the missionaries challenged Moshoeshoe. After a long discussion on the subject, Moshoeshoe said (according to Casalis, who does not react at all to the king's irony): 'Ah! polygamy; – you are attacking there a strong citadel: I greatly fear you will not be able to shake it, at least in our time ... [I]t took a long time to get the white men from whom you are descended to content themselves with one wife ... We will talk of this again. It is certainly annoying there should be this difference between you and us. Without that we should soon be Christians.'

After eight years of working among the Basotho, Casalis converted and baptized two of Moshoeshoe's wives. They immediately asked for divorce. The king refused, saying that these women would be treated as outcasts by the community if he consented, as there were no rules in place to protect or provide for them. This compelled Casalis to draft documents stating that in the event of divorce the women were allowed to keep the land they lived on, as well as their cattle. Only then did the king agree to the divorces.

Mrs Casalis, called Ma-Eugène by the congregation, brought a new dimension to the mission. Basotho women approached her more easily than they did the male missionaries, and she extended the ministry to teaching them to read and write, as well as how to administer first aid. Sarah Casalis proved a great help and comfort to her husband, who consistently writes about her in exalted terms.

Apart from studying Sesotho, the missionaries also recorded and classified the language into a grammatical system. Casalis was fascinated by the word the Basotho used for God: *Molimo*, which is composed of the prefix *mo*, which belongs to intelligent beings, combined with the word *holimo*, meaning 'in the sky'. *Mo-holimo* therefore translates as 'the intelligent being living in the sky', the one who has always been, who exists in an incomprehensible manner. Casalis concluded from this that the Basotho must have long had the concept of God in their framework of understanding: 'in spite of a universal perversion, which probably dates many centuries back, truth has reserved itself a witness in the vocabulary of these people'. The missionaries did not hesitate to adopt this venerable word and imbue it with Christian content.

Fifteen years after the missionaries' arrival, the Paris Evangelical Missionary Society had established nine stations and baptized more than 2000 Basotho. Their services were attended by 2300 people, and 600 pupils went to schools run by the missionaries' wives. Much of their success can be attributed to the fact that, whereas other African leaders barely tolerated missionaries, Moshoeshoe was the patron of the church.

chapter seven

Berlin: 8/9 October 2007

It was past midnight. My suitcases and overflowing hand luggage
were parked in the passage of the flat. I took off J.'s coat and scarf and
switched off the lights, sitting down on the nearest sofa to cool my
arms and my buzzing head for a while, releasing my swollen feet more
than twenty hours after boarding an aeroplane in Cape Town. I sat like
that, motionless, for a long time, feeling the frenzy of marking exams,
last-minute emails, frantic cellphone conversations, must-do lists,
precarious money matters, burglar alarm arrangements, insurance
payments, all slowly drain away from me.

I must have fallen asleep.

When I woke up, it was into a delirious autumn light. I got up and
stepped into the present tense: I am in Berlin.

The windows of my flat are thrust, like a glass tree-house, deep
among leaves of ochre, vermillion, mauve and dark copper.
Somewhere, behind it all, I have a sense of water shimmering,
bringing a dazzling feeling into the flat that is to be my home for the
next nine months, while I am here on a research fellowship.

My head is empty. Light. Memoryless. I stare into the autumn – as
one should stare into an autumn like this. On a patio below, red and
golden shawls of fallen leaves have been thrown on the garden furniture.

I open a door. The cold bites, yet inside it is warm. I'm sheltered. Unreachable. Safe. Inconspicuous. Looked after. Words I have not used for a long time. The windows are double-glazed, the front door can be locked twice, two soldiers sculpted from sandstone guard my study window with spears, heaters radiate throughout the flat, there's food in the fridge, a carpet under my feet.

The autumn glowing through the glass kitchen door is so beautifully fierce that, when I switch on the kettle, I feel as if I'm standing in a heart of fire. When the first smell of coffee rises from the filter, I think that my throat wants to burst with light and happiness, but what comes pouring out, unexpectedly, are harsh choking sounds of relief.

Liewe Ma

Disbelief! Total disbelief about where I am. Up until now, every visit to Europe has simply confirmed alienation, an irrefutable Africanness and, above all else, my Third World-ness. Until now. Poring for long hours over small scaffoldings of words seldom results in being wanted for nine months at a place like this, where one is supported by thirty other fellows, maintained, fed AND set free to do what one does best.

Spinning through my head is the word 'trust': I have never been so trusted and am battling to get rid of my South African habit of thinking like a criminal to pre-empt. E.g., the library is open twenty-four hours a day. One takes out a book by signing a card. Don't they realize how much one could steal? How family and friends could secretly live here in the library for many months on fruit and drink from the small coffee area, even reading newspapers and the *London Review of Books*. In fact, one could bring all the squatters from Cape Town and say, Go for it here!, and lots of everything would still be left in Berlin.

13 *October 2007*

I saw a piece (it's not a play as it has no characters; it's not a musical performance as it has no musicians) with the string mechanisms of three upright pianos, playing by themselves, three flat water basins (shifting and pouring water or paint), screens and speakers from which various languages and human sounds flowed. No linear progression. 'Every part of the piece evokes its own context,' the programme notes explained. I sat with a clearly avant-garde audience (next to me a man in bright yellow tails and yellow bowler hat ringed with mink), riveted for an hour. The next day I read that it takes three days for the piece to be set up, therefore it could be performed only once in Germany and not for three consecutive nights as in Switzerland, because the German unions do not allow theatre workers to work two or three nights in a row. The piece couldn't be developed in Germany, as the shift of theatre workers ends at three o'clock in the afternoon and a new shift would simply destroy a morning's carefully calibrated coherence.

18 *October 2007*

To get to Grunewald Station I have to cross the Hertha Lake via Hasensprung. This afternoon, suddenly, as if by a movie cue, two extraordinary large swans swam towards me as I stood on the little stone footbridge, their feathers touched into an ice-blue white by the wintry light, their necks arching as if they understood that it was exactly there, at the curve, where their eternal majestical beauty was embedded. For a few seconds they blessed me with this view, then gracefully turned around and swam away. I felt as if I was standing on holy ground.

The biggest privilege here is that one doesn't have to constantly reorganize one's priorities. At home I would think: I need to read this book, and finish marking that assignment, attend to my emails and then go to the university. Then a child arrives or a beggar comes to the door and you think, okay, I will first go and buy groceries, then do the emails, then go to the university ... Here all of that is taken care of.

I get up early. No newspaper, no radio, no television, no spouse to discuss anything with (in fact, this weekend I talked to absolutely nobody, from Friday to Monday lunch!). I start working, no cellphone – no one knows my number or new email address. Inside, the flat is warm, I see the individual autumnal seeds twirling down from the trees, I can follow up on references, I can check information as I am writing, I have time to rewrite, I can explore other options, other viewpoints. At half past twelve I am given food that I did not think about for a second; during my walks or at night I come up with ideas on how to explore further something I am working on. In the evenings I read African philosophy for two hours, German for an hour and then an hour of Thomas Mann before I go to bed. This whole weekend I read poetry and *Die Zeit*.

The best thing of all is that, for the first time since I was a student, I have time to daydream. I remember reading a book on creativity which said that daydreaming is crucial in order to discover the new. The creative brain has to have enough free time and space to test the connections between unlikely entities and concepts of the impossible.

Apart from clothes and an Afrikaans dictionary, I have brought nothing. My life here must be as completely different as possible from the one I left at home. (This, of course, can happen only because J. is looking after this left-behind life!) I sit for hours looking at the trees, listening to the stillness around me.

I can't remember when last I felt so safe, cared for and WANTED despite being white. I know we live a highly privileged life in South Africa, but I hadn't realized how harsh my life in reality had become. It is not because one can walk alone through Hasensprung at one o'clock in the morning without the slightest notion of fear, but because one is shielded from people who are poor, hungry and cold. I am protected in my flat from the poor. I see them only on a poster at the station. In Cape Town they are on my doorstep three or four times a day, at traffic lights, on the streets, on television, in the post, next to highways, near the office. The poor mark the most breathtaking vistas and the most desolate horizons in South Africa. Here, where I live in Berlin, the poor is a theory.

Liewe Ma
I bought groceries this morning and saw on the shelf: rhubarb yoghurt! Yes, Dr Oetkers Onken Joghurt mit Rhabarber-Vanille-Geschmack – Gutes aus Milch!
My new Gothic diet!
Your daughter Blodwyn Galswintha

CONVERSATION ONE
LINES OF FLIGHT

I am sitting opposite my discussant in one of the smaller sitting rooms at the Institute for Advanced Studies in Berlin. He is a philosopher and has kindly agreed to engage in a series of conversations with me about what I am trying to understand. He has many things in my eyes that should disqualify him as a possible discourse partner (white, male, teaching Western philosophy in Australia), but I have read a provocative paper he wrote on the concept of becoming-animal in J.M. Coetzee's novel *Disgrace*, and it is this concept of 'becoming' that I am interested in. Not becoming-animal or becoming-woman as in Coetzee's book, but becoming-black.

I explain to him that in order to understand something I have to write it; while writing – writingly, as it were – I find myself dissolving into, becoming towards what I am trying to understand.

'Tracing the lines of flight is what Deleuze calls it.' The professor is a translator of some of Deleuze's work.

'I am not fleeing! This is why I am having this discussion. I'm staying, but I want to understand with what I am staying.'

'Not flight as in fleeing, but flight as in going in a particular direction. One moves from an established known identity by transforming oneself. But transformation always moves in a particular direction and writing is often the best way to trace these directions. Expressed in different words: the aim of good writing is to carry life to the state of non-personal power.'

I quickly write this down on the cover of the thick manuscript file bearing words in bold letters inspired by *The Satanic Verses*: 'BEGGING TO BE BLACK'. The professor notices my blunt working title and responds somewhat curtly.

'Tracing lines of transformation is fine, but blackness/whiteness ...,' he says. 'You're not going the essentialist route, are you? A core that makes somebody white or black, or Jewish, or female?'

'No. And I am not busy with difference either, I think. I want to ask two questions. Firstly, I live in a country that for nearly four centuries was interpreted and organized via Western or European frameworks. Since 1994 I have lived with a black majority that asserts itself more and more confidently, as well as the many black people from the rest of Africa who stream into the country. So I find most of my references and many of my frameworks of understanding to be useless and redundant.'

'As in how?'

'As in how to understand the "reading" of Robert Mugabe both by the South African government and by the Zimbabweans themselves, for example. I do not want to have a Western perspective on Mugabe; I want an African perspective. I am trying to work out what that is. Is Thabo Mbeki's muteness the perspective, or is Archbishop Tutu's criticism the perspective, or the crowds who always cheer Mugabe? Or are these reactions all based on something else which makes them not contradictory, but moral and sensible but diverse interpretations of the same world view or philosophy?'

'Isn't that derogatory, at least to Tutu? You must remember that colonizers are always trying to "understand" the colonized in order to colonize and dehumanize them even more effectively. Are you not trying to understand so-called blackness as amoral, or a farce, or simply theatre, in order to keep an ingrained racism more sensitively and subtly alive?'

'I want to be part of the country I was born in. I need to know whether it is possible for somebody like me to become like the majority, to become "blacker?" and live as a full and at-ease component of the South African psyche.'

'Now what is an at-ease component?'

'If Angela Merkel or the Australian prime minister says something, you do not sit dumbfounded, thinking: God, where did that come from? There is a traceable logic from within your framework to understand, even if you passionately disagree with them, the most inane and gross comments even of George W. Bush. At times when my president, Thabo Mbeki, speaks, and he is an intelligent man, I sit like somebody in complete darkness. It's not necessarily that I don't understand what he is saying; I do not know *where* it is coming from, from within what logic it wants to assert itself as "right". I want to understand him and all the many utterances that daily try to turn me into a racist. It feels to me wrong to simply say, yes, we are now mos all liberated and equal, while in actual fact I have known only the white part of this new constellation. It is like saying: black people should now stop their nonsense and become like "the rest of the civilized world" – meaning they should become white. But, actually, black people are in the majority and it is I who should be moving towards a "state of non-personal power" within blackness.

'How do I "flee" towards black, to use your term, if I have never cared to know what black means? So my first question is this: is it possible for a white person like myself, born in Africa, raised in a culture with strong Western roots, drenched in a political dispensation that said black people were different and therefore inferior, whether it is possible for such a person as myself to move towards a "blackness" as black South Africans themselves understand it?'

'With all its hurts and Fanon-identified harms?'

'Yes. And then, secondly, I want to look at the way in which black people challenge Western paradigms that insist liberal values are the only possible framework for a modern state. If we ignore or gloss over this, is that not simply apartheid and colonization in a new guise?'

'Let's summarize: you accept that all life is changing, is becoming, that black people have been and still are profoundly affected by powerful influences from both inside and outside Africa. But you are saying: because you lived in this apartheid bubble which tried to keep itself whites-only and Western, that this has stunted your own changing and becoming?'

'Yes. So, I am not necessarily interested in African philosophy versus Western philosophy, but rather in what kind of self I should grow into in order to live a caring, useful and informed life – a "good life" – within my country in southern Africa.'

'Are you talking about a kind of entanglement?'

'No. It's not about mingling, or the entanglement of roots, but how one root can become or link to another.'

'A synapse.'

I smile. 'Perhaps that is the word.'

---

26 October 2007

'I want to understand German *Wurst* and German pork,' my brother says as he enters my flat in Berlin. He is still glowing robustly from the South African rugby triumph in Paris. I take him and his wife to the impressive foodstore KaDeWe, where he systematically works through the *Wursts* and hams. When the women behind the counter, concerned at this over-focused carnivorous attention, try to get him interested in *Kartoffeln oder Rotkohl*, he shakes his head emphatically and says: *'Nein. Fleisch!'*

28 October 2007

This morning I see that my electronic alarm clock has lost an hour: so much for buying cheap German electronics, I think. We dress quickly and rush to get to the Sunday-morning chamber music concert featuring Daniel Barenboim, but are blocked by a closed Unter den Linden Strasse. The street is covered in sand, and old coaches and people dressed in nineteenth-century costumes are parading past. My brother taps an official firmly on the shoulder; the man turns around and says somewhat reverentially: *'Effi Briest.'*

My brother turns to me. 'What the fuck is Effi Briest?' he asks, but not softly enough, because the official and the Germans around us look at him with borderless pity.

'A famous German novel,' I whisper, 'about a very young woman, a girl actually, forced into marriage. Her miserable affair and the pedantic morals of the time destroyed her.'

My brother rolls his eyes at the word pedantic, but I point at my watch: if they don't let us through we will be late, and we have already paid for the tickets! With a desensitized determination that would have made our apartheid forebears proud, my big, broad-shouldered brother breaks through the barriers of police, film people and crowd control and forces his way into the Staatsoper.

To our surprise there are hardly any people in the foyer, although we have been assured that the concert is sold out. I can't believe what I am seeing: the rubbish of the previous night's concert is still lying around. Good God, I think to myself, the Germans are falling apart right in front of my very eyes, but we storm through. At the final entry point a man stops us. 'You are too early,' he says calmly. 'It only starts at eleven o'clock.'

'Yes,' I retort sarcastically but with rising voice, 'it is now ten minutes *to* eleven; when do *you* think would be the appropriate time to enter?'

He grins as if to say, I got you! 'We are now in winter time. It's only ten to ten.'

We are stunned. Of course: they change the time here! We go to have tea at the Opernpalais, contemplating the influence it must have on a psyche to change time. What notions of relativity or other possibilities does it create when one realizes as a child that time can be changed? My brother snaps his fingers: like that!

Liewe Ma

Did you know that the Berlin municipality actually has an 'Autumn strategy'! As Berlin is the city with the most trees in Europe – 400 000 deciduous trees, spread over an area of 890 square kilometres – the city has 1 000 'leaf workers', each with a broom, working double shifts until December to gather the leaves 'as quickly as possible' (!). First the main arteries are cleaned, then the rest. People in orange overalls collect 100 000 square metres of leaves and fill the municipality's 350 vehicles with 2600 loads of potential compost. Special attention is given to moth-infested trees: they are cleaned thoroughly (one sees people shaking trees, using ladders and special sucking pipes), taking care that the contaminated leaves do not stay behind to spread the infection. This, yes, is where I am living.

Liewe Ma

I am quite a phenomenon in the German class for speaking long fluid comprehensible sentences (based on Afrikaans vocabulary and word order) but with every single word wrong in terms of gender, tense and case-ending. Cannot help wondering what effect such a complex structured language has on a child's IQ. Read yesterday a sentence in a newspaper consisting of seven sub-clauses. Quite normal, says the German teacher. One can do it because the gender, tense and case throw up little red flags in every clause to indicate time, gender and subject. Many of these sentences would not be possible in English, and my Afrikaans translation ground to a halt when I reached about the third sub-clause. But it is such a beautiful language. I made a literal trans-lation of what you described to me as probably the best-known poem in German: 'Autumn Day' by Rainer Maria Rilke:

> God: it is time. The summer was enormous.
> Lay down your shadows on the sunhours (sundial),
> And on the plains, let the winds run loose.
> ...
> Whoever has no house will not build one any more.
> Whoever is alone now will stay alone for long,
> Will wait, read, write endless letters
> And will wander through the streets
> Restlessly, as the dry leaves are driven.

I saw part of this poem in a newspaper advertisement for home loans. Do we have any poem in South Africa that would speak to all of us about houses? Would any advertisement use good poetry?

4 November 2007

Every Tuesday we have a colloquium presented by one of the fellows. Today somebody spoke about ageing and evolution. Some interesting remarks:
- Humans are the only primate that ages so visibly.
- Human females are the only primates that do not die when they are no longer fertile.
- In America black people die 5 per cent earlier than whites. Such a constant difference cannot be blamed entirely on financial circumstances. Man's body has the capacity to look after itself. It regulates its resources so that your heart pumps, the virus you have just breathed in is blocked, you remember to change gears, look in the rear-view mirror, stop at the traffic lights, etc. But when a person is under constant psychological stress, the body becomes so busy dealing with that that it doesn't have extra resources to scan itself for harmful cells. Could this mean that black Americans experience more stress than whites do?

Questions and remarks are thrown at the fellow. Research has shown that stress is good, one of the scientists says. Rats that are shocked at regular intervals live much longer than rats that are never shocked. Rats that are irregularly shocked have the shortest lifespan. Apparently the people who live longest are professionals with executive stress.

Liewe Ma

If only you could have been here last night. Or rather: if you could have been my German teacher again and read to us in that dusty classroom with enormous clouds gathering far out over the plains: '*Kennst du das Land, wo die Zitronen blühn.*' I remember how strange your mouth became when forming the words '*Im dunkeln Laub die Gold-Orangen glühn.*' I can still hear the strong aspiration of the h-sound in your throat: '*Die Myrthe still und hoch der Lorbeer steht?*'

But it was when you read '*Es schwindelt mir, es brennt / Mein Eingeweide. Nur wer die Sehnsucht kennt, / weiß, was ich leide!*' that something else, something *unbestimmt* entered your voice, something that made my body, as young as I was, turn cold, a sound that I never heard from you ever again, but maybe am spending a lifetime now finding its source for you. Your daughter.

CONVERSATION TWO
PETRUS'S STORY

Transcribing a conversation makes one acutely aware of how often and how easily people talk past each other, of how a discussion can drift along and then suddenly hit upon a crisp and powerful interactive patch, only to loosen up again, to meander on, as if preparing for the next moment of entanglement. I transcribe the words of the professor:

'Before you continue I want to make a few comments, if I may. If Deleuze forms the context of our discussion, then we have dealt with essentialism and difference in this sense: plants and animals, inside and outside, and even organic and inorganic, cannot really be told apart. All these things are themselves, *yet* on another level they are transforming towards one another. Things continue to become the other, while continuing to be what they are, if you understand what I mean.'

'Are transformation and becoming then the same for him?'

'Deleuze uses several words: multiplicity, for example, which is already a process of becoming-other, but I think becoming-minor is the most accurate. Minor in terms of becoming-child, becoming-animal, becoming-woman, becoming-black.'

'But I think I am trying to do the opposite. I am not trying to become-minor, because black is not minor in my country. And although there is a global, largely Western world view that everybody has to function in, within the country itself I feel a presence that is overwhelmingly black, and I don't want to flee or retreat into whiteness; I want to change towards what I am becoming aware of. I don't want to formulate my life as J.M. Coetzee's Lurie does in *Disgrace*: "Too close, he thinks: we live too close to Petrus. It is like sharing a house with strangers, sharing noises, sharing smells.'"

'All becoming is minoritarian, because you diverge from the standard or norm which defines the majority. In other words, becoming-majoritarian is not *becoming* in the real sense of the word.'

'Are you suggesting that my interest in becoming-black is precisely because black is, despite majority rule and a majority black continent, still a minority?'

'Minority in this sense has nothing to do with quantity. It is argued that the majority is represented by the "standard", and that is always the adult-white-heterosexual-European-male-speaking-a-standard-European-language. Although there are, for example, more females in the world, men appear twice: once in the standard and once in the group from which the standard is extracted.'

'So why should one then want to become black and part of a non-standard minority?'

'Many women, children and black men want to become the standard and therefore never present in themselves real change. But others are constantly refiguring the standard through inventing in a piecemeal way new forms of life and different modes of existence. They believe that these different forms of minority-becoming provide the impulse for change to a fairer dispensation. Deleuze says that it is precisely these desires for new pivots that eventually carry the potential for "new earths and peoples unlike those found in existing democracies".'

'I'm suddenly reminded that Njabulo Ndebele said that white people in South Africa have a unique opportunity to remove themselves from under the umbrella of the international sanctity of the white body and share the vulnerability of the black body. But still, in order to do that, I need to understand ultimately the vulnerability of the black body.'

'I think you have established some solid lines. You have formed a pact, a certain kind of relationship between yourself and what you want to become towards. So you could begin to move beyond your given state of being and form an inter-individual assembly or assemblage. One is defined by one's capacity to affect and be affected by what amounts to the other side of the pact.'

'In order to move, one needs to know in what direction. How does one know the other side of the pact?'

'By listening. To stories, to others.'

'Are stories good enough?'

'Stories have different characters and threads and plots; they leave space for variety. Stories are boundary crossings, making it possible to move, justifying different kinds of behaviour and also behaviour that is not necessarily justified – no single line holds things together, because the spaces contain contradictions in which one variety is as valid as the other.'

'Going back to *Disgrace*. I am reminded of those haunting sentences by Lurie about Petrus's side of the story. "Doubtless Petrus has been through a lot, doubtless he has a story to tell. He would not mind hearing Petrus's story one day. But preferably not reduced to English. More and more he is convinced that English is an unfit medium for the truth of South Africa."'

'As an Afrikaans-speaker, what do you say about that?'

'I think it is an important moment in our discussion. I think I can now formulate what I am trying to say: Petrus is indeed telling his story all around me, but his choice was long ago removed to tell it in a language other than English. English has become the language that confirms and judges our existence and the quality and weight thereof. But Lurie is right; this is absolutely the problem: English cannot tell the truth of South Africa, because the language itself imposes a particular framework in which what Petrus is saying about himself cannot be heard. Although Petrus may assert the right to exist in English as told by himself, his story, his relationship with his family and the moral content of their raping, plundering and caring, is relentlessly framed and interpreted by that which forms the fibre of English. So Petrus's story, Sunday after Sunday in the newspapers, is framed as one of deep-seated, mindless, generic corruption, rung through with indigenous howls like: Why would we throw a loyal cadre to the dogs …, We will kill for Zuma …, We didn't join the struggle to stay poor … – but these are not read within the assumption that Petrus has a story that he is telling within his frame-work, but as indicators of the devastating depth of his depravity.'

'So what is Petrus's story?'

'I hear Petrus saying: I function within an ethic that is communal to the core. The benefit to the community, whether they are the living, the living-dead or the still-to-come, is what determines whether something is good or bad. The deed is not per se good or bad – it depends on who the community is and what and for whom the benefits are. A deed is not intrinsically wrong; its rightness or wrongness depends on who does it to whom and from which level of status. But I, Petrus, am being held captive within an ethic that is individual and Christian-based to the core. Confined by these bars, scorched by this relentless interpretative gaze, I drive along the road with this resentful Professor Lurie next to me, smug within the belief that what he believes in is the only right belief. I speak to him, I lift one sentence after the other up towards him, alive with formulations on the complexities of caring within a globalized commu-nity, but behind his ears he wrings their necks and throws them on the enormous trash heap in his head of African failures.'

PART TWO

*Understandings,
Assumed Understandings
and Non-Understandings*

———

chapter eight

One of the many misinterpretations of Moshoeshoe's words by the missionaries concerned his request that the Basotho assistants at the mission station, including his two sons, should not be paid for the work they were doing.

> 'If you do,' said he, 'you will spoil everything. They will forget that you are our benefactors, that you are here not for your advantage, but for ours; and they will end by demanding that I also shall pay them when I want them to do anything for me.' This last word was quite a revelation to us. On making inquiries, we found that the natives, though great bargain-makers in matters of sale or purchase, did not recognise manual labour as having any price.

This small paragraph about work in exchange for monetary payment touches upon one of the most profound and destructive initial differences between colonizers and colonized. Moshoeshoe's request was interpreted as that of a king who expected his people to work for him for free, and of course the missionaries, claimed Casalis, would and could never be *that* exploitative. It also posed a dilemma: how could their self-sacrificial offer, that they would look after themselves – one of the first things they promised Moshoeshoe – impress the king and his people if this very pagan community already had a notion of 'building' oneself through voluntary labour?

Over many years, African philosophers have pointed out that person-hood in a communitarian African world view is not bestowed on some-one simply through birth. Who you are, what and how you are, is built by you over the years of your life through caring interconnectedness. This is significantly captured in Sesotho vocabulary, in which a human being is made up of body/*mmele* and two souls: *moya* (soul) and *seriti* (spirit). *Seriti* is what makes one human; the image that you see when you dream of someone is their *seriti*. It is located in one's personality and dignity and must be continuously protected and strengthened through 'building', which can be achieved by working in ways that benefit the community.

In the Setswana poem 'Sempe a Lešoboro', by M.O.M. Seboni and E.P. Lekhela, the speaker says: 'Mme, I'm being killed by this man-changing thing; / I am killed by this ox called work.' ('*Mma, ke bolawa ke ditšhentšha banna; / Nna ke bolawa ke kgomo ya pereko.*') This is the cry of a young man who feels that the work he is doing dehumanizes him, not because it is hard work, but because it does not build his *seriti* – he has learnt, like the white man mentioned elsewhere in the poem, to do as little work as possible in exchange for as much money as possible. At the end of the poem he buys himself a calf in order to 'humanize' the money he earned.

Was Moshoeshoe concerned that working for money would make his sons spiritually dead for the Basotho community? Some chapters later Casalis indeed notes that he observed a different work ethic among the Basotho, but in his eyes this system thwarted progress: 'When it was wanted, they would ask for a helping hand from their neighbours, as, for instance, in building a hut, in finishing their sowings, or getting in crops which might be a little late. It was understood that the same services would be rendered in return when required … At first sight we were reminded almost of the golden age; but there was here, after all, no element of progress. By following these customs … [i]t would be impossible to create workers capable of aspiring after anything better than the first necessaries, impossible to establish trades, to create industries.'

These non-understandings stretched into other areas as well. When Emma, Casalis' eldest daughter, died of measles, Moshoeshoe sent a request that she should not be buried until he had seen her corpse. Before the coffin was closed, he interpreted the trouble the family took in adorning the little girl as a sign that, like the Basotho, the missionaries also did things to accompany the body to the 'other side': 'We see that you believe that Emma will rise again, and that death is but a stream that man crosses to go to God.'

Shortly after Emma's death, one of Moshoeshoe's main wives, Mantsane, also fell ill with measles and gave premature birth to a lifeless baby. Grief-stricken and in a fit of delirium, she jumped down the cliffs of Thaba-Bosiu to her death. Casalis was immediately summoned by the king, because 'this day of mourning would probably be a day of strife also'.

It became, in fact, the day the king was forced to choose between his followers and Casalis. The prominent Fokeng family of the deceased wife (of which one of his senior councillors, RaTšui, was a member) were strong opponents of the missionaries' teachings and wanted her to be buried in the traditional Basotho way. A thousand oxen had been assembled at the appointed place, and a grave had been prepared at the wall of the cattle kraal, in which she would be buried in a sitting position. Moshoeshoe, draped in a heavy kaross, asked Casalis to conduct the funeral, but the missionary, who had set a Christian cemetery aside some time before, refused: 'I should be unfaithful to my Master if I acceded to your desires.'

The angry family demanded that the funeral should take place according to traditional customs. 'On what are these customs founded?' Moshoeshoe demanded of them. 'I should like to see the book where they are enjoined: the Missionaries give us the reason for all they do. Man dies, because he has received in Adam the seed of death; the dead should be buried in the same place, because it is a beautiful thought that they lie together in the long sleep of death. Man is only alone as long as he remains in his mother's womb; when he sees the light of day he clings to the breast of her who has given him birth, and from that time he lives in the society of his fellows.' Without responding to the innovative manner in which Moshoeshoe embedded the new teachings within a communal way of being, Casalis records the family's response: 'We are silent, because we will not yield.'

Challenged to argue the point, they said: 'We will speak, when the Missionary is gone.' This angered Moshoeshoe, and he ordered the traditional pit to be refilled. According to Casalis, Moshoeshoe then turned to him: 'You have conquered: the wife I mourn shall go and sleep with Tseniei, and I, also, will one day rest with them.' He was referring to the first convert to be buried in the Christian cemetery. During the singing of the last hymn at the funeral, Moshoeshoe's father, 'greatly incensed by the departure from the customs of the nation', burst from the crowd and demanded that Casalis be put to death. Moshoeshoe managed to defuse the conflict.

Over time the confrontations between the missionaries and sections of the Basotho – with the king caught in the middle – became sharper as the missionaries attempted to gain control over the terms of the relationship. Moshoeshoe, aware that the gospel came with potentially harmful as well as advantageous results, tried to control the space within which the missionaries worked, but, as they became more and more secure, he had no effective recourse as they framed their own instructions, not in accordance with the will of the king, or accommodating the Basotho in general, but in accordance with the will of an Almighty God.

Moshoeshoe seems not to have got on as well with Arbousset as he did with Casalis. The young missionary expressed less admiration for the king's qualities than Casalis did, and in his account of his time in Basotholand he records a greater number of open clashes. On one occasion he brought some guests to Thaba-Bosiu, where Moshoeshoe received them 'in a state of semi-nakedness', which was frowned upon so clearly that Moshoeshoe withdrew apologetically and changed into European clothing. The king got his own back, though. Arbousset and his fellows were summoned to Moshoeshoe's stone house, to a room filled with his councillors, where it became unbearably hot – 'heavy with the fetid reek of sweaty bodies' – but when one of the white men, feeling faint, suggested that the meeting be held outside in the *kgotla*, the place of assembly, Moshoeshoe refused.

Having heard of the magnificent waterfall and rock formations deep in the Blue Mountains (as the western foothills of the Maluti were called), the young Arbousset decided in 1840 to explore other parts of the kingdom. Moshoeshoe, always hungry for more knowledge, joined him. In his account of this excursion, Arbousset records several remarks by the king, and because the words attributed to Moshoeshoe differ so profoundly from those of the missionary, both in tone and structure, one has the feeling of being closer than ever to what the king actually said.

On the journey the two men climbed the Pulane Mountain, where they sat on an enormous rock and observed the vast landscape, Thaba-Bosiu just 'a smudge lost in the sky'. Moshoeshoe 'exclaimed painfully' that during the lifetime of his mentor, Mohlomi, 'these fertile and spacious valleys were covered with men, just as they are today covered with stones. War, that is the great evil of this country!' Arbousset then writes: 'After having spoken in this manner, the son of Mokhachane brought his hand over his eyes and kept a deep silence.'

Because everybody was now quiet, Arbousset used the opportunity to admonish Moshoeshoe about the evil hearts of men, which had caused these wars. The country where Mohlomi had ruled was now empty, he said, because one 'horde' said they wanted to be the only master, and then another 'horde' said, no, *they* wanted to be the only master. Ignoring centuries of European wars, not to mention the wars started recently by white men in southern Africa, Arbousset argued that when a man gives his heart to God, he becomes less selfish and more prepared to share. After holding forth with words that fill half a page, the missionary gave Moshoeshoe, his eyes still covered by his hand, a chance to speak.

> Shaking off his drowsiness, Moshoeshoe raised his head. He again let his eyes wander over the plain, and he spoke more or less as follows, as if he wished to recite poetry, although it was only history:

'My friends,' he said, 'works that are produced by mortal hands will themselves also perish: works created by hands that do not grow old, remain. These skies have not changed; over there the famous mount Hlohloloane [near today's Clocolan] rests still on its original base; and between it and ourselves, the Phuthsiatsana river winds today as it has always done. Is the grass in the valleys less green this year than the previous year, or are the waters of our springs less sweet and less good?... Mohlomi was a great king, a wise and gentle king; under his government, men grew like the grass; they were as numberless as the animals of the fields. He has faded away; a deluge of Matebele swept over his people. Oh, what an unfortunate country ours is! The tempest struck the father, and the flood of waters carried away the mother and her child. See in the distance the shadow of the clouds blown by the wind: it ascends, it draws near, it is before our eyes, it has passed; and there another shadow of cloud rises from the horizon: it scuds along, floats, and passes away; it is the picture of our tribes. Did our ancestors know that their dwellings would remain widowed after them, or did they foresee that their great-nephews would tear the flesh of their fellow men with their teeth? Did they know that white men existed? Would Peete (Moshoeshoe's grandfather) believe his eyes if he came out of hell right now and saw that man sitting beside us, and heard him speaking in our language about a thousand things that are all true, but new?'

One may wonder whether Moshoeshoe would so easily have consigned his beloved grandfather to 'hell', but this monologue, despite certain fingerprints of Arbousset's, reaches a poetic quality and philosophical contemplativeness that the missionary himself rarely accomplishes in his narrative. Moshoeshoe's anxiety breaks through all the entanglements of time and space as he expresses his deepest awareness of the mortality of humanity, its deeds and its wisdom. He articulates how humanity short-sightedly seeks only destruction, unaware of and uninformed about the beauty of an immortal universe.

A few pages further in his account, Arbousset notes in a remarkable sentence, mixing compliment with insult, how peacefully the Bamokotedi clan chose Moshoeshoe's father, Mokhachane, as chief instead of the rightful elder brother. 'In any other country, endless wars would have followed; but here, where no-one fights a war for a principle, the outcome seemed natural.'

During the journey, one evening around the fire, Molapo, one of the men accompanying them, formulated succinctly the destabilizing effects of what is today termed the colonial gaze: 'I am ashamed of myself in front of my moruti: I am also ashamed of myself when I am alone; sometime[s] his word kills me.' In reply, Moshoeshoe provided an extraordinary philosophical analysis: 'When a man is alone, there is council within him; a feeling occurs, then another; it is a real meeting of consciences (*pitso e matsoalo*). An utterance which I have heard for a long time from the lips of my white man comes back to my memory sometimes when I go to bed, and it occupies me for part of the night: does the soul like sleep? its sleep is thought.' This description of the self, in conversation or 'in council' with the self, could have stepped out of the philosophy of Socrates and later Immanuel Kant and Hannah Arendt.

In his narrative Arbousset recorded a public clash between himself and the king. One day, when he went to Thaba-Bosiu to preach, he found Moshoeshoe in his most distant hut in the midst of a circle of his subjects.

A young woman stood before him, sad, silent, and yet resolute and assured. The chief spoke to her in a rather excited way, and I heard him say to her two or three times: 'You have done wrong.' I asked someone who the woman was, and I was told: 'It is the wife of one of the BaTlauka [Bahlanka] of the King.' 'And what has she done?' I continued. 'Her husband is dead, he has left a child, and she wants to keep it, but Moschesch claims it.' I then listened more carefully, and I heard the following debate. 'Mother of Maklobo,' said the MoSotho king to the young woman, 'who is your mother?' 'So and so.' 'And your father?' 'Letsebele.' 'Who married you to your man?' 'You, my Lord.' 'And to whom belongs the child whom that man has given you?' 'To whom else but to me, because you married me to my husband

and not to my child,' replied the poor woman, and the conversation ceased for a moment.

Soon afterwards, it started again. Moschesch, perceiving that I was by his side, was embarrassed; he did not want me to speak, because he knew well what my feeling would be about this difference. But I believed it was my duty to speak, raising my voice to make myself heard: 'You, woman, keep silent,' I said to the MoSotho, 'and you, Moschesch, listen; I too want to add a few words.' There was silence. 'Son of Mokhachane,' I then said to the chief, 'You have married this woman to one of your BaTlauka [Bahlanka]?' 'Yes.' 'That's good. And the MoTlauka [Mohlanka] is dead?' 'Yes.' 'According to the law of the BaSotho,' I continued, 'this child should belong to you?' 'Yes.' 'But this is a hard custom, very hard. According to the law of the whites, when a husband dies, leaving children, if the mother survives him, the children belong to her and she has the right to enjoy them.' 'But that is not our custom.' 'I know that, but your custom is very cruel. Indeed, who suffered the pains of birth to bring this child into the world? Moschesch or this woman? And who suckled it, and who took care of it?' 'Sir,' replied the king, 'it is I who nourished the mother *and* the child *and* the father, with the milk of my cows.' 'That's very good; you've acted like a good chief, you've shown yourself to be their father. But now your MoTlauka is dead, your cows have been returned to you, this woman has only her child left.' 'He's not hers, he belongs to me.' 'But once more, is he the son of your womb?' Upon hearing that argument, the MoSotho king began to laugh and I kept quiet.

However, the matter did not end there. Soon the dispute started again, but I no longer took part. On both sides people get hot and excited; one of the friends of the widow takes her part and speaks rather lengthily in her favour, when suddenly Moschesch violently throws a stone at him, hurls himself on him across the crowd, batters his body and tries to kill him, which he would have done except for some friends of the wretch who pull him from his clutches and drag him outside; but their chief follows them, and I am left alone with a son of the king, not knowing what to do. He, frightened by the cries, says to me: 'Go, sir, stop my father, he will kill that man.' I then work my way through the crowd, I reach the chief. 'See, Moschesch, you the king, the father of the BaSotho, see what you are doing.' At that moment, the hapless man is taken away by his relatives; but the chief still follows them armed with stones (for Moschesch, more than any other person, does not know himself when he is in a temper); then however he returns on his tracks, agitated, eyes flaming, altogether beside himself. Unhappily he finds the young widow who was flee-ing. He throws her a severe look, and points her to the entrance of the hut, then he seizes a stick to hit her. The poor woman offers these few words as her sole defence: 'Calm yourself, my father,' and she glides promptly into the hut, where Moschesch strikes her twice in the back with the stick, until finally I tear it from his hands, crying to him: 'Moschesch, Moschesch, what are you doing?'

Making provision for biased perspectives from either side, this is a dis-turbing scene which shows the king resembling as never before the young boy who murdered those who refused to obey him. On the other hand, Moshoeshoe must have been immensely irritated by the presence of Arbousset, the white all-judging ear, as well as by the interference of the church in matters of governance. Arbousset was not only mimicking the way the king was speaking to one of his underlings, saying 'you, Moschesch, listen', but was also openly challenging his authority in front of his people. Even more problematic was the way in which he com-pared Basotho custom unfavourably to white people's law, describing it as cruel, blissfully ignoring the abuse of children and colonized people under the very same white man's nineteenth-century law.

It was clear that clashes between two distinct world views were becom-ing increasingly unavoidable. What was the content of these two 'distinct world maps'? According to anthropologists John and Jean Comaroff, Western culture saw matter as neutral and man as the prime mover in his interaction with his surroundings, while the Basotho continued to speak openly of a world, 'connected and continuous', in which the inert has the ability to affect the lives of the living.

The Basotho had contact with many other indigenous groups, but meeting Xhosas or Zulus simply confirmed that the world was populated by different peoples with their own value systems, spirits and proven knowledge. Meeting the missionaries and witnessing the zeal with which they asserted their message, the Basotho were confronted with the unfamiliar view that there could be only one 'true' way of knowing and classifying the world.

Moshoeshoe spent many hours explaining to the missionaries the sensible value of customs like polygamy, lobola, initiation and rain-making in weaving a community together, but he always came up against the whites' inflexible belief that the Western way was the only worthy way of living on earth. Those outside this 'true' way were inferior. They *could* enter the privileged domain through conversion, but black people quickly realized that conversion made them 'like whites' but never equal to whites.

This is perhaps on the deepest level the reason why Moshoeshoe refused to be converted. He demanded to live intelligently within his world view, while at the same time claiming the freedom to move confidently into other world views when and how he saw fit. Becoming a Christian would not only give the missionaries power over him, but would force him to admit that the Western way was the only 'true' approach to life. He would then have to accept the judgements of these two somewhat self-righteous youngsters on his life, kingdom, rulings and philosophy, while he would for ever remain a stranger to them within their framework. By refusing to convert and thereby accept their belief system as the only valid one, he prevented the missionaries from projecting him as their sinful opponent to be transformed into a lower and 'guileless variant' of themselves.

Moshoeshoe defied conversion, but he engaged in the missionary sphere with confidence and curiosity; many of his people resisted in more sullen ways. Among those taunting the intruders were the powerful presences of the king's father, Mokhachane, his brother Libe, and some of the king's senior councillors. Casalis records how Mokhachane would publicly scoff at their words or would 'amuse himself by pinching our noses and ears ... till Moshesh at length became indignant; and ... turned the conversation on the subject of reading. "Lies! Lies!" cried the stubborn old man. "I will never believe that words can become visible."' Moshoeshoe asked some of the best readers to withdraw and told Mokhachane to think of something and tell him what it was. Casalis wrote its name in the sand and, to the utter astonishment of the old man, when they were recalled the village scholars 'read the marks on the sand'. Casalis mentions how people overwhelmed the missionaries with demands to be taught how to read.

On the face of it one might think that the missionaries were succeeding, but the Basotho were clearly much more interested in the practical advantages of missionary teachings than in conversion. They resisted preaching by leaving the village for the mountains the moment a preacher arrived, or by dancing and singing in the traditional way, which they knew the missionaries detested. Some would openly carry out rituals such as sacrificing sheep. Casalis ruefully records that some Basotho accused the missionaries of cannibalism for eating and drinking the body and blood of Christ.

Protest also came from Moshoeshoe's favourite diviner, Tsapi, who presented such a forceful artistic expression of his concern one day that it must have shocked and haunted everybody on Thaba-Bosiu. He painted half his body white with clay and half black with carbon. Then he approached the palace shouting that Peete and the recently deceased 'Mamohato had appeared to him. While Peete had wrestled him down, the old man had given him a message for Moshoeshoe: 'The children of Thaba Bosiu die because Moshoeshoe is polluted and because the school of the *Moruti* [missionary] and the evening prayers offend the *Barimo* [ancestral shades].'

Casalis' account of this event is peculiar. True to his theological training, he usually provides an interpretation of whatever he describes. His memoirs were, after all, an attempt to inform the French- and English-speaking worlds about the lives of the Basotho. Tsapi's demonstration, however, is presented without any commentary or any attempt to assist Moshoeshoe in dealing with such a strong message from the ancestors.

Initially I assumed that Casalis, secure in his link to the king, simply found the incident harmless, but while I was working in the archives at Morija, a telephone conversation floated down the corridor: 'Research suggests that, but I will not say it on national television ... Why would I want to besmirch the founder of my nation?'

I felt my stomach churn. Although I hadn't thought about it for years, I knew immediately what they were talking about: oral evidence suggesting that Moshoeshoe killed 'Mamohato. I remember how, when I first read this claim, my brain simply jettisoned it. It is not and cannot be true. Oral sources say that when Moshoeshoe returned from an expedition, he found that too close a relationship had developed between his first wife and a commanding officer in his army. The king beat 'Mamohato so severely that she fell ill and died some time afterwards.

Why are both Casalis and Arbousset silent about this? Is it not a mere oral conflation of the beating described by Arbousset and the wives who died after childbirth or measles? Some researchers suggest that the killing of 'Mamohato was deliberately kept away from the missionaries, but within a society split among believers, non-believers and an unconverted king, it is highly unlikely that news of that kind would not reach the Sesotho-speaking missionaries.

If the oral evidence is correct and the missionaries did know, then Casalis' exposition without interpretation of the event makes sense. The two voices speaking through Tsapi are significant: a man eaten by the biggest abomination the Basotho had ever produced, and a woman killed by the best the Basotho had ever produced. Peete's message to his grandson was clear: You, who are our best, have become polluted by the missionaries. You have angered the ancestors. In a way Casalis need not say anything more: he perhaps also thought that the king was polluted, but by Basotho tradition.

That night in Morija I reread the words that Moshoeshoe spoke to Casalis years later, at the funeral of the missionary's wife: 'Today you are a man ... you know all the trials through which a man may pass ... You believe that because Moshesh is a polygamist he cannot understand what you suffer. For me there has never been but one woman, and since

Mamohato left me [died], I walk as a solitary man in the midst of the crowd.' At this point, according to the memoirs of Casalis' daughter, Adèle, the king started to sob loudly. Why would Casalis not mention this in his memoirs? Unless he found the link the king made at the funeral, between grieving for one's 'other half' and grieving for the woman whom one killed, too unbearable to contemplate.

chapter nine

Liewe Ma

When I have my four o'clock coffee, it is pitch-dark outside. One starts to appreciate the rituals that Europeans have created to make their long, dark winters bearable.

Last week, after Berlin opened its impressive museums for free one night, historian Philipp Blom pointed out that Western culture has entered a phase in which it honours the old simply because it is old. Earlier, he wrote in *Die Zeit*, museums were places where one could go for the new and the strange, from exotic animals to dragons and scientific discoveries.

But from the nineteenth century museums became obsessed with classification. Curators were appointed and everything had to be classified and labelled. The wonderful, the inexplicable, was banned. 'We have lost our borderless belief in culture and soul. It was effectively murdered in Auschwitz, the Gulag, in Vietnam,' Blom writes. 'We no longer believe in the reign of the soul or in beauty. The middle classes have triumphed, a class without end.' The word 'antique' entered the German language only during the middle of the nineteenth century, and the desire to display the uncategorized was lost. 'We are anxious about climate change and see in every old soup ladle the imprint of an intact world,'

Blom says. While rainforests disappear, walls of the Renaissance are restored. 'We would not ask Frank Gehry to build a computer-generated steel façade for the Cathedral of Chartres ... No, we stand like the team of worried scientists around Lenin's embalmed body: this mummy, all covered in make-up and pumped up with chemicals, is our proof that our genial epoch did exist once upon a time.'

Even in the Louvre, Blom says, one finds helpful directions towards the Mona Lisa and the Venus de Milo; the rest of the artworks are mere background to the way of salvation. 'It would make more sense to take the Mona Lisa directly to the Disney World in Paris and save the many tourists the troublesome detour.' He begs Berliners to rediscover the link between creativity and mortality.

Imagine, dear Mother, such an article over three pages in the *Sunday Times*!

Liewe Ma

Did you know that the biggest Northern Sotho department in the world is at Humboldt University in Berlin and run by a beautiful young Afrikaner woman? I attended an event at the modern South African embassy where her students did a presentation of their research visit to Northern Sotho regions. Blond, energetic, innovative, fluent in Northern Sotho, they showed films, sang songs, danced. The black man next to me whispered: What on earth do they think they can *do* with this language? When asked this during interval, the students looked surprised: Research, translation; did we not know that an exceptionally large collection of documents by Northern Sotho missionaries is here in Berlin, still to be properly looked at and digitalized? The Lesotho ambassador was also there and invited me to a reception for the Basotho queen 'Masenate Seeiso, the wife of King Letsie III.

Liewe Ma

Do you know that pedestrians here actually *wait* for the green man to flash, even when there is not a single car on the horizon? Is this the meaning of a law-abiding citizen? I find myself in petrifying angst at traffic lights: if I wait, I feel completely illogical; if I cross while it is red (and there are no cars), I feel the eyes of the Germans bore into my back: Go on, you Third World scoundrel, this is why you and your ilk are in such a moral quagmire.

Yesterday I went for a haircut in Schlüterstrasse. Without appointment. Yes, said the man at reception, disapproving of such an oversight, there was still *one* place open – he emphasized the singular number with a transparent forefinger. I was shown to a chair. A young, nerdy man who looked as if he had been cultivated under corrugated iron walked up to me and gave me a firm handshake. Stressed out and over-controlled, his movements seemed as if somebody had just given him therapy: Come on, shake her hand, you can do it, come on! But then it happened that even the woman who washed my hair introduced herself with a firm handshake. Anyway, Mr Neurotic put his fingers through my hair: 'Zu dick, it is zu dick at ze back. It looks unsophisticated.' I sat there, astounded. A hairdresser with a vocabulary! Then he meticulously clipped a leather pouch with his tools to a small stainless-steel table, put on a leather apron (perhaps he is a closet blacksmith!), took out a pair of scissors as small as my thumb, and before my eyes, indeed, unsophisticated became hypertensely sophisticated. The procedure was painful. A comb slipped out of his hands; he picked it up with a tissue and threw it away. He used a tape measure to measure the distance from my shoulders to my hair. He removed cut hair from my jersey with tweezers.

Liewe Ma

I discovered a shop that states blatantly: We only stock excellence. Not mincing matters, a pamphlet says that they are not interested in 'Biohandel', omitting certain old-fashioned ingredients because they are regarded as not 'green' enough, and pretending that mediocre is excellent. The shop stocks only the 'hallmarked, the authentic in the true sense of the word: that which is good, proper (*ordentlich*), belonging and familiar, sedate and filled with integrity ... For us it is not about the false appearance of animal-protecting, eco-friendly, landscape-beautifying, workshopped insight', but about the preserving of qualitative difference based on the multiplicity of cultural activities. The shop expresses its concern that the 'strangling net' of so-called harmless products in the end will smother the subtle differences brought about by living one's life in a way that is as unique as one's fingerprint.

Jirre, Ma! One may be ambivalent about the sentiment but the articulation is fantastic. Is it because the majority of South Africans function in our second or third languages that one never comes across this kind of succinct and imaginative articulation? Is it because our lives are not fed by a rooted literature of quality built up over centuries encompassing all variety that we express ourselves best in dance? (I'm reading Goethe's *Faust* – in German, with an English version for reference, and I keep on thinking: when this man wrote this immense work exploring the content of evil, questioning the existence of God and ignoring Jesus, my forefathers were draying around in southern Africa in ox wagons.)

Anyway, I bought a pencil of cedar wood at the shop, a toothbrush of pig hair (wondering what our germ-obsessed grandma would say about her grandchild, not removing, but actually *putting* pig hair in her mouth), a vest of camel hair, and soap made by nuns living in lavender fields. This was put in a bag on which was written: *Es gibt Sie noch, die guten Dinge* (One does still get them, the good things).

CONVERSATION 3
IMAGING BLACK

'I don't think I know how to talk about social imaginings. I think I am experiencing a racial awareness crisis. Whereas I can imagine myself poor, ill, scared, beautiful, strange, powerful, I can't even *begin* to imagine myself black. Why is that? One stood up against apartheid because one believed that all people shared a common humanity and that discrimination was wrong. In other words, I think I can imagine the indignity and hurt and empathize with that, but I can't imagine the being-blackness.'

'Do you know or suspect why that may be the case?'

'Part of me is terrified that it is an indication that, somewhere, somehow, the residues of as yet unrecognized reflexes of racism are still smouldering. That I cannot imagine myself black because I actually despise black.'

'You suggest that to imagine yourself black would be for you the final proof of your non-racialism?'

'Maybe. But maybe I simply don't *know* enough about being black to imagine it. Again the story of Petrus. I think I do not hear it properly enough to say: now I can imagine myself with a black voice. On the other hand, maybe whiteness is unlaydownable and I just have to learn to care for it?'

'I really feel a bit uncomfortable with your black/white divisions. You suggest that blackness is more than skin-deep, to use the cliché, and this is essentialist talk. Trying to argue intelligently about it is a waste of time for me. We're sitting here in a country and in an institution and with people that are still staggering to make up for those very consequences of racist essentialism.'

'Okay. You're right. You're right.'

'And this is not to deny that a group of people's inner psyche had been overwhelmingly formed through the colonial and apartheid principle of race. But race deserves more serious thinking than skin colour.'

'We still have twenty minutes.'

'No, let us continue next week. I also have to point out that you should be careful not to let blackness become a voiceless group that you privately observe and define, instead of a varied, multiple people with which you should have multiple-way conversations. In other words, don't keep on talking to whites about blacks. Talk and listen to blacks.'

Somewhat unsettled by this stern admonition, I walked back to the flat.

Oblivious to the trees and the long, quiet street, my inside was searching for a word. A milk-near word. Something rising through all the remnants of past hearings. How was one to break through all these dividing borders? 'Suture,' I think. Perhaps 'suture' is the word that can wash this world. Carefully, to stitch, to weave, this side to that side, so that border becomes a heart-hammered seam.

---

10 December 2007

I am trying to understand why I experience such an extraordinary sense of well-being here. I remember how terrified I was, the first time I travelled overseas in 1986, that I would arrive in Holland and suddenly realize: *This* is where I belong! My whole life and so-called Africanness have been one big misunderstanding; this is actually who and what I am. The fear was in vain. It took barely an hour to become completely convinced that the industrious, ironic Dutch were not even vaguely familiar to my soul. I knew blindingly, like lightning: in the deepest, most intimate sense possible, I functioned to another rhythm; I was Third World, specifically African Third World.

So why do I feel I function so well here in Berlin? Even my body is surrendering shamelessly to the dark greens, the cold air, the truncated sun. But day by day I begin to suspect that it is not *only* the product of the exceptional, generous support systems provided by the *Wissenschaftskolleg*, or the safety and comfort of the surroundings, or my self-disciplined solitude, but because this place forms part of a larger German coherency to which I as an Afrikaner have access – being from a post–Anglo-Boer War community which modelled itself on the only anti-English nation-building group in Europe.

(In the weekly German classes I took, we read *Biedermann und die*

Brandstifter, a play about how an ordinary man allows a disturbed arsonist to live in his attic. At one stage the characters in the play get drunk and start singing: '*Fuchs, du hast die Gans gestohlen.*' As the German teacher sang it, I sang along. She was aghast. What else do I know? '*Muss i' denn*,' I ventured. Her hands covered her face: These are Nazi songs!)

I experience, for the first time until now, coherence. For example: on my way to the woods, I walk along Furtwängler Strasse. I know who Furtwängler is. At home I have a CD on which he conducts the Berlin Philharmonie performing a Brahms symphony. During my stay here, Furtwängler was the theme of a cultural programme on rbb Kulturradio one morning, part of a newspaper article a month later, part of a museum exhibition about the choices of musicians during the Second World War, part of German history taught and written about, available as a biography in a book or CD or DVD in the bookshops, part of a documentary on late-night television, part of a street address on somebody's business card, and part of a conversation about the bus stops along the route of the M29. Furtwängler, an extraordinary musician, is woven into the fabric of the culture that intersects daily in many different ways with the lives of ordinary people in the streets and shops: there is coherence between the life in your head and the physical life around you.

The coherence in Germany also extends to the shop windows in Kurfürstendamm. One week they display clothes and shoes for workers at hospitals, roads, construction sites, factories and cleaning sites. The following week they display dresses from the Prussian period for Christmas, then soccer gear in German colours, then artworks built on Greek and Roman mythology.

In South Africa we all live an incoherency. It looks like this: the area I live in has a name only some people can pronounce (be it Oranjezicht or Qunu), its meaning lost to most of us. Many provinces, areas, towns and streets had other names prior to their current ones, so one will find some people still using the previous name, others the one before that. Some use the correct pronunciation, others a new anglicized version of the correct pronunciation. (Some of the taxi drivers talk of Orange-cyst.) Apart from Mandela and Verwoerd, we do not really know the people who appear as statues on pedestals, or the people honoured by naming or vilified by renaming. No part of our history is without its exclusion and destruction of some part of the population.

Every day, most South Africans jump with stretched-out legs from one solid knowable stone, hoping to land on another – but they are mostly out of reach. If one misses, one wades in an unknown morass until one reaches something recognizable to stand on for a while and catch one's breath. I always think of Gloria Gotyombe: when she comes once a week to clean the house, she must ask herself: What on earth could this white woman be doing on a computer that is so important that she and her husband can generate enough money to pay for a house and a car and clothes and the abundance of food in the fridge?

Workers' clothes would never be displayed in our shop windows, because work was racified and is therefore despised. Nobody wants to be a worker. We all want jobs, but not work. The clothes on display are suits for the bosses. Actually, we all want to be bosses, non-working bosses.

Most of the organized events in South Africa exclude, either through place or form, theme or reference, framework or cost. On our national holidays (Heritage Day, Reconciliation Day, Youth Day) we realize we have nothing in common – not what we read, not what we speak, not what we write, not what we sing, not whom we honour. Nothing binds us. Our daily Third World lives are broken into hundreds of shards of unrooted, incoherent experiences. (Visiting Jakarta with a group of Dutch and Flemish writers, one of them remarked how they navigate with difficulty through the streets checking for 'undesirabilities' – unequal surfaces, unexpected holes, open sewers, pedestrians, bicycles, etc. – while I seem to walk the streets with a different sensibility, as if I know the geography beforehand.)

Of course incoherence is not new to southern Africa: centuries ago the First Peoples found their way of life splintered by black groups moving south, and after that all indigenous groups were violently invaded by white settlers. But the thing about colonialism is that the colonizers often manage to produce their own coherency, so the world in which I have grown up was a completely closed coherent world in which the first time I came across a black man with a university degree was when I was twenty-two years old. For half my life I functioned entirely in Afrikaans, from bathing my children to writing a complicated dissertation. The new South Africa changed that. Afrikaners found their way of life forcefully splintered by a gradually self-asserting black majority, and the majority of Afrikaans-speakers turned out not to be white and started claiming the majority space in their language. So Afrikaners, who have so easily appropriated the land and the continent, found themselves in a new kind of post-colonial dynamic and are still reeling and deeply resentful about the incoherence of their lives.

Liewe Ma

J. has arrived. He brought into the flat our stressed-out lives from South Africa. I shifted to my 'official' side of the bed, made space in the cupboard, learnt to adjust the shower and asked for a television.

We saw our president-to-be dancing in skins, takkies and sunglasses at his wedding. Then, picking up his legs as I've seen younger men do, he falls backwards on the people behind him. The BBC played it at least five times during the day and every time I felt the embarrassment spreading in my neck. The worst, however, was the wife-to-be: she sat in her traditional clothes plus white bra with a submissive demureness that is quite frightening. And one thinks of the impressive presences of our recent first ladies. J. tells of power failures called by the misnomer 'load-shedding'. He says he is going to vote for the political party that is *not* dancing. Watching BBC or CNN, it seems the only business in Africa is dancing, dressing and, it has to be said, dying.

126

Coming down Hasensprung on Saturday, there it was: snow. Real, big, soft flakes of snow. I put down my bags and just stood there, feeling it on my face, my heart wanting to burst. I learnt that snow has a smell, and that at night it glows into the flat as if a big, cold moon is hanging outside.

When I passed the Hasensprung on Sunday, the pavement had been scraped clean. I was aghast. Somebody had actually cleaned Hasensprung on a Saturday-fucking-afternoon! Can that be? On Monday morning, something crunched under my shoes. Gravel! I was almost moved to tears: to think that somebody *cared* enough that others might slip there? It's beyond my understanding, coming from a place where we kill each other for twenty rand.

15 December 2007

At a table next to me in Kreuzberg, a group expressed their disgust at how the consumerism of West Berlin had overrun their lives. It was shocking that the shops were open on Sundays. Nobody went to museums or parks or to visit family; no mental activities any more, no, everybody shopped! Except that they used the word 'consume' and not 'shop'. They sat at the table with simple, slightly out-of-fashion, clearly well-worn clothes and seemed somehow embarrassed by their own critique. One woman said that the pressure to consume daily bewildered her neighbours. Fights broke out regularly between older and young people, because the young wanted to consume all the time. And, did you hear, they want to rebuild the palace! 'We demolished the palace because we wanted to say we believed in equality. Now the West wants it.' 'Of course the West wants it – consumers even of their own history of inequality. Communists now suddenly have nothing to show their children of all those years of comradeship, you know!' 'Except the sculptures of Marx and Engels.' 'Yes! Background now for tourist photo shoots. Because the West "won", it suddenly makes us all spies and murderers – completely without ideals of a better world. Twenty years ago one could plan a simple life for the good of the people, now everything is gone.' 'Except consuming!'

Liewe Ma

We sat the whole day watching television, trying to glean what is happening at Polokwane. It is so weird. All news from Africa, whether it's Zimbabwe or the election in Kenya, or now the ANC conference in Polokwane, is presented as if there is no context and no logic behind it. The journalists reporting from the Middle East often have a desperate passion on their faces as they try to *make* the viewer understand what is happening there. But reporters from Africa stand like figureheads of order against unfathomable chaos, or interview with condescending indignation a blocked-out face. What on earth is happening at Polokwane? My country seems un-nuanced and illogical. By the way: homeowners here are compelled by law to make the pavements in front of their houses safe. If someone falls there they can be taken to court!

Liewe Ma

You had me in tears when I took out your first letter to me here in Berlin from my pigeonhole yesterday: in the handwriting that I know so well from the times we still wrote letters. I looked for a long time at how you wrote my name. Yours was the handwriting on my first schoolbooks, the writing on the letters I had to take to school when you complained about a teacher's spelling, the writing that arrived in my room at university admonishing me not to become distracted by what you called 'pseudo-political activities' on campus. When I turned the envelope to open it, I saw it was wragtiewaar one of those envelopes that Pa had printed decades and decades ago with *W. Krog Middenspruit Kroonstad* on the back. Oh my God, then I sommer cried blindingly. We needed no post-box, no postal code, no gender – only four words to say exactly who and how and where we were. How invincibly contextualized we felt ourselves once upon a time!

Liewe Ma

J. and I walked down Lassenstrasse with your grandson Philip, who is visiting us. Coated and gloved, and far away from where we imagined you – surrounded by all your other children and grandchildren during long, warm summer evenings with watermelon, salads, the sounds of swimming and ice cubes in long drinks. In the Grunewald Kirche we heard the well-known carols – sung in God's language, as you used to say. A few minutes before midnight, the minister gave time for silent prayer. We bowed our heads as the lights were switched off and the doors opened. We held hands. And so we sat, us three, from so far away, mentally and physically, and yet, looking at us from outside, nobody would guess our Africanness. That broke my heart. At twelve o'clock the church bell started tolling and with it those of the whole city – encapsulated we were by the enormous ringing pulse of Berlin.

Liewe Ma

We had an exquisite Christmas dinner at the Schlosshotel in Brahmsstrasse, tasting many things, laughing a lot, feeling free and lovely and somehow pastless. I imagined Rilke coming down the famous wooden lion steps of this beautiful Pannwitz house while J. and Philip were picturing Paul McCartney and the Rolling Stones. Afterwards we listened to the Missa Creola in Kreuzberg. There are so many lights and so much heat in KaDeWe that they keep their doors open in the snow and it's like passing an oven. I go to Hackescher Markt every Saturday to eat a crêpe with Nutella and drink a glass of pomegranate juice. These sound like ordinary sentences, but, oh boy, how far away from you this all is.

I also, finally, let my grey hair grow out. To be grey in South Africa means to be redundant and muggable. To be grey in Berlin means to be a survivor.

Your greying daughter.

chapter ten

'You ask me to *cut the ground*?' the king of the Basotho reportedly exclaimed to some white men who had settled on his land.

The slow invasion by white emigrants moving in from the Cape Colony had begun to destabilize further the power relations on the Highveld. In 1836 Louis Trigaardt passed through with seventy wagons, and two years later Piet Retief was sworn in as leader in the vicinity of what later became Winburg. Those who moved to Natal caused the end of Dingane; those who moved north forced Mzilikazi to flee beyond the Limpopo. Soon as much as a fifth of the white population of the Cape Colony streamed across the border, and the fluffed hills and large plains, lush with red grass and game, stretching away from Thaba-Bosiu must have seemed irresistible.

Like so many before and after them, these white men addressed by the king were absolutely determined to force him this time to agree to a border, a line of demarcation traced between themselves and him, to ensure the exclusive possession of the territory they had invaded.

'Listen,' said Moshoeshoe, 'to a story which is, I am told, in your great Book: It happened once that two women disputed about a child before a very wise king. The latter ordered the child to be cut in two, and half to be given to each of the women. "It is quite just," said the pretended mother! "Let it be divided instantly!" "Oh, no!" cried the real mother, "I would rather lose it entirely!" ... You, my friends, who are strangers, you think it quite natural that my ground should be cut. I, who am born here, I feel my soul revolt at the thought. No; I will not cut it! Better lose it altogether!'

Casalis does not describe the outcome of this incident, only the way in which Moshoeshoe occupied the moral and intellectual high ground.

Several options were open to the king as a response to the request to divide his land. He could have given the men a lecture on Basotho ownership, sharing and land tenure; he could have explained how land could be allocated to strangers only through a democratic decision taken at a *pitso*; he could have told them how land, like the sky, could not and should not be owned; he could have told the famous Basotho story of the devouring dragon Kholumolumo.

He did not tell them any of these, but chose to tell them *their* story – to give them, as it were, their own story back – as if he realized that those in front of him were incapable of understanding anybody else's story. He would force himself, by whatever means, into the world of those who assumed there was only one 'true' way to understand the world.

Although the issue was land, by using a non-land story from the Bible, Moshoeshoe achieved several things: he had immediate access to his listeners; he framed his claim to the land in terms of divine providence; he expressed his biological and emotional link to the land by using the image of a mother and child; and he played off the real history of greed and appropriation against a biblical history of integrity and willingness to sacrifice. There also might have been some cynicism behind his argument: let me use the language they pretend to believe, he could have reasoned, because, despite the humble and exemplary lives of the missionaries, these white people have tried to get the Basotho to accept a gospel they themselves discard whenever they please.

With the words 'You my friends, who are strangers, you think it is quite natural that my ground should be cut', Moshoeshoe was stating that this meeting was not merely about a contestation of land, but that 'strangers' were assuming rights they did not have.

Although Moshoeshoe was displaying remarkable diplomacy and

insight into the frame of reference of white people, he was also experiencing a triple tragedy. His foreboding that he was soon to lose (how
much of?) his land, as had other chiefs around him, must have been
greatly aggravated by the fact that he had to use his enemy's story to
convey his deep and legitimate claim to the land. The biggest tragedy,
however, was that, unlike in the Bible story, there was no 'very wise king'
to judge his case.

It was precisely this king, this Solomon, that Moshoeshoe began to
look for in earnest, because after the destruction of the great kingdoms
of Shaka, Dingane and Mzilikazi, it was only a matter of time before the
white trekkers would attempt to destroy him as well. He needed this
'king' – who would turn out to be a queen.

Casalis soon perceived a pattern in these more and more pervasive
land-grabbings. While the newcomers (some of them black like the Barolong chief Moroka) were 'few in number', they usually 'gave no offence'.
'They seemed so humble, so submissive! they merely asked permission
to sojourn in the thinly populated parts of the country, and their stay
was to be but temporary.' But the moment they found their number
sufficiently 'augmented', they would 'throw off the mask'.

This ugly face of Europe, Casalis felt, slowed down the growth of
Christianity considerably: 'Our converts thought that war ought to
cease entirely where the supreme authority of the Word of God was;
they imagined that they had nothing to fear from the white race ...
[But] the encroachment of our race ... led many of the natives to see
in Christianity nothing more than a series of precepts without practice,
and theories without application.'

Moshoeshoe had hoped that the missionaries would be able to
strengthen his diplomacy against other whites. This hope must have
been severely crippled when he saw the suspicion, rancour and disdain
with which the trekkers treated the missionaries.

During Moshoeshoe's fifty-year rule, the Basotho would systematically
be robbed of their land. It started as early as 1833, when Moroka and his
missionary James Archbell asked for a place to settle in order to escape the

droughts and attacks from Mzilikazi's Matabele. Moshoeshoe, joined by Sekonyela, whose land bordered on the area, agreed on a piece. Archbell drafted a contract, which the two illiterate chiefs signed. A gift of eight cattle, thirty-four sheep and five goats was sent to Moshoeshoe.

The king strategically placed Moroka at Thaba 'Nchu to form a buffer between his people and the Korana marauders who lived beyond. For several years the newcomers fulfilled his expectations. Raiders ceased to penetrate and Moroka joined Moshoeshoe in driving away an invading Nguni chief. Moshoeshoe gave Moroka a firearm as a present and Moroka adopted the bravest of Moshoeshoe's sons, Masopha, who earned himself the praise name of The-golden-falcon-with-fierce-eyes-glaring, to live with him. Moroka was invited regularly to attend the Basotho's *pitso*, and although he was living in the land of the king, he was treated as an equal, in accordance with Moshoeshoe's diplomatic protocol.

But Archbell resented being accountable to Moshoeshoe rather than to the docile Moroka. Demanding secession, Archbell produced the signed contract and insisted that, because livestock had been exchanged, the land of Thaba 'Nchu had not been lent to Moroka, but sold.

Moshoeshoe was furious. Moroka knew as well as he that land was communal property. 'No one – including chiefs – could sell land,' writes Casalis. The livestock given by Moroka to Moshoeshoe was mere *peho*, given in gratitude and acknowledgement of having been well received in Basotho territory. Moroka's demand for ownership of the land took up years of quarrelling, and finally, after official intervention from the Colony, it became Moroka's land – today's Thaba 'Nchu.

Moshoeshoe, who had signed the wretched document before Casalis arrived in his kingdom, used the young man extensively to dispute it. As other negotiations and demands piled up, the king and his missionary developed a way of working together that turned them into a formidable combination. The gospel Casalis preached might have disappointed Moshoeshoe, but his loyalty towards the king, who made his being-a-missionary possible, was irrefutable. Between them they worked out a remarkable strategy of representation. Some letters sent from Thaba-Bosiu were in Casalis' handwriting, but were written in Moshoeshoe's voice, in the first person, and signed by him with an X. Other letters were written on the king's behalf, but referred to him in the third person and were signed by Casalis. A third kind of letter would be signed by Casalis and written in his own voice, as if it were a personal, and therefore very honest, aside from the missionary, a conversation between white people, as it were.

Although the ideas and arguments in all these letters and documents were believed to come out of debate between the king and his councillors, the fact that Moshoeshoe could make use of a direct and an indirect black voice as well as an indirect white voice made extensive diplomatic manoeuvring possible with people who the Basotho became increasingly convinced were without *batho* (humanity).

The choice of voices when interacting with whites was carefully calculated. If the king was speaking in the first person, the message was: this is the king speaking, but there are educated people here with me who will detect any dirty tricks you might be contemplating. If a letter was sent by Casalis with the king as a third-person presence, the underlying message was: an educated white man has written this, so your response had better satisfy him first before it comes to me. If it was only Casalis speaking, the premise was: between you and me, we who understand and abide by the same codes ...

This kind of relationship was only possible because, on the one hand, Moshoeshoe, being neither arrogant nor insecure, selected with insight the kind of white person he could trust. On the other hand, Casalis had not only learnt Sesotho in order to come as close to the Basotho as possible, but had thrown his lot in with them and fully believed in the righteousness of their cause. He also realized that his continued missionary work would be possible only under the man who had initially chosen him, in accordance with God's plan.

While Moshoeshoe was fighting and negotiating ceaselessly to protect his territory and his people, he was also trying to modernize their living conditions and achieve sustainability by introducing agricultural developments such as ploughs and different kinds of grain. By 1838, when the main thrust of the Great Trek began, Moshoeshoe had stored enough grain in the weatherproofed baskets on Thaba-Bosiu to last seven years. Through effective trade systems, most people nearby, including the passing trekkers, bought their grain from the Basotho, and the traders at Morija sold merchandise to the value of £3 700 over a fourteen-month period.

By 1842 Moshoeshoe was at the height of his reign. Despite humble origins and barely a decade of relatively safe living on Thaba-Bosiu, he concentrated around him a prosperous following that is estimated to have been between thirty and forty thousand people. At any given time he could assemble between twelve and fifteen thousand subjects on Thaba-Bosiu within a single day.

In the 1850s he decided to make use of the missionaries' printing press, the first in the interior of southern Africa, and promulgated a law forbidding the sale of spirits. Moshoeshoe was a complete abstainer himself; he did not even drink the mildest form of beer. A notice was printed and distributed to educate people about the dangers of alcohol and to forbid the introduction or sale of 'spirituous liquors' throughout Basotholand.

Five years later he again used the press to send out a warning about land claims. This time he was blunt; no biblical story, but a straightforward message that his land was not for whites: 'The trader who fancies that the place he is sojourning in belongs to him, must dismiss the thought, if not, he is to quit; for there is no place belonging to the whites in my land, and I have granted no white man a place, either by word, or by writing.' This sentence does not reject white people, just those whites who refuse to live according to the Basotho world view.

As part of his modernization campaign, Moshoeshoe also employed the printed word to enforce his rejection of some of the consequences of witchcraft: '*When anyone is killed in a case of witchcraft, the murderer will be most severely judged, and sentenced to death.*' To underline that it was not merely his personal whim, the text confirmed that the ruling was 'assented to by Letsie, by all my brothers, and by all men in the tribe, who spit on the lie of witchcraft, and cover its face with their spittle'.

The king did not follow the Zulu military system, with its standing army and regiments based on age, and the positive effect of living in what can be described as mostly peaceful circumstances soon became clear. The first census, twenty years after Moshoeshoe became king, showed that the average Basotho family possessed nine head of cattle, one horse, and twenty-one small stock. There was one plough per ten families and each family exported four bags of grain in a year. Moshoeshoe himself was by far the wealthiest man in the country, with most of his livestock looked after by others in his kingdom.

But Moshoeshoe saw all too clearly that he had become the only person able to mobilize significant resistance against a widely dispersed white population, ten thousand strong. He actively began to mount his defence by devising four strategies. First, he skilfully pitched the Boers, who were hungering after his land, against the British, from whom they were fleeing – the same tactic he had used to get Shaka to attack a bothersome Matiwane. Second, Moshoeshoe put on a display of power and claimed the full range of his land by conducting a *letsolo* (hunting expedition) across the Caledon River, with several thousand men on foot armed with assegais and five hundred horsemen armed with guns.

Third, with the assistance of Casalis and the excellent contacts of Dr Philip in Cape Town and London, Moshoeshoe made his first serious request for British protection. He sent a letter to the Cape governor, Sir George Napier, saying that he was 'increasingly convinced that the existence and independence of his people are possible only under the protective aegis of the Sovereign whom you represent'.

Fourth, through Casalis, Moshoeshoe wrote a letter in the first person to the British authorities regarding three hundred farmers who had simply settled in his territory and claimed ownership of the land. 'My subjects go to your land; you do not drive them away, and when they return they do not bring with them your ground (land) clinging to their sandals.'

His letter provided, as he had planned, the excuse the British needed to move beyond the borders of the colonies and conclude the Napier Treaty, which acknowledged Moshoeshoe's territorial integrity and demarcated his land, distinguishing it from that of the Griquas. The treaty, realizing Moshoeshoe's long-cherished dream of a group of allied African states, was signed by him and Griqua leader Adam Kok in 1843, giving the Basotho jurisdiction over the land between the Orange River and twenty-five miles to the north-west of the Caledon. Of course Moshoeshoe insisted that the treaty add twelve extra miles to incorporate Moroka at Thaba 'Nchu, and, thereafter, to protect these legal boundaries, he quickly installed his son Molapo as well as his nephew and half-brother, with their followers, in the north; his allies Moletsane in the north-west; Moseme near Thaba 'Nchu; and his brother Posholi in the south at Vegkop.

From that point on, the Napier Treaty was regarded by Moshoeshoe as the only 'real' treaty relating to the border of Basotholand.

Many documents from the time refer to Moshoeshoe as 'wily', 'insolent' and 'sly', portraying him as a shrewd monarch buying time in a difficult period by producing and manipulating border inconsistencies. The very strategies that made Moshoeshoe a remarkable leader, namely his attempts to accommodate everybody and to reach consensus by means of rigorous discussion, were used to describe him as sly and without principle. Hardly any recognition was given to the fact that his kingdom was subjected to a significant number of destabilizing pressures. It was surrounded and interspersed by indigenous and coloured groupings such as the Griqua, Korana, Basters and Khoisan; it was subjected to various religious systems ranging from Protestant and Catholic to traditional African; it experienced political interference from Afrikaner trekkers and British civil servants with their own clashing imperial and republican aspirations; it had to tolerate the various strategies of neighbouring black groups trying to survive their own ordeals; and, last but not least, Moshoeshoe was regularly confronted with the irritation of his own people for not according them enough say in his strategies towards whites.

Whites interacted with Moshoeshoe through letters and documents or one-on-one meetings. Because they assumed that he had despotic powers, irritation and accusations flared when the king insisted on a consultation process at a *pitso*. Moshoeshoe walked a tightrope – how tight it was can be gathered from the remarks of Jean Fredoux, the son-in-law of one of the missionaries: 'This remarkable person ... on his mountain of the night still wearing his old costume; owning two good European-style houses and living right alongside in gloomy huts; today seated close to his missionary and tomorrow perhaps consulting some pagan prophet; going to listen to the teachings of the Gospel in church and maintaining a numerous seraglio at home, – Moshesh shows himself to be at the same time the man of the future and the man of the past.'

The first significant loss of land (Moroka's claim had not yet been conceded to) occurred in February 1848, when large tracts were simply annexed by the British, without any consultation. In an act of profound contempt and arrogance, the Governor of the Cape Colony, Sir Harry Smith, decided to put an end to the 'trouble' brewing in the interior. Describing Moshoeshoe to his superiors as a simple-minded savage, he admonished the king in a letter to accept the Christian faith and prepare for eternal life. Moshoeshoe ignored the letter. Irked by a lack of response, Smith summoned him to a meeting at Winburg. In front of the Basotho and British delegations Smith simply told the king that all the land up to the Vaal was now under British sovereignty, and he tore up pieces of paper to demonstrate that former treaties were now worthless. The whites could stay (Smith called the Boers 'my children') and the black people could rule themselves, because, he said, raising one hand a foot above the table, 'Moshesh is like this', and then raising his other hand a foot above the first, 'but Her Majesty is as this'.

No gesture could have indicated to Moshoeshoe more powerfully that this authority, Her Majesty, was precisely the 'very wise king' he needed to judge and defend his cause in order to keep his land.

As a result of his tutoring by Mohlomi, Moshoeshoe probably believed that goodness would bring its own reward, that kindness would not only generate justice, but would outwit and outlast megalomania and greed. When the missionaries arrived, they seemed to confirm that to be good and fair was also to be right in the eyes of the wider world. But as parts of his land were simply swallowed up, Moshoeshoe must have realized that the attributes sprouting from the good would not outlast anything.

He threw himself into a last intense effort to save his kingdom and did so on all fronts, modern and traditional, local and global. In the face of the building threat, Moshoeshoe re-established all the institutions he had neglected at the request of the missionaries: he publicly encouraged initiation schools again; he took new wives; he performed sacrifices, purifications and ancestral rites; and he regularly consulted a diviner, a woman named Mantsopa. He traded huge quantities of grain for guns and ammunition, and took in white men to repair these guns. With all his horses, he had the largest cavalry in Africa at the time. He allowed his men to conduct cattle raids along any border that was imposed on them in the hope that people would move away, making the borders more porous.

The second loss of land happened in the same year, after the battle between the Voortrekkers and the British at Boomplaats. Being on good footing with the Boers, Archbell's Moroka quickly moved in to convince the authorities to draw a border between themselves and Moshoeshoe's territory, thereby establishing the deeply resented Warden Line, named after Major Henry Warden, the British Resident to Trans-Orangia. The British authorities got Moshoeshoe to put his name on a document robbing him of almost all his arable land and more than a hundred villages 'without the consent of my people'. Without being specific, some historians say that Moshoeshoe was 'coerced' or 'induced' to sign the document. In a bitter and disillusioned mood, he confessed to Casalis that he had previously hoped that black people were different from whites, but through Moroka's action, he now realized that black people also looked after their own interests only and did not mind trampling the rights of others. When the king's son was asked whether he accepted the Warden border, Letsie replied: 'Yes, as when a dog consents to walk after him who drags it with a rope.'

Moshoeshoe is reported to have said: 'When we drive the Boer's cattle, sheep and horses in war, or before their fearing faces, they call that stealing. When they drive ours, they call it soft names, they say they recapture or replace their stolen ones ... [A]ll property reared and nurtured on land stolen from us, on our own stolen land remains our property ... [Y]ou white people do not steal cattle, but you do steal whole countries.'

The loss of land had a disastrous effect on the missionaries' Christianizing activities. When the Basotho officially lost Thaba 'Nchu, Moshoe-shoe's second son, Molapo, the missionaries' most important convert, left the church, starting a stampede in which rising numbers of Basotho abandoned the Christian faith.

In 1851 Warden decided to attack the Basotho in order to inflict 'a severe humbling' by stripping Moshoeshoe of military power to eliminate him as a possible partner to the destabilising forces mounting in the Eastern Cape. The desperation of indigenous groups under the vicious onslaught of Sir George Grey was already manifesting in diverse calls to mobilize the ancestors to overthrow colonial rule, a process that would culminate in the cattle-killing movement following Nongqawuse's prophecy later in the decade. Moshoeshoe was not only well informed through his various networks, but was even accused by authorities of being the force behind the power of the young Nongqawuse and her uncle Mlanjeni.

Before Warden's attack, Casalis tried to intervene by writing several letters to various powers, because he saw from his house how bands of keen armed and mounted Basotho were assembling into regiments, incited by prophecies about 'the end of white people'. Moshoeshoe's own diviner Mantsopa prophesied that 'the enemy would come, and would be almost destroyed in a contest so sharp, and of such short duration, that it would be called the Battle of Hail'.

The battle against Warden, who was assisted by Moroka's Barolong and the Korana, took place on Viervoet Mountain. It was described by the missionaries: 'The assegai, the battle axe, and the rifle wraught terrible havoc in the ranks of the Barolong and Korannas, who fought bravely. Those who did not fall under the blows of these arms, were hurled into the awful gaping abyss around them. At the same time the artillery ... was repelled by Moshoeshoe and forced to retire in great confusion towards the camp. On the following morning the British Resident began his retreat in the direction of Thaba Nchu.'

A year later Cathcart took his turn. He arrived at Platberg in 1852 with artillery and two thousand men, and demanded a meeting with Moshoeshoe. The king refused. He said he was old and that the river was too full for him to cross, and sent in his place his sons Sekhonyana and Masopha, the latter having studied at Zonnebloem College in Cape Town where many of the chiefs sent their royal sons. This was an instance where Casalis sent a letter written by himself as himself, providing an additional explanation: that Moshoeshoe was willing to come to the meeting, but was physically prevented by his followers because they were afraid that he would be taken prisoner by Cathcart, as the British had done with Xhosa chief Sandile. Neither explanation placated the Governor. He issued an ultimatum that Moshoeshoe should hand over 10 000 cattle and 1 000 horses within three days as compensation for his people's cattle raids.

The Governor's demand was not only impossible, but insulting. The sixty-six-year-old king then crossed the swollen Caledon River with a small escort, this time including Casalis and his brother-in-law, Hamilton Dyke (Sarah Casalis' brother), to explain that retrieving so many live-stock within three days was impossible. Cathcart bluntly refused to allow extra time.

'I would ... recommend you catch the thieves, and bring them to me,' he is reported to have bellowed, 'and I will hang them.'

'I do not wish you to hang them, but to talk to them and give them advice,' Moshoeshoe replied; 'if you hang them they cannot talk.'

'If I hang them they cannot steal, and I am not going to talk any more.'

Moshoeshoe approached the thieves in the same way he approached the cannibals: changing them by being humane towards them, by talk-ing to them. Cathcart, on the other hand, probably thought that he was asserting the rule of law by refusing to talk. For the king, this signalled an abdication of humane behaviour.

Back home, Moshoeshoe raised a general levy, took a large portion of his own herds and sent 3 500 cattle five days later. Cathcart's response was to take the cattle but, in addition, immediately to seize everything he saw grazing on the Berea plateau. Then he attacked the Basotho. They were well prepared, and it was an exhausting fight, only broken by nightfall. Moshoeshoe's mounted and armed soldiers, under commanders Molapo and Moletsane, not only managed to protect Thaba-Bosiu and kill five or six hundred soldiers (according to newspapers published in Cape Town), but also recaptured at least some of the cattle sent to Cathcart.

Lying in his bed that night (says Casalis), Moshoeshoe thought it the ideal moment to end the battle. He got up and deliberated with his councillors. In the middle of the night, Casalis was woken and informed of Moshoeshoe's decision by one of the sons, Sekhonyana. A letter was written, first in Sesotho, then translated into English for Cathcart (note how the typical diary style of comma and dash, so loved by Casalis, was used): 'I beg you will be satisfied with what you have taken. I entreat peace from you, – you have shown your power, – you have chastised, – let it be enough I pray you.'

The king's insight into human nature proved effective. Cathcart, worried about the enormous loss of life, the large numbers of armed Basotho and the impenetrability of Thaba-Bosiu, was pleased that he could save face. 'I have received your letter,' he wrote in reply. 'The words are those of a Great Chief, and of one who has the interests of his people at heart ... I have taken the fine by force, and I am satisfied.'

Nine months after he allowed Cathcart to feel that he had won, Moshoeshoe decided to make a show of force by launching an attack on Sekonyela. Moshoeshoe had seen his power and cruelty grow from year to year, and decided to appear for the first time in the unusual role of a military commander. According to Casalis, the attack revealed him to be a master.

Moshoeshoe described his unwillingness to go to war in the following way to Casalis: '"To what purpose am I thitherwards bent?" said he as he was about to depart.' Always the pedagogue, he added, while indicating the window in Casalis' drawing room: '"Were I to grasp a cudgel and to rain blows, right and left, on that, what beauty would there be in my deed! And how the wind and the rain would rush in through the wreckage which I would leave!" Never before had the son of Mokhachane seemed more interesting to me than in this moment of intimate struggle which, had it not, however, revealed itself in his features, he alone could describe.'

The king solemnly prepared himself and his soldiers for the assault on Sekonyela. A 'priest of war' declared that the divining bones showed the enemy to be prostrate and dead with its head turned towards the setting sun. Moshoeshoe was ordered to sit on a particular rock while one of the chiefs shot an arrow at the mountain that they wanted to attack. After this, a 'witch of sorts' predicted that the fight would take place 'in stormy weather; your enemies will perish in deep waters'. Moshoeshoe's last preparatory task was to be secluded in a hut with his father, Mokhachane, receiving the old man's words and being purified by his hands. Then he mounted his horse and led his army towards Sekonyela.

Before the attack, he gave precise instructions: they must mark their faces with white chalk to avoid killing one another; they must leave women and children in peace; they must not take any of Sekonyela's cattle, 'for it is there that his darts would fall upon you'; they must not shout while fighting but let the guns talk. On the summit of a mountain facing Sekonyela, Moshoeshoe launched a brilliant strategy which at one stage involved the Basotho climbing on one another's backs and scaling the mountain from every angle. In the aftermath of their victory Moshoeshoe again showed his mettle. A captured uncle of Sekonyela begged the king to kill him because he had no reason to live any more. Moshoeshoe refused, and ordered him to have 'a nobler courage than to know how to die; live on!' Women, children and prisoners were provided with food, warriors were allowed to return and protect their corn, nearby white farmers could come and remove their own stolen cattle among the booty, and the mission stations were all protected against looting, apart from taking 'a little salt with which to cleanse the wounds of the injured'.

When the chiefs under Sekonyela were brought before the king, he explained his plan in practical terms by taking a piece of copper wire and forming it into a circle around the Basotho chiefs who were with him. Then he called the other chiefs into the ring, saying that they would remain united in the same way that their heads were within the ring. '[Y]ou shall abide as quiet as you are at present, but each at home, diligently tending your flocks and tilling your fields. When the harvest is over, we shall meet again here and then we shall settle all matters concerning the country which the war has just devastated.' Sekonyela despatched three deputies to Thaba-Bosiu, offering a full and unconditional surrender, and Moshoeshoe 'granted him peace'.

The king (closely observed by the surrounding groups) had re-emerged as a powerful military force, his people regained confidence in his strategies and the booty made up for what had been lost to Cathcart.

The main hero of this conquest, however, was Moshoeshoe's son Masopha. Praise songs describe how, 'while the snow fell hard on their shoulders', he stormed Sekonyela's stronghold. Masopha was the 'grass hat' of his father and, the song goes, although he was punily built (his thigh was like an oribi's), woe to the one who says 'he's not a man, but a little man'. Yet he was humble: 'he doesn't give things to himself … the seboku grass speaks of him'.

Despite these momentary flashes of a coherent framework enabling its participants to function with confidence and fairness in both internal and external affairs, it was not able to prevent the final burst-in of another civilization. The new British Commissioner, Sir George Clarke, officially cancelled the original Napier Treaty torn up by Harry Smith but cherished and honoured by Moshoeshoe, on the grounds that the wars between the Basotho and the British broke all pre-existing treaties. Deeply upset, Moshoeshoe set off to Bloemfontein in an effort to re-negotiate.

As Casalis was ill, the missionary Pierre-Joseph Maitin from the Berea mission station was asked to accompany the king. He joined the entourage at Platberg, where to his surprise he was provided with a fresh horse and saw how a boiler, strapped to the back of a Mosotho, was taken down and placed on a fire especially to make coffee for him.

Moshoeshoe had decided, in a move as unexpected as it was true to his style of diplomacy, to take Moroka with him. When they met at Thaba 'Nchu, Maitin wrote, it was 'a most affecting scene, to behold two chiefs and their subjects, formerly mortal enemies, giving one another reciprocal demonstrations of joy and of the pleasure which they felt at meeting in peace'. While they were there, a letter arrived from Clarke, informing Moshoeshoe that he would not be able to see him in Bloemfontein, as various matters required his attention. Moshoeshoe responded: 'I am proceeding to Bloemfontein. I have no desire to turn back or to make any alterations in my plans. If Sir George does not wish to receive me, I have to come to terms with the new government which he leaves behind and to know on what footing I stand with it.'

On they went. Maitin pointed out that the people of Bloemfontein might get the wrong impression when such a large group descended on the town, so the missionary was despatched to convey their peaceful intentions, and Clarke had little choice but to send a word of welcome. Moshoeshoe's entourage stopped and camped overnight a visible distance away, and several messages were sent to invite the king to enter the town.

At six o'clock the next morning, dressed in suit and hat, Moshoeshoe arrived at the Commissioner's house. He was asked in for breakfast and given four oxen for his entourage to slaughter. Afterwards Clarke agreed to a meeting, but demanded to speak to Moshoeshoe alone before Moroka joined them. Without wasting time, the king explained inimitably the possibilities of beginning anew, this time using a universal simile: when one marries, one expects only good from one's wife; as time goes on, one gets to know also the bad. If one marries a second wife, however, one again expects only the good – so the failure of the first to live up to expectations need not contaminate the expectations of the second. Although their interaction was amicable, Clarke didn't make any commitment to changing the boundaries. When Moroka joined the meeting, Clarke said that he had other business to attend to and gave them a letter in which he undertook to compensate the white farmers who were vacating Basotho territory.

That afternoon Moshoeshoe gave an address to the members of the new government. He stressed how keenly he desired to see blacks and white people living together in harmony. He reminded them that there was a book of God that should enjoin them to be just in their dealings with blacks as well as whites. Then, says Maitin, the king suddenly exclaimed with fervour: 'Fear drink! Let the drunkard be tolerated by none, whether Black or White!'

The British officials were astounded by this speech. Maitin records that one of them enquired: '"Moshoeshoe is a Christian, is he not?" – "I wish I could reply in the affirmative, but I cannot." – "Is he then a hypocrite? Does he not believe what he told us?" – "Moshoeshoe has told you nothing but what he believes to be the truth." – "If that is so, he will be saved, do you not think so?" – "I trust he will, for I hope he will be converted, but he is not yet so." I concluded by saying that, heathen though he may still be, I believe that Moshoeshoe is nearer to the kingdom of heaven than many who call themselves Christians. Everything I had to say was listened to in a serious and friendly manner.' In Clarke's absence, the government speedily agreed to send officials to finalize the boundaries that Moshoeshoe had clarified with his people.

At that moment, Sekonyela, who was taking refuge in Bloemfontein after his defeat by Moshoeshoe, entered the chamber. Immediately Moshoeshoe stood up and held out his hand. The two withdrew to a seat in the courtyard 'to converse'.

Moshoeshoe, in one impressive reconciliatory swoop, had embraced Moroka, Sekonyela and the white government. But, yet again, his actions earned him nothing in return.

~

After twenty-one years in Lesotho, Ma-Eugène died. Although she had been ill for quite some time, she insisted on going to Morija after the infant son of the Arboussets died. At the station established by her husband, she fell seriously ill, and within two weeks a message was sent to Thaba-Bosiu that she was dying. Moshoeshoe saddled his horse and with some of his sons and councillors left for Morija, where hundreds of people were already waiting. Casalis took him by the arm and led him to the bed where a long line of Basotho women were filing past. The king, weeping, kissed her hand, after which Sarah Casalis sank into a heavy coma and died soon afterwards. She was buried under the trees at Morija.

Her death forms the end of Casalis' memoirs, because it also signalled the end of his road with the Basotho. Calling Sarah 'my help-meet and my joy', he writes: 'It may be felt, possibly, that "these recollections" of my missionary life stop too abruptly, arriving at nothing definite even in what concerns Moriah and Thaba-Bossiou. The truth is, I have found it simply impossible to continue them beyond that day of mourning which brought so great a change into my life.'

Casalis left the Basotho and South Africa shortly afterwards. His last letter to the High Commissioner written from Thaba-Bosiu on behalf of Moshoeshoe concludes: 'After having thus transcribed the sentiments which Moshesh wishes to convey to you by this letter, I have the honour to subscribe myself, Your Excellency's obedient and humble servant. (Signed) E. Casalis, V.D.M.'

In his book *The Basutos*, written many years later, he permitted him-self to describe the surroundings where he had lived with Ma-Eugène in much the same language that he used to recount his dream on the ship. This time it was not Daniel guiding him, but Casalis who takes the reader to a hilltop, from where the breathtaking mountains and valleys of Lesotho are visible, with peaceful grazing flocks and slender columns of smoke. 'And then – what means this silence? This African silence, which is only interrupted by the hoarse croaking of a crow, or the flight of a solitary crane! … Turn your eyes from these silent scenes to seek the station. You will discover at the foot of a hill, in the shadow cast by the mountain nearest you, a few simple, though well-built houses, whose white fronts are turned towards large orchards and cultivated fields.'

Although he was leaving after twenty-three years, this vision of peace-ful civilization, planted by him, signalled that he had fulfilled his promise to the prophet Daniel – he had earned his place in the palace of his Saviour.

chapter eleven

It is a spellbinding dusk.

I'm dining on a wooden deck. On the opposite cliff, fast losing a last lisp of light, hundreds of bald ibises flutter to claim their spaces on the basalt ledges for the night.

I'm the only diner at the stone lodge built on the banks of the Senqunyane River in Lesotho from which, a few kilometres from here, plunges down the highest waterfall above sea level in the world. On the table are slices of hot, flat potbrood, baked on top of a stove, and a soup of roughly chopped tomato and dhania leaves. I wonder whether these ibises perpetually changing places on the ledges are those described by Arbousset during his journey to the Blue Mountains as *ibis nudi collis*?

Eating slowly, I become overwhelmed by sound: the river clattering on the rocks below me, the crisp hoof-clops of horses as riders, blankets flapping and heads bobbing just below the deck, hastily tripple across the low bridge, the tongue-claps of young cattle herders hurrying troops of donkeys laden with white bags of mielie-meal, and mothers calling, far away.

On my table lies the bill. With a kind of pleasure that borders on awe, I take out the maloti notes from my purse: on every one is the well-known engraving of Moshoeshoe in traditional clothing next to the Lesotho crest of two horses and a crocodile. The motto: *Kgotso Pula Nala* (Peace Rain

Prosperity). On the back of some of the notes are the famous Maluti peaks, on others a man wearing a grass hat and blanket, or a woman with mielie cobs and stone huts.

As I walk to my cottage, there is a soft footfall behind me in the dark. I stop. It's the friendly young waitress.

'Look' – she points to the sky – 'a special night!'

In a perfect line, close to one another, radiate Jupiter, Venus and a water-white ravel of moon. The date is 1 December 2008. I remember reading that when this magical conjunction happens again, I will be dead.

Late in the night I'm awakened by a thunderstorm. I open the door and it feels as if the thunder growls, not from heaven, but from deep down under my feet. It is true then, that the ground can rumble biblically. With fierce platinum and green lightning tearing into the stone cliffs, the whole harrowing day-long drive, through these enormous mountains and near-inaccessible passes, is reduced to this stroboscopic moment: standing – touching the sandstone of the door frame to balance – in what feels like the authentic heart-chamber of the earth.

~

The dark patches of moisture ciphering from the stone flanks and the extra clarity of sound as cattle and herders cross the river are the only indications of the rain of the previous night. Next to the enormous Cape willows at Semonkong Lodge waits my guide, Clement, and two horses. I sign an indemnity form and climb onto a nameless horse from the verandah wall. Clement is on a smaller horse that I suspect is quite a bit older, as she farts boisterously every time we go uphill.

We climb the river embankment and cross a small hill. We do what Clement calls 'walking pace' and I realize I have forgotten how the living rhythm of undiluted animal power, wedged into the centre of the body, dictates a peculiar thrilling abandon in a saddle. One has no separate life, only this eternal moment – melted into, surrendered. We come onto a plain and the landscape spaces itself dramatically. (I note that since leaving Maseru the day before, I am using the word 'dramatic' more and more.) The wide plain is an intense green, rimmed by low fraying edges of hills and faraway grassy mountaintops. Until now in my life, mountains had stretched up, ascended away from me into the sky. Here, now, it feels as if things are opening downwards from my feet, as if I am on the flat top of the world from which mountains reach down through colossal cracks, gullies, ravines. From here the world forms itself, from here its rivers wash, its seas fall away, its earth bends.

We encounter several groups walking or riding in the opposite direction. 'Mielie-meal,' says Clement. Out of nowhere a memory returns of a friend telling me that her grandmother had died a month before. She formulated the loss in an exceptional way: 'It's hard for me. My mother used to work in the city, so my grandmother raised me. We shared the same bed. At times my mother would bring the youngest baby and then it would sleep between us until it was big enough to move to the floor with the others. Then it was again only us on the bed. You know, I knew my grandmother so well,' she shook her head slowly, 'so well … I knew her heartbeat.'

Peacefully, my nameless horse ambles along, the reins loose between my fingers. I still think about this formulation in astonishment. I absolutely do not know anybody's heartbeat. Not even the man I have shared a bed with for more than thirty years. I know him well, yes; I know from his eyes, from his mouth, from his body language everything he cannot tell me, but I will never ever say that I know his heartbeat. The only heartbeat I know is my own.

Clement points out the blankets of the other riders. Despite the hot sun, almost everyone is dressed in rubber boots, loose pants or skirt, and a blanket. He turns the corner of his own blanket to me: a *Seanamarena* of pure wool and made to the 'Original Royal Quality'. As people pass, he identifies a variety of designs and colours, mostly mielie cobs, feathers, the patterns of playing cards, one with a British crown and cross. (Later, in the Semonkong shop, I saw blankets with Spitfires and other aeroplanes.) Can it be? That in this era where most people cannot tell a sweaty plastic blanket from a woollen one, there are people, as poor as they are here in Semonkong, who would spend the money of several salaries in order to own a blanket of real traditional Basotho design and made of pure wool?

Not a duvet, but a blanket? 'That is what most people own here,' says Clement. 'A horse, a pair of rubber boots and a blanket. Most of the older generation also still wear the traditional cool grass hat.'

Suddenly there's a shift, but I cannot pinpoint it. (I notice that I also start using the word 'suddenly' a lot.) It's not the grass plains, or the horses, but another awareness arises as we move closer to something that I first assumed to be a donga but which turns out to be a canyon. Slowly we are being sucked into a focus, our pelvises gently swaying with the horses. First there is the sound and then, suddenly, the view. The Maletsunyane waterfall plunges and falls with ferocious foam ruffles and wild trimmings, the one endlessly chasing the other down the fissure until everything disappears in a veil of smoke and mist. 'It is a sheer fall,' a traveller once wrote, 'at a single bound, with no interruption and all of a piece. It crushes out all suffering, all weeping.' Flocks of swallows dive as if mesmerized in adoration. The waterfall is not about power or scale, but is slender and breathtakingly beautiful, like a long, delicate throat encircled by jagged stones. From the opposite side we see how the river water on top gathers in a still pool before slipping over the stone lip into a blue-white lint of milk, beaded and braided with foam and smoke falling, falling, abandoning all eyes that have ever rested on it over the years, the centuries.

'Although we live some distance from the waterfall, we are always aware of it. We know when it picks up, when it becomes frail. We know the sound; the amount of smoke indicates the rain. In all of human memory it has never dried up. The waterfall is here' – Clement's voice becomes high and thin – 'right at the back of our heads.'

It appears that the local population believe that a snake resides in the misty pool at the foot of the waterfall, and they are concerned about the recent establishment of abseiling facilities by white tour operators. One Semonkong inhabitant assured me that the abseiling will anger the snake so much that it will want to relocate. If the snake ever moves from the Maletsunyane waterfall to one of the many other waterfalls in Lesotho, it will be accompanied by winds, storms and tornadoes that will destroy everything in their path.

'It was also the whites who let a man in a cage down into the pool below. The first time he saw nothing, the second time he said he saw something that looked like a snake from the back, the third time he went down, the rope suddenly became light and neither the man nor the cage were ever seen again. After that we had years of drought.'

On the way back my whole body has taken on a lightness. As Clement recites the Moshoeshoe praise poetry he learnt at school, blossoms fill my lungs as all these name-awake sounds suddenly become hearable in my mouth. There is language to be stuttered after.

chapter twelve

1 *January 2008*

The fellows who were not away for New Year had a party on the third floor of the library. From as early as six o'clock, crackers began to sound. Everywhere in the quiet streets of Grunewald were groups of young people with kitbags full of fireworks. And unlike South Africa, where the focus is on the display of light, the focus here is on the noise. Even the packaging suggests: *Die Original Harzer Knaller* – the original hard explosion. Many of these crackers slithered like noisy snakes along the streets. From eleven o'clock it was as if a blitzkrieg was taking place, with every single yard around the *Kolleg* being shattered.

Rockets were taking off from the Martin-Luther-*Pflegehaus*. Even the old-age home was shamelessly shooting away thousands of euros and the reigning sound was a deep, destructive *duffff!*

J. looked at me: 'There's a serious problem with these people here; you do realize that of course?'

Shortly before twelve we all went out onto the balcony of the library to see in the New Year in the cold and open air. We clinked and chinked and *prosit*ed and *gesundheit*ed and cheered. But while we were standing there, in high spirits, suddenly, around the corner, fully lit, came the regular M19 Grunewald bus, with not a soul inside apart

from the driver. Exactly on time: four minutes past twelve. I was
overwhelmed! Such dependability! Such safety! I lifted my fist into the
air: *Viva Grunewald bus, viva!* I was elated! For the rest of my life I
would remember this moment when the bus came, swinging on its
axles, around that corner. What a life one could lead with so much
dependability, so much safety, and a word I cannot find in English:
geborgenheid – something between being rescued and being kept safe
by people (or a God) who care.

As we slowly walked home at one o'clock, and approached the
Grunewald bus stop at the Rathenau corner, something strange
happened. I suddenly felt nauseous. Of course, it was all the wine and
food, I thought as I sat down on the pavement step. But as I looked
along the deserted street it was as if tableaus of dead bodies slowly
unfolded in front of me: hundreds of thousands of pale, muddied,
dead bodies from the Franco-Prussian War tumbling in Koenigsallee,
millions from the Napoleonic Wars, 20 million from the First World
War, dropped as if unloaded by big trucks, 72 million from the Second
World War in heaps as far as the eye could stretch. Some were spilling
over the blue bridge into the Herthasee, bloated bodies in uniforms,
face downward in mud, mats of hair, and on top of them pale, dry,
emaciated bodies scraped together in bundles and bundles of
scorched bones.

I started to vomit. The earth seemed unearthly.

I dare not walk, I thought over and over; walking here would be like
walking on bodies obdurately seeping through this continent; I dare
not breathe; breathing here would be breathing the air from trees
grown green from these ash sponges of death. It felt like I was sitting in
the heart of whiteness. And shivering. From my half-baked but
intended Africanness (a continent where 'only' twenty million people
were killed during the twentieth century), I could simply say over and
over, 'The horror! The horror!' at some image, at some vision, at that
thing producing the Grunewald M19 bus.

My husband had no time for what he called my 'nonsense' and
dragged me home, muttering: 'It was not the wars that produced that

M19 bus, it was the absence of safe transport for ordinary people that brought those fucking wars!'

I awoke much later that night and it was absolutely still. Very still and still dark; the room filled with a strange blueness. Through the glass door I saw it was snowing. As if blessed, we lay under the thick feather duvets with their sturdy white linen, gazing at the soundless large flakes. *'But as I lie in darkness / None can touch you as I did then.'* / *'You hide your lips in jasmine snow, / and on my lips a snow is felt'* (Pasternak).

We went for a walk in Grunewald. *'Not a twig, not a pine needle stirred in the whole glittering brightness. Everything was silent. Neither of us said a word ... It was strange when a branch, a twig or a piece of ice fell near us; one didn't see it, or where it came from, one barely saw its lightning fall to the earth ... If something amongst the trees gained only an ounce of weight, it could fall, the tips of the pine cones like wedged slivers to the ground'* (*Die Mappe meines Urgroßvaters*).

CONVERSATION 4
BEEN THERE DONE THAT

'I don't know what Europe or India or South America is and is not, but I do know that, living in a South Africa properly embedded in its continent, I need to understand this world view or philosophy of interconnectedness fully. Apparently the Batswana believe that the moment a person starts living according to the each-man-for-himself principle, then "the light of the mind is darkened and character has deteriorated so that it may be said that the real manhood is dead, though the body still lives".'

'You must bear in mind that Western philosophy has ample examples of philosophers who emphasized the importance of interconnectedness. Spinoza, Feuerbach, Levinas, Freud ... Some would say that Jewish culture has that characteristic.'

'There is always a Westerner saying this to me. The West is like a vacuum cleaner, sucking up everything, mauling it to pieces within the debris of its own failures, and then it tells you: But we have already said this. Nothing can be said in the world that the West has not already said.

What I am trying to describe has NOT been grasped by the West, and if you think what I am saying is the same as what these other philosophers are saying, then it simply means we from Africa have not yet properly managed to articulate it succinctly. And it is hard: we have to use Western tools. It is as if we have to help you eat braaivleis with chopsticks, or dhal with a knyptang – the equipment makes you miss what makes the food the food it is.'

'This sounds like exceptionalism. South Africans have been accused of thinking that they are always exceptional – encouraged especially by Tutu. African philosophy does not live on an island. It speaks to Europe and the West out of its lived experience with Europe and the West. So it is always a two-way dialogue. When a non-African tries to understand an African, he or she needs equipment to cross the boundaries between different cultures. Africa's text is being written by Africans, but it is also addressed to a world outside Africa. All of Africa's diasporic voices are entwined with North or South or Arab or Jew, and virtually every European who has a colonial history with Africa.'

'I think that is precisely what I mean: you don't hear us through our own voice. You keep on hearing us only through *your* voice.'

Liewe Ma

I suddenly remember the majestic thin-nosed face on the painting against your wall. You told me that it was a self-portrait made by a German painter while he was interned during the Second World War. It would have been his task after the war to make important-looking paintings of the new Afrikaner leaders freed from British rule by a victorious Germany.

For a time he hid down at the river on your farm. Every second day, you were sent on your horse to take him food and paint. When he was later caught and interned, he sent you this self-portrait, with one eye blue and one green, as well as a small painting of the river that now hangs in my house in Cape Town.

The letters in Gothic script in your bottom drawer – did he write them? The poems? Is this how your extensive German library, collected over many years in our godforsaken town, started? Is that why you studied German at university?

I don't know how to ask you how you bring together in your mind this beloved German waiting in the veld, and the Jewish record dealer in town phoning to say that '*etwas neu*' had arrived. And then you would go to his shop and he would play for you your first Schubert lieder, Schumann, Wagner, pointing out what to listen for. Sometimes he was moved, you said. What did he make of this seventeen-year-old Afrikaner girl who was his only client listening to and buying German *Lieder*? This we do not talk about, nor about the language in which the longings of both these men, one in hope, one in despair, were lodged thousands of kilometres away from Germany.

P.S. The Christmas light tubes on Unter den Linden run parallel with the branches, emphasizing stem not bulk.

Liewe Ma

Strange how soon one becomes aware of how everything here reeks of unlodged guilt. How, from behind the naked moss-tinted stems and branches and the very earth out of which they stretch, different layers of grief emanate from Berlin.

When sitting on the sofa in my flat, I overlook the Herthasee. On the opposite side are two tall, slender aspen tree trunks, bent at a point that makes them look like two frail silver-white legs, or a tuning fork guiding the silent agony of the piece of land they are growing in, land that once belonged to the Mendelssohn family. There where my eyes rest every day, a history of Aryanization, arrests, re-appropriation, bombing, rebuilding, renaming played itself out. A few yards from there is the unadorned stone commemorating the assassination of Walther Rathenau. Here? On this ordinary corner where the rain falls so softly? Rathenau is described as the first victim of National Sozialismus. '*Ich habe und kenne kein anderes Blut als deutsches.*' 'I have and know no other blood than German. If I am expelled from German soil, I will stay German and nothing will change that.'

In Berlin alone, seven thousand Jews committed suicide, and forty per cent of all Jews lived here in Grunewald. This means that in these big, silent, beautiful houses, on their big, wooded plots, several thousand people could have killed themselves.

On the pavement in front of the house where we have German classes are two tiny copper plaques giving the names of the two Jewish people who were removed from that particular house as well as the camps where they died. These plaques are called *Stolpersteine* (stumbling stones) and are found right across the city, marking the names and places of the disappeared, daily confronting neighbours who claimed they hadn't noticed.

Entering the Villa Jaffe, I always feel as if somewhere behind the peaceful surfaces of plants and trunks and wooden doors, a big unfathomable grief is slowly turning its sad head to listen to my footsteps.

I found a book about the Second World War in which a woman wrote that, after she had finished her shopping at the corner shop, she came across a long queue of Jewish people walking in the streaming rain through the city towards the Grunewald station (close to my flat): 'Quite a long queue it was. The people on the streets who saw them were actually ashamed.'

There are several memorials at the station, but the absolute desolation and complete *verlorenheit* of the remembrance plaques at Perron 17 is unforgettable. One sees the numbers engraved in hard russet steel plates as one walks up and down:

Date: 13.8.43
Number: 1003 JUDEN
Place: from BERLIN to THERESIENSTADT

Then 1000 the next day, then 996, then again 1000 three days afterwards, right through the years, through the forest's autumnal fires, the cold, windy, rusty howl of winter, through the swirls of pink blossoms, the mad, soft fragrances of summer, lindenduft and candles, they were sent.

Now and again, coming back by train, I hear neo-Nazis shouting there, another time soccer fans, and one evening a wondrous blackbird. But nothing erases the rows and rows of never-ending numbers that humanity chose to dispose of.

Coming from a country where the copper *Stolpersteine* would immediately be stolen, why do I find it unsettling to think of similar projects in South Africa? Perhaps because every single thing in our country already portrays injustice, reminds us of the ongoing injustice. One need not pull it out of the past through plaques and memorials; it is walking around, mortally wounded, poor or corrupted, the perpetrators and the victims. The shame belongs to a colour – that colour is the reminder.

chapter thirteen

On the first day of the court case, *The State v. Reggie Baartman, Jantjie Petrus and Dudu Mofokeng,* dealing with the murder of George Ramadikoe Ramasimong, also known as the Wheetie, there are demonstrations outside the Supreme Court in Bloemfontein. The trial has been preceded by months and months of postponements, attempts to secure proper defence lawyers and raise money for legal fees, endless articles in the newspaper, and harassment of witnesses. J. and I try to follow what is happening in the newspapers. We read that placards in the street demanded the release of 'our' heroes.

'I wish they would publish some proper photos of the demonstration,' J. grumbles. 'I bet they've all been bussed in from Kroonstad.'

Expert witnesses describe the Three Million, formerly known as the Americanoes, as a group of men who first became known for wearing smart suits and parading in the streets. They quickly became popular, attracting more and more members, because they offered protection against the criminality that is endemic to impoverished societies.

Through the various testimonies one picks up that, while there have been times of close cooperation between the Three Million and the comrades, there has mainly been conflict, resulting in several murders. When his brother was threatened by the ANC, the Wheetie went to Reggie's house to ask that the attacks be stopped. Reggie went with the Wheetie and his brother to negotiate with the comrades to leave the man alone. Three Million members testify that the comrades murdered not only the Wheetie, but also his youngest brother and other members of the gang. Shortly before the Wheetie's murder, Reggie delivered a letter in person to the Wheetie's house in which he requested peace. Despite this request, two comrades, Simon Bloem and Abessinië Buthelezi, both related to Reggie, were killed by the Three Million. On the weekend of the funerals, three grieving and angry relatives, Jantjie, Hankan and Dudu, decided to kill the gang leader. According to Reggie's defence, he tried to dissuade them and gave them money to go back to Johannesburg, and only afterwards, waiting at my house, did he become aware of what they had done.

According to the first state witness, a Mr Lebeko, the Wheetie had been in court that day, and was walking back with his brother and sister when they saw someone with a gun approaching. Lebeko shouted, 'Watch out, George!' but the first shot had already been fired and was soon followed by the second.

At this point in the evidence, as I read in the court transcript later, the judge intervenes: 'Mr du Toit, while we are at the second bullet, would this be an opportune moment to take a tea break?' After the 'teeverdaging', the defence advocate, Mr Naidoo, tries to prove that the witness was too tired and hungry during the shooting to be accurate in his memory.

NAIDOO: You were tired from sitting the whole day in court, you were
    weak with hunger, Mr Lebeko, is that correct?
LEBEKO: Yes, I was tired, but not so tired that I could not see what was
    going on around me.
NAIDOO: Were you hungry as well?
LEBEKO: No, I was not hungry. That is my habit: when I had something
    to eat in the morning I will eat again in the evening.
NAIDOO: So after court, reaching the bus stop, you felt a little hungry?
LEBEKO: No, I did not feel hungry.

The Wheetie's brother, who now has lost two brothers in this vendetta with the comrades, testifies how, after the three shots, he stormed towards the body: 'I tried to touch his head but it was bloody, he was covered in blood. I tried to pick up his head and blood fell out of his mouth. I stood there until the police came.'

STATE: How did he lie?
RAMASIMONG: He lay on his back.
STATE: Do you think he was still alive when you reached him or was he dead?
RAMASIMONG: He looked dead to me.

After this gruesome testimony, the court chooses once again to ask that most significant of questions: 'Would this be an opportune moment to adjourn for lunch?' (A 'middagete-verdaging'.)

To my utter surprise, Mishack's affair with the Wheetie's wife becomes part of the evidence.

STATE: Mr Ramasimong, do you know how this vendetta between the Three Million and the comrades came about?
RAMASIMONG: Yes I know. There is a person with the name Mishack Daniels; he was a member of the ANC. He had a love affair with the deceased's wife. A dispute was created. During those times, if a man had an affair with another man's wife, then it was standard practice to take them to the comrades.

It soon becomes clear that the defence of the accused killers, Jantjie Petrus and Dudu Mofokeng, are doing as J. suggested they would: blaming it on the dead guy. They harass the witnesses to try to make them confuse the three coloured cousins, so that the one murdered near the school, Hankan Petrus, can be identified as the one who fired the shots. Unfortunately for the defence, both Jantjie, who fired the gun, and his cousin Hankan grew up or spent lots of time in Kroonstad and were quite well known in the community. Besides, the witnesses are also much too well schooled in the finer details of coloured race gradations to be confused.

NAIDOO: How can you say you recognized him by the hair? How does Jantjie's hair differ from Hankan's hair?

WITNESS: Jantjie's hair looks 'soos die van die kleurlings'.

NAIDOO: But they are built the same.

WITNESS: Not at all. Hankan Petrus is lank op sy been [long on his leg] en fris en hy is nie so lig van kleur nie, u edele. Jantjie se gelaatskleur is lig.

COURT: How could you see that his face was light when he was wearing a balaclava?

WITNESS: I saw his arms.

COURT: But then you talk about skin colour, not facial colour; gelaatskleur means the colour of the face, see.

KUNY [Reggie's advocate]: How would you describe him?

WITNESS: I would describe him as brown.

KUNY: Light or dark brown?

WITNESS: It is dark brown; the colour of Hankan's skin was darker brown than that of Jantjie.

Another witness is also asked to comment on Jantjie's colour.

WITNESS: What I can say is that he, and his father, who is today here in the court, they are of a lighter colour than the other people of that same race. I would say that they are even lighter than comrade Reggie, who is of the same family.

And yet another.

WITNESS: Hankan had my colour.

DEFENCE: What is that?

WITNESS: Jantjie had a far far lighter skin colour than I.

This is confirmed by the last witness.

WITNESS: No, Jantjie, accused no. 2, is not slightly lighter, he is much, *much* lighter than Hankan.

As the case progresses, terminology changes: the murdered man, whom I got to know as the Wheetie, becomes Diviti, and later on Diwit. The pieces of evidence that were in my house acquire their own dynamics as well. The balaclava, whose colour varies from black to navy to dark brown, is first described as a *coppa-head*, later as a *copper head*, while the state and the court stick to the old-fashioned Afrikaans word *klapmus*.

The same happens to the red T-shirt. The first witness says that the person who pulled the trigger was wearing a 'maroon skipper' with sleeves just below the elbows. The state then rephrases: it could also be called a sweater, or a shirt, or a T-shirt or a skipper. Yes, says the judge, let us call it a skipper, 'wat dit ookal mag wees' – we have grown used to the (un-Afrikaans) term 'skipper' here in court.

At one stage even the state gets confused and describes it as a rose-coloured polo-neck jersey.

COURT: You describe it as 'rooskleurig'?
STATE: It is red or rose-coloured, my Lord, or something along
    those lines.

On the day of the murder, the killer walked past the Wheetie's sister, Makhetha, who had hidden near the toilets when the shooting started, so she is able to identify the skipper.

STATE: On the basis of what do you recognize the skipper?
MAKHETHA: I recognize it because it has longish sleeves, but I noticed
    when he passed me that the sleeves had been cut off and that there
    is not a seam where it had been cut.
STATE: Do you mean this … yes indeed, see here, these sleeves of the
    skipper. Your Worship, perhaps the court should look at this.
COURT: I will ask the learned assessor on my left because she would
    perhaps know better what a seam should look like.
STATE: As it pleases the court.
COURT: Yes, she says that the seam had not been stitched and it is
    therefore without a seam and I also now see it myself.

Just as the police had tried to explain my actions in terms of fear, so the defence introduces the idea of fear when the Wheetie's sister is cross-examined: her testimony can not be trusted because she was frightened. But they are in for a surprise!

NAIDOO: And seeing that there was this chaos, this shouting and the person running towards this point with a gun, were you not at that stage frightened?

MAKHETHA: My conscience was dead.

NAIDOO: I beg your pardon?

MAKHETHA: My conscience was dead, I was not frightened ... I was brave enough to stand there because I wanted to see what was happening and what would be the ultimate end of it.

~

One evening I get a phone call from a woman who once taught at the same school as me but who has since moved to Bloemfontein. Denise has been attending the trial because she knows just about everyone involved. 'Denzil testified today,' she says. 'Oh, my heart bled for him! He sweated so much that by the end of his testimony he looked as if he was standing in the rain.' Apparently the accused stared menacingly at him while their family members made all kinds of noises. 'But in a way it was also tragic-comical, you know. When he was asked why he didn't attend the funerals of Reggie's relatives, he said: "I was involved with a rape case; the daughter of my aunt was raped and I helped out there." Now what does that *mean*? Nobody follows it up; its just one of those things. Then they asked him: When you were arrested, what were you doing? He said: I was busy fixing my false teeth. I mean, how can you accuse a man of lying when he is prepared to say all of this?'

According to Denzil, who drove the car, they dropped the two accused and then waited for them in Stasie Street. There Hankan Petrus got out of the car to buy apples. 'You know,' laughs Denise, 'picture this. Here you sit in a car. Two guys have jumped out to kill somebody. Do you sweat? Do you try to peer through the crowds to see what is happening?

No, you get out to buy apples. Not naartjies, apples. I can't get over it! Apples make mos this hollow sound, sien jy? Ek klap sommer iemand as hy appels in my ore eet, but one can actually see Denzil chomping away behind the wheel. Waiting. I said to my husband tonight, I wonder what happened when the killers ran full speed back to the car? Did they throw the apples out and turn up the windows? Or did they let them fall like hot coals?' I read in the newspaper that Denzil also confirmed the (my?) lie that he was arrested when he went to fetch the pistol and balaclava on my stoep two days later.

The evidence of Pieter Claassen, who runs a business that he asks not to be named in court, links Denzil to the event. At five to five that afternoon his staff were preparing to leave and he was on the telephone, looking out of his window at the taxi rank. He saw a dark-grey Honda Ballade stop, the back doors thrown open so that two people could jump in. Then the car drove off quickly. Because it all looked suspicious to him he wrote down the registration number of the car.

In the newspaper that week, a photograph appears of my stoep and the pots with the yucca and palm tree where the gun and balaclava were hidden. Captain Potter said that he received a phone call in his office from his 'beriggewer' (informer) that Denzil would remove the evidence from the stoep of Anna Samuel.

Who is this 'beriggewer'? The two of us never discussed this on the phone!

A photograph is shown to the court of what J. calls the most photographed stoep in the Free State, with a constable pointing his finger at the exact place where the gun and balaclava were found. The judge says, 'I cannot see clearly whether it is a periwinkle or a wandering Jew or what kind of plant it is in the photo … was it under the plant or behind the pot?'

During my own cross-examination much later, the plants would become very scientifically precise: 'Evidence was found on your stoep behind the *selloum*, the pot with the *selloum* plant, *Philodendron selloum*.'

Not only race, but also language is a marked point of power relations in the court. As most of the accused and witnesses are either Afrikaans or Sesotho, an interpreter is used. Valiantly, the three lawyers from Johannesburg start in Afrikaans and are of course praised by the judge for its good quality, but for the rest of the hearings they are emphatically encouraged to continue in English. But when a coloured sergeant is called to testify, the tone is different:

WITNESS: I am Sergeant Samuel Atherfold Smith.
COURT: What? Repeat please … only give us your full names.
WITNESS: Samuel Atherfold Smith.
COURT: Atherfold?
WITNESS: Yes, Your Honour.
COURT: Smit or Smith?
WITNESS: Smith.
COURT: Mr Naidoo, let us hope that a person by the name of Atherfold would be able to follow your questions in English.
WITNESS: Your honour, I actually prefer that the questions be asked to me in Afrikaans.

The court records state that after I dropped the group at Tau's shop, the three accused got a lift to Rosettenville in Johannesburg. Here they hid in somebody's flat, where the police arrested them a few days later.

~

The evening before I have to appear in court, I go to see Saunders, the man I originally gave the red T-shirt to on what feels like only the day before. The meeting is short. I tell him that if I'm asked in court about the gun on the stoep, I'll tell the truth. I'll say that Denzil came to fetch it that night and they told him to put it back the next day. The reason I will tell the truth is precisely why I'll be standing in the witness box: doing what I believe is right. If I start lying in the very next sentence, it negates the whole principle.

He looks at me in amazement. He doesn't know what I'm talking about, he says. As far as he's concerned, they caught the deputy head on my stoep with the gun the following day.

'But that's not true,' I reply.

He shrugs his shoulders – there are various witnesses to support his evidence. Besides, Denzil's case is already on thin ice. If I say he's lying, they'll charge him for being an accessory; then it will be *me*, and not the other comrades, who ensures that he loses his teaching job.

It has become impossible to navigate through the tides of wrong and right.

~

Next morning I drive the endless drive to Bloemfontein. My thoughts are tired of questioning and answering; they look for tiny spots of simple shade to lie down. At the court the police officials are over-friendly in an obvious way – destroying any claims of integrity that I might privately have had. With cold shock I recognize Reggie's lawyer as a well-known poet who compiled a famous anthology of liberation verse while in exile. His advocate is well known for saving the lives of many ANC activists. I feel ashamed to be in their keen and genuinely kind presence. But would I feel proud to be sitting over there with the three accused, feeling I was doing my little bit for the liberation of my country? Reggie looks impassive; I hardly recognize the other accused. The one who stood with me at the counter buying cooldrink must have cut his hair. I can look at them only with great difficulty.

STATE: How do you know Mr Baartman?
ME: He is on the board of the school where I teach, his daughter is in my class, she sings in the choir that I accompany, she plays in my hockey team, we are in the same Mission church, our children were confirmed on the same day and I have very good contact with his wife.

And then I begin, telling the story again. At one stage during cross-examination I move my toes and hear a squelching sound from the sweat in my shoes. I have been asked what I did when I realized that the red skipper belonged to the killer.

ME: I went home and waited for my husband and we realized that I had been faced with this terrible choice: if I keep quiet I became an accessory to murder, while one of the reasons why I joined the ANC was precisely because, unlike the apartheid government, it respected everybody's life and not only that of white people. Or I can go to the police and work with the people who are responsible for this tension between Reggie and the Wheetie. This was a terrible choice for me.

STATE: How did you feel about the murders that had been committed between the two groups?

ME: If I was in any way consulted about the murder of the Wheetie, then I would have said that killing him is playing into the very hands of those who want to eliminate the ANC. If you kill the Wheetie, apart from solving nothing, you become like them. Since then, as you know, several murders happened, so that was clearly not an answer to the issue.

STATE: Your feeling towards the ANC and the coloured community as such – did it change or do you still feel the same about them?

At this point, the judge intervenes.

COURT: Mr du Toit, look here, the answer of the witness might be interesting for some people. You will have to explain to me, however, what relevance it has to the whole case before I will allow you to ask that question.

STATE: Your Honour, the only purpose is to establish whether the witness is now hostile to the accused, whether she (*intervenes*)

COURT: But then you can frame the question in terms of the accused; why do you want to refer to the coloured community in general? What does this have to do with the case of justice?

STATE: Your Honour, I assume from the testimony of the witness that she was involved in the coloured community and provided support in so far as it was possible for her. I want to establish whether this is still the case … or whether she has withdrawn herself.

169

COURT: Mevrou, do you want to answer this question or do you not?

ME: It doesn't matter. It feels to me important today, in all political parties, to make a distinction between the principles a party is standing for and the deeds of the people who are members of that party. If one important ANC person does something that I find unacceptable, that does not mean that the whole party or its principles are to be rejected. The principles of the ANC and what it fought for are those with which I identify.

STATE: Has your attitude changed towards the coloured community?

ME: No, not at all.

STATE: And towards Mr Baartman specifically? Is there animosity between you or is the situation still the same from your side?

ME: No, it feels we will have to have a few cruel conversations one day, but his family is very close to my heart, and in a way I can also understand why he did what he did, although I do not agree with it.

Reggie's famous advocate is friendly and asks me everything, except – thank you, dear God – about the gun on my stoep. I am relieved: my integrity as a witness has not been tested. Coming out, I see the police doing a sort of hop-skip with satisfaction and making thumbs-up signs at me. I want to vomit myself out of myself.

We find out about the sentence from the newspaper: In a packed court-room with some people hurling cries of rage at the police and others singing 'Nkosi Sikelele', Reggie was found guilty of defeating the ends of justice and fined, Jantjie guilty of murder and, with mitigating circum-stances, sentenced to fourteen years in jail. His mother burst out crying in the court: 'He's twenty-three, he is only twenty-three!' Dudu Mofokeng was found not guilty.

The newspaper reports that the judge has credited me and the other white state witness for the successful solving of the case. Therefore officially, in black and white, in legal language, I am partly responsible for the fact that a young man is sitting in jail and that Reggie's political career has been destroyed by a criminal sentence.

Years later I scan all the available material in the court transcript in order to find some indication of moral language that could assist me in distinguishing right from wrong. The sentence, all eight pages of it, is wonderfully simple and consists of a spelling out that the court should be fair and apposite in its punishment and satisfy the 'responsible members' of the community that the punishment is proper and will hopefully lead to rehabilitation. The only scale used was the law. Because you broke the law against murder, you did wrong. It feels as if the sentence is suggesting that to kill or to steal or to lie is not wrong because it harms others per se, but wrong because it is against the law – as if to confirm that in this country laws mostly do not develop from moral beliefs.

So it became possible that an activist like Reggie could decide that, because he was fighting against those who initially *made* the unjust laws that took away his freedom and trampled his human rights, he could despise these laws and function outside them.

There is only one paragraph that draws the judge into a kind of moral statement:

> The truth is that your attempt at defeating the ends of justice could have resulted in the police being unable to track down the guilty. In fact, despite your attempts the police succeeded commendably (*lofwaardig*) in tracing the guilty within a few days. It easily could have been a different story. If it was not for the perceptiveness of Mr André Claassen and the conscience (*gewetensoortuiging*) of Mrs Antjie Samuel, you could have been the only source to lead the police to the killer. This is where your moral blameworthiness lies and for which you have to be punished.

I really have nothing more to say about the event. Except that every small fibre of the sort of non-racial life that I was trying to create in Kroonstad, in order to open up some space to live humanely in this inhumane land, had been destroyed by this murder. From the coloured community, there never came a word of judgement. Not about me, not about Reggie either. Nor a word from anybody in the ANC. I remember that way back in the eighties an old black man pitched up at my door one morning. He introduced himself as Gabriel Setiloane and asked to speak to me privately. 'You are getting involved with a problematic part of the ANC,' he said. 'Do not do that. This is all I want to say.' And he left. I dismissed him outright as being part of the old AF group who resented the power of the Young Lions. Some years later I looked him up in his house behind a luscious hedge of roses in the township to talk about his book on the concept of God among the Sotho-Tswana. With a faint smile, this remarkable African philosopher and theologian accepted my apology for not taking him to heart that day.

After the court case, Reggie lets me know through a journalist: he and his wife forgave me long ago – although he always said I would never give evidence against them, he knows me; although he was shocked and disappointed, they've forgiven me – and we should now let bygones be bygones. I am aghast. I haven't *asked* to be forgiven. In fact I do not even think I am sorry! I feel guilty, but it is a guilt more rooted in confusion than in conviction about wrongdoing.

~

Three days after the end of the court case, I drive to Cape Town to take up an editorial post at *Die Suid-Afrikaan*. Unlike Lot's wife, when I drive out of the town on the N1, I don't look back. For more than a year the murder has taken up just about all the space in my head, as I have tried to find a way towards an honourable position.

After three months, J. and the children join me in Cape Town. We're glad to see each other. At dusk we stand among the boxes and furniture of a rented house and look out at the embrace of the mountain, bathing in the blueness.

'We should never have gone to live in Kroonstad then,' I say.

'Don't lay the blame on a town, my dear,' says my own true J. 'We could have lived in dozens of other ways in Kroonstad, but you wouldn't. With heart and soul you went to dig this life out of the townships. Under the cover of causes you went and wormed your way into places of which you understood neither the undercurrents nor the codes. You wanted to live like that, and you worked us into a poor working-class suburb, worked us into the Mission Church, worked the children out of their schools in the town; ultimately you worked yourself out of a job, you worked us out of friends, so that day by day we became like strangers in the town where we were born – full of contempt for whites, while you had to bend over blackwards to be accepted in a community that actually saw you as nothing more than a convenient curiosity. And there was also something seductive about it – look what an exciting life we have here on the platteland. And something missionary – look how good we are. In that way you could also be the most knowledgeable person in the township – you could be the expert in Afrikaans, in music, in hockey, in politics – the nice madam that you can call by her first name. Only, you didn't want to be the madam, you wanted to be one of the oppressed, one of *them*, but the moment you were treated like one of them, boom, you wanted to be the madam again.'

He throws a sheet over the bare floor, and he and I and our four children sit down cross-legged around a box of Kentucky Fried Chicken.

chapter fourteen

I am joined at my dinner table by three government officials overseeing a (more than welcome) road-building project near Semonkong. They tease me about my government that is so Africa-obsessed that it has become Africa-confused. They laugh loudly at my suggestion that Lesotho should become part of South Africa. The Free State should rather become part of Lesotho, they suggest, and so restore Moshoeshoe's land to the Basotho.

'What are you reading there?' one of them asks, pointing to the book next to my plate.

'*Litsomo tsa Basotho*, and specifically the story of Kholumolumo. But because I have to look up just about every word, it goes slowly.'

In bits and pieces, and with great energy and overlaps, they tell the famous story to me. 'Once upon a time, or, as we say, when the world was still young, there was a gigantic dragon called Kholumolumo. (No, it was not a dragon; it was a monster! Yes. A kind of leguan; remember the tongue!) Anyway, this monster ate people. (No, not ate; he didn't chew them, he swallowed them alive.) By the time he was finished, the dragon had swallowed everybody. (The whole nation! – except one woman.) Only one woman escaped. She was pregnant, and out of misery at being the only survivor, she covered herself with ash. When Kholumolumo came near, he thought this strange shape was a stone. Because he had eaten everyone else, he was so full that he got stuck between the mountains and couldn't move. (It was a pass between the mountains! No, I never heard anything about a mountain or a pass; he was simply lying there too full to move. It's a Lesotho story, you moron; there must be mountains!)

'Then the woman gave birth to a boy. She went to pick up dry dung to make a soft bed for him. (Hey man, please, we are civilized here, dry dung for a soft bed! Come on, be serious. Hey, brother, crushed dry dung makes an excellent insulator.) Shut up now, I am trying to tell a story here. When she returned, she saw a young man with a spear and a blanket. "Where is my child?" she asked. "It's me, Mama," said the young man. "Now where are all the people?" His mother answered, "Kholumolumo ate them. He swallowed the cattle, poultry, dogs, people, everything!"

'Then the young man sharpened his spears at a whetting stone. He cut wooden pegs and sharpened them too. Then he went down to the stream, where the tip of Kholumolumo's tongue was licking the water. The tongue was so long that the young man couldn't see the mouth from where it came. (Senkatana! The young man's name was Senkatana!) Senkatana hammered the first peg into the tip of the tongue – *ki-ki-ki-ki* – and nailed it to the ground. (It was two birds that told him to use the pegs! Nonsense! The birds come only at the end of the story. My version says he simply cut the monster's throat!) I continue: then he hammered in another peg a bit higher up: *ki-ki-ki-ki*. And another. When he reached the monster's mouth, it was already dead, strangled by its own pulled-out tongue.

'Then Senkatana saw a lot of movement in Kholumolumo's stomach. He pushed a spear into the stomach and heard a cow lowing, "Don't stab me." He stabbed elsewhere and a goat bleated, "Please don't stab me." Another stab had a dog barking. At the fourth stab, Senkatana heard a human voice saying, "Auw, you are killing me!"

'Then the young man cut the stomach open. People spilled out and jubilantly ran with their arms in the air celebrating their release. They ran to the places they came from and began rebuilding their houses.

'Then some of them suggested that the one who liberated them should be their king. But others said: Only a witch could have conquered that dragon. Let us rather kill him. (You see, this is our problem: always PDO – pulling down others!)

'First they tried to throw Senkatana in a big fire, but a cloud came down to confuse them and they threw somebody else in the fire. (Where do you hear it was a cloud? It was simply a scuffle and they grabbed the wrong man. No, you miss the point; the cloud suggests that the hero has supernatural powers!) I continue: Senkatana asked: "Why do you want to burn somebody?"

'Then they tried to make him fall down a big hole covered with grass. (You're messing up the most brilliant part! When he was asked to sit on the grass, Senkatana said: No, *you* sit where you want *me* to sit!) I continue: a cloud came down and confused them so they threw another man into the hole. Senkatana asked, "Why do you want to throw somebody into the hole?"

'Lastly they tried to throw him down a high cliff. Again a cloud confused them and they threw another man. Senkatana went to resurrect the man. "Why do you want to throw somebody down the cliff?" he asked.

'Finally the people set fire to the place where Senkatana was sleeping. He got through the smoke and fire, but as he was still dazed, they killed him. At that moment his heart stormed out of him and fled into two birds. (In my version the cloud now comes and takes him away. In my mother's version there is a cow, called Tolodi-phatsoa, that helps Senkatana to escape. Finally his mother tries to feed him poisoned meat, but the cow warns him. The father then eats the meat and dies. Then the cow says: You see, your mother didn't love you.)'

'The monster is a metaphor for what?' I ask.

'Some academics have suggested that it could mean Western civilization of the last few centuries.'

'AIDS?' one suggests.

'But what I find interesting is how the version that I grew up with differs from this. At the end of the story in the *Afrikaanse Kinderensiklopedie*, the editor wrote in brackets: "(When we read this tale, we immediately think of the story of Christ.)" So Senkatana, with his desire to save his people, assimilates Christ.'

The main teller of the story shakes his head. 'That is a Western framework. In a play based on this story, written I think by S.M. Mofokeng, Senkatana has a long monologue about how life, when lived as an individual, is not a life worth living.'

(Later I found the text:

> Where is everybody? Where are the eyes of all the others
> Needed to admire with me this beauty?
> ...
> No happiness is complete when man is by himself.
> Every one of us has been created to be with others,
> To admire with one another the things that make us happy,
> To be delighted with one another, to live connected.
> Without one another freedom is empty,
> Without one another freedom is not freedom!
> But a painful rope that incarcerates.)

'So, you regard Senkatana not as a saviour, but as somebody who liberates people because he needs them to live his life?'

'To live a fully human life.'

'But then why are those he saved from the monster so terrible?'

'Remember that Senkatana conversed with animals and humans; he was assisted by clouds. He led a fully intact life. But those who went through the monster's digestive system became tainted; they never recovered fully.'

We toast with our last dregs of beer.

~

I am in Lesotho because of Moshoeshoe, but in Semonkong because of a student. Bonnini was pointed out to me when, on a campus where English, Xhosa and Afrikaans are largely spoken, I was looking for someone to perform Sesotho poems in the original language with English translation. I asked her to work with me and she said, yes, sure, 'a better Sesotho accent you will not easily find'. I was delighted, not only because of her good accent but because she could read the Lesotho orthography. (*Kholumolumo* instead of the South African *Kgodumodumo*, *Moshoeshoe* instead of *Moshweshwe*, etc.)

Bonnini has this lion-coloured skin, called *tau-tshehla* in Basotho poetry. For our performance that first time, she had her hair braided with red-copper-coloured strings and stood next to me on the dark stage like a golden glow. 'She speaks the king's Sesotho,' the interpreter from parliament complimented afterwards. 'Of course,' Bonnini said coolly, 'I come from the centre of Lesotho.'

How central and how far-flung the place is where Bonnini grew up, I learnt only yesterday, driving up from the bustling Maseru, past the neatly kept university estate at Roma, with the Madonna hoisted into what looks like a blue painted vagina in the sandstone crest of the mountain above the Catholic school, past the little village of Moitsupeli where the tar road comes to an end, past Ramabantha (Place of Belts) where the taxis come to an end, and on along an impassable road littered with petrified onion-bubbled stones, sharp basalt fissures and steep lava outpourings. I drove so slowly that for three hours I didn't get out of second gear, the same flies sat on my windscreen all the way, even the Maseru bus overtook me, people working in the fields waved in boredom, '*Dumela*,' and then, seeing a woman anxiously perching *on* the steering wheel, they exclaimed, ''*Me!*'

And yet, what dramatic, breathtaking vistas fell open from one terrible steep crawl to the next! In the pure air the colours were unusually sharp and clear, with spittle-thin waterfalls linking stone bowl to stone bowl, or threading like slender sinews from the rocks. After nearly an hour and a half, the road left the stone huts and running blanketed children behind and everything became pure spectacle. The mountains were so huge that they felt alive with prehistoric knowledge. They seemed to have raised majestic sandstone necks unreservedly.

So I would whine up an impossible slope past cream or orange portals, my hands sweating, my whole body aching the car uphill, just to become suddenly aware of the sun catching a golden-coloured dolerite dewlap to my right under scabs of soft green grass. At the top, I would stop and feast my strained eyes, only to go down, again standing on the brakes, seeing young boys on horses or waving from boulders against wild patterns of red solidified lava on the other side of an immense abyss.

Arbousset explains the blueness of the northern part of the Maluti as follows: '[T]he summit of the mountains is composed of a coarse, granular, and brittle grit stone of a dirty grey colour, which is partly responsible for the bluish tint of the range to which it owes the name Blauwbergen or Blue Mountains.'

On one plain I turned off the engine and got out of the car. The whole wide bowl was embedded in imposing, suffused-into-blue mountains and was absolutely without any movement of human or animal, an ancient, undisturbed landscape – I felt like the only primate alive in the breath of this grassy plain. Standing long enough, with just the sounds of the car cooling off, I became aware of the changing reflections of clouds and space in the broad, slow-flowing river that cut the stillness with absolute stillness.

~

'The only non-Western story I grew up with is the one about Kholu-molumo,' I say to Bonnini, who is sitting opposite me on the lodge deck with a Maluti beer.

'Which version?' she asks.

Despite the thick crusts of mud on her smart boots from the foot-path leading down the embankment to the lodge, she is cheerful, waving and greeting people she knows in the same loud banter that they direct towards her. Although her striking regal body language is still apparent, small play-acting movements have crept into her interactions, as if she forms part of a generally known game of teasing, in which everybody can read the important subtexts.

The Semonkong Lodge was Bonnini's keyhole to another life. To entertain tourists visiting the Maletsunyane Falls, a group of youngsters were at times asked to perform on the deck. So it happened that one day a husband and wife spotted Bonnini among the others and volunteered to pay for her schooling. Their choice could not have been more apt. 'Since I can remember I was ambitious. I wrote poems in Sesotho and simply stepped into the road here in Semonkong, stopped whatever car was passing through and said: "Here is a poem on this piece of paper and I am going to perform it for you." Some people waved me away, but mostly they listened and gave me money.'

Through the funding from this couple, Bonnini could successfully finish her schooling in Semonkong and a degree at the University of the Western Cape, but between Semonkong, a village with a few houses, about four general stores, a school and a prefab clinic, and a university in Cape Town lies a world few can negotiate or even articulate.

~

Bonnini and I walk up the steep road – the word 'road' is hyperbolic. Donga, boulder, rubble, scree and dark clay stratification is more accurate in this case. God knows how my car got down here, and I suspect only prayer and thank-offerings will get me back up.

Semonkong lies where the embankment flattens out. We go to one of the shops to look for Basotho blankets. At the door, on a tin drum, sits a Chinese man picking his beard. He is watching everywhere: behind the counter where a Basotho girl and an older man are doing all the transactions; at the back where the mielie-meal is being weighed. He watches who comes in, and who leaves.

'People are complaining about these China people,' one of Bonnini's friends tells us. 'They cannot speak English or Sesotho. They do not speak to anybody, let alone look properly at a person speaking to them. That man sleeps in this shop. After three years living here he only knows one word: *Suka!* – meaning *voertsek*. He takes our money, and up until now has not shared a single gesture or meal or walk or word with us. He lives like that here, among us, but as if he is dead.'

We stroll past some houses and the large cattle pen in the middle of the village until we reach Bonnini's mother's house, where she grew up with eight siblings. It is a two-roomed structure. No fence. No garden. Spotless, neat. Inside, her mother is cutting up freshly picked *maroho* in a bowl and there is no doubt where the daughter got her looks from. Golden-skinned, with the same shiny stone-wet eyes, the woman invites me into her livid blue house with decorations painted in dark pinks. She speaks in Sesotho and Bonnini translates, with lots of explanations in between, such as: This is not my mother's opinion but it is generally believed in the village; or: I do not know why she answers your question like this.

After a suitable time I am offered pap, *maroho* and a glass of water from the water bucket, which has obviously been carried from somewhere. 'My mother is sorry that everything is cold, but she thought we would be coming already this morning.'

I keep my eyes on the plate. How do I do justice to such a gentle and beneficent gesture? Everything on this plate or in this glass has been gathered or processed with great trouble, plus the knowledge of how bodyness will pick and shred and stir and taste and give itself. The perfect texture of the pap, the amount of salt in it, the sharp taste of the *maroho* that pierces my mind with memories of sitting long-legged with black women under a tree eating from the same pot, the cool water in the scratched but surviving glass. At the same time, it feels as if the gesture is not about the food, also not about *giving* at all, but about sharing a physical generosity. It is as if the skin containing my body has become porous, as if I am dissolving into a delicate balance with this woman and her daughter, their offered food and all the places it comes from.

Maybe it's also even more than that: in this house where a rural mother sits with her university-qualified daughter, unable even to begin to guess the complications of her life, the meal is shared within the context of a deep trust that whatever is shared, now, with me, is not only worth sharing, but confirms what has always been known here: being part of. Not of some thought-out or yet-to-come imagined space, but part of something that *is*, calibrating heartbeats.

chapter fifteen

SNOW Phase One

Everything in Berlin is covered in a feather-soft layer of fluffy snow.
The biggest immediate problem is to recognize dog turds – because
a shoe sunk into an Alsatian turd stinks as much below zero as above.
On the lake one can clearly see fox tracks and one knows that those
nine ducks on the little island are not so noisy at night now because
they are bloody cold. Just before the first big snowfall, a woodpecker
hysterically pecked a hole in the branch in front of my window.
One could immediately see that he was not pecking haphazardly.
No, he was stiffening his neck to get his head at a specific angle so he
could moer his beak like a drill in one spot. Someone skated on the
lake and left ugly tracks. I find myself thinking that snow should be
left unhumanized. Apparently one may not venture onto the lakes
until the police give clearance after testing. Police have time to test
the thickness of ice on ponds? 'Of course, ze police are keeping
ze citizens safe, ja?' says the person at the bus stop. There is snow for
the first time on the roofs, so everything starts to feel seriously
'snowed under'.

SNOW *Phase Two*

Okay. What I didn't know is that there is a phase two in snow. Today is minus three. They say that a '*mächtiges Hochdruckgebiet über Norden Russlands*' now brings to '*Mitteleuropa kalt trockenes Wetter mit Schneeflocken*'. God, everything sounds colder in Deutsch. We are learning the difference between snow (which is white) and ice (which is transparent) and iced snow (which is white as snow but hard as ice). To keep balance one walks the pavement wide-legged, as if there is an ice *Kegel* in one's pants. Anxiously we hold hands. At times you think you are stepping on snow but it turns out to be ice and your shoes get wheels. In Snow Phase Two the dog turds are obviously sorted out; in fact they are so sorted out that dog-owners stand bending over in order to prevent the turd from freezing to the arse. How does one walk then? Wonderful people (obeying the law) sweep the pavements or strew ash on them.

Initially J. refuses to wear a beanie. ('I cannot think up into a beanie,' he says.) However, today is so cold that he buys one, but now he complains that it is made for young men whose little ears are still tight to their heads, and not for the dreary, elongated ears of old men. We eat *Currywurst und Bratwurst* like we eat biltong and chips in South Africa. J. had *Blutwurst* the other day: two gigantic things that you cannot describe without being politically incorrect peering out from under an avalanche of *Kartoffeln*. Potato mash is so tasty here that one cannot really call it mash – we even had *Kartoffeln* with grated truffles, parmesan and a dash of cognac. We've eaten *Leberwurst* from glass bottles, *Wurst* in soup, *Wurst* on bread, we've discovered *Rotkohl*, we've had *Gans mit Kastanien*, and by eleven o'clock in the mornings we've already downed our first *Glühwein*. It is cold. Bloody freezing cold. And, as the snotty travel book says, German food only makes sense in the middle of winter. And this is where we are, in the middle; and God, does this food make fantastic sense!

CONVERSATION 5

INTERCONNECTED WITH WHOM?

'So, if you have established that there is indeed a particular African philosophy present behind the actions of black people in, say, southern Africa ... by the way, why not Africa? If England, Sweden and Italy are European, or Australia and the States are Western, then this interconnectedness can surely be African?'

'A white South African cannot, yet, really name something African, I think. Besides, when I read about the Nigerian gods and deities, I think, Jesus, maybe not, and when I read that the missionaries were perturbed when they arrived in southern Africa because they found "no idols to shatter, no altars to seize, no fetishes to smash", in contrast to the rest of Africa, then I think, maybe the particular kind of interconnectedness I have come to know is confined to the southern part of the continent.'

'Would it not have come from the north with the black people moving down?'

'I thought about that, and my guess is that this all-encompassing philosophy, this interconnectedness with "the wholeness of life" – religious and secular, spiritual and material, which can never be compartmentalized or understood in isolation from one another – was inherited from the First People population, which lived mostly in southern Africa. Especially because it implies a cosmological dimension, a human and non-human world that encapsulates plants, animals, a spiritual god and ancestors. There is enough evidence in the records about the San and Khoi suggesting such a sophisticated world view. I believe that just as much as their click sounds have survived in our African languages, so this broad philosophy of an interconnectedness towards something more spiritual, more whole, more towards the potential power of everything, has survived in the minds of the speakers of those languages.'

'Needless to say then that you obviously do not go along with the Hegelian notion that some civilizations are on a lower scale in terms of development than those of "a more advanced spirit" (*der höher stehende Geist*). So let's continue: you have established this world view; now what do you want to do with it?'

'I want to say: what makes Nelson Mandela such a special statesman is the fact that his political acumen is embedded in this world view. It is because he, in contrast to the whites, regards white South Africans as part of his interconnectedness. But white people battle to understand that; we treat Mandela as an exception and ignore for convenience's sake that he himself keeps on saying that he is what he is because of others. The same with Tutu. What makes his theology and actions so remarkable is not the Christianity but that his Christianity is embedded in this world view. He redefines his Christian community in terms of interconnectedness. The remarkable work of Pumla Gobodo-Madikizela on the psychology of victims and forgiveness could find its remarkableness precisely because it was embedded in this world view. The brilliant book by Njabulo Ndebele about Winnie Mandela is unlike anything else published in South Africa because it treats the phenomenon of Winnie within this context of embeddedness, not only in perspective but also in form. No main character, no hero, no linearity. And so I can go on. I want to insist that we impoverish ourselves by ignoring this embeddedness. To say blacks and whites are all the same is an impoverishing experience.'

'It reminds me of Carol Gilligan's "ethics of care". Her research indicates that it is not a sense of justice, but a sense of interconnectedness that guides people in general and women in particular as a moral force. Despite some problems in her research, she found that women think about morality in terms of their responsibility towards the people they care for.'

'If I understand Kwame Gyekye correctly, I think the community in African terms is more fluid and more inclusive, with its variety of simultaneous links and networks woven through clanship, cattle, marriage, initiation and rituals. But of course there is tension. African intellectuals like Tiyo Soga complained already in the nineteenth century that "wholeness" was destroyed by the entry of Christianity into southern Africa; note: not through Christianity itself, but because Christians *excluded* non-believers from their houses – albeit on missionary orders.

'A century later, writer and scholar A.C. Jordan insisted that the idea of community should include strangers. He said that interconnectedness is what takes place between the community and the stranger. One not only becomes a person through one's community but also through the stranger. To avoid the disasters of the past, Jordan said, the figure of the stranger ought to be continually reinvented, and it is the specific task of the intellectual in a society to be an advocate for the stranger – to insist on responsibility for the stranger as constitutive of collectivity itself.'

———————

SNOW Phase Three

Mink. Yes, in phase three one begins to think deeply about mink. About animal. One feels that only a full-blooded animal can pull one through this cold. J. stood for a while at a stall next to the Spree River where they sell thick Russian mink hats. 'It's only the knowledge that my children will kill themselves laughing that's preventing me from buying one, because really I feel my brain shrinking this morning into a nut.' We went to Dresden by train, and in my whole life I have never been so cold. The wind cuts through anorak, space-blanket top, camel-hair vest as if it's gauze. Blowing one's frozen nose while wearing gloves is pure guesswork-and-mercy about what should be wiped and what should be blown where. So we burst into the Gemäldegalerie Alte Meister, our noses watering, our glasses fogged up, our faces frozen into Parkinson's-like expressions.

We see people with babies in prams. 'Taking one's child out must be like preparing for a life-threatening expedition,' I say, as we watch small children standing patiently while their parents put one layer of clothing on top of the other.

Back home the street is like an ice rink. We hang onto each other. Suddenly, while we are crossing the road under the light of the little green walking man, a car starts to slip. One can see the driver pulling the wheel, but it has no influence, and the car comes straight for J. We are caught in the same inertia – trying to run, but not succeeding on the slippery snow. After it just misses him, J. yells, lifting his fist: 'Boemsen! You bloody boemsen!'

'What on earth does that mean?' I ask.

———————

'Don't you remember *Cabaret*?' he says. 'Liza Minnelli teaches the young man the German word *boemsen* for "fucking".'

Oh, but the absolute joy of entering the warm but uncluttered flat! We hang up our coats and scarves, take off our shoes, put the radio on rbb Kulturradio and make Tchibo coffee. Life is perfect.

SNOW Phase Four

This is snow mud. It is dirty, and it goes *ggorts-ggorts* when you walk, and you need waterproof shoes. It is heavy walking in a substance consisting of anything from dog turds to dead birds. 'How do birds die?' I ask J. 'Do they sit on a branch until they keel over? Or do they fly down to die?' But the thread of the conversation is lost when a cyclist falls in front of us in the treacherous mixture of gravel, ash, ice and snow. Mucus shoots in silver threads from his nose and his thin hands claw like lobsters in the slush. Before we can stop ourselves, we burst out laughing. Hurt and angry, the cyclist looks up, but we helplessly hang onto a lamp post and scream our heads off. Snow Phase Four reduces the city to a dirty, merciless hole.

chapter sixteen

Moshoeshoe once explained his view on all the treaties. He took a table, covered it with a tablecloth, placed a desk on top of the table, a letter on the desk, and a hat on the letter. The table, he said, was the (preferred) Napier Treaty, the tablecloth the Maitland minute that succeeded it; the bottom of the desk was Harry Smith's minute, and the upper part of the desk the High Commissioner's words; the letter was Sir George Grey's words, and the hat the current proposal by Moshoeshoe. 'Suppose the treaties are said to be dead,' he said; 'they are like grandparents in their graves, but their descendants are alive still.' In this way Moshoeshoe demonstrated something more than simple hierarchy, suggesting an inclusive convergence of all the proposals with the animating influence of the past upon the present and future.

But the wolf was at the door.

For nearly ten years, Moshoeshoe regularly appealed to the British for protection. Although he had proven himself a reliable ally, Cathcart, Warden and the latest British Commissioner cancelled and dishonoured signed treaties and agreements as they pleased. As all his efforts came to naught, he found himself facing his biggest threat, the Boers, alone.

Within four years of becoming a Republic, the Free Staters decided to get rid of Moshoeshoe. The forces sent to attack the Basotho first burnt down the mission station at Bersheeba. At Letsie's village they came across

Boer body parts taken either as trophies or as war medicine to strengthen Basotho warriors in battle. Infuriated, they burnt Letsie's village to the ground as well as Arbousset's manse at Morija, destroying twenty-five years of documentation and research. Then the chase was cut to the impenetrable heart of the Basotho: Thaba-Bosiu.

On the morning of 5 May 1858, the mountain was rocked by cannon and rifle fire while the Boers were storming up Khubelu pass. The Basotho, hidden behind rocks and ramparts and in crannies, opened fire. According to one eyewitness, 'Bullets came down the hill like rain.' Some Basotho swept round the south-eastern part of the mountain, threatening to cut off the Boers from their camp. The Boers retreated, and their defeat subsequently became celebrated in Sesotho praise poetry.

> The children of Moshoeshoe chased the whites
> *Qhala-qhala* they dispersed
> They scrambled everywhere
> They hid anywhere among the stones on the hills
> Sugar and beer spilled – hastily thrown away
> Only coffee dregs stayed behind on the plains
> Yes, their wagons fell into the Caledon River
> As they tried to swim across
> When they turned back
> They saw their own people killed
> They saw birds flying low over the ground.
> …
> One of them was stabbed by an assegai
> Later the crows dragged him to and fro
> Insects crept into his eyes
> Vultures tore his beard
> Ravens pecked right through his tongue
> …
> Yes, the buttocks of the brave ones shuddered
> Horses ran away with saddles strapped to their backs
> In other places and far away countries
> Women and children turned towards Lesotho and cried.

Sir George Grey was sent from the Colony to intervene in what was to become the first of three wars between the Free State Republic and the Basotho. Expecting the worst, Moshoeshoe made an unusually cynical remark: 'Yes! Sir George is the fifth great man who has come here to make matters right between me and the Boers ... and such arrangements have always ended by a piece of country being lost to my people.'

By now, Casalis had returned to France, which was a huge loss for Moshoeshoe in his interaction with whites, as there was no other missionary who matched Casalis in terms of loyalty, insight, finesse and trust. The king, close to seventy years old, with failing physical and mental powers, and without his favourite missionary by his side, was acutely aware that he had not yet secured the future of his people. He told Commissioners Joseph Orpen and John Burnet in 1862: 'What I desire is this: that the Queen should send a man to live with me, who will be her ear and eye, and also her hand to work with me in political matters. He will practise the Basuto and gradually teach them to hear magistrates, while he is helping me in political matters.'

Although the term 'indirect rule' had not been invented at the time, it was exactly what Moshoeshoe had envisioned. Casalis had originally helped Moshoeshoe to formulate this concept and to convey his new diplomatic intention in correspondence in English.

Commissioners Orpen and Burnet said of Moshoeshoe to the High Commissioner: 'He has not the slightest confidence in anybody, British, Colonial, Free State, or Basotho, save only in himself. "I am Basutoland."' Burnet reported separately: 'He will never be anything but a great humbug, an old liar and deceiver, without one particle of truth, faith, honesty or sincerity.'

The king was desperate. For the first time during his reign, and to the surprise of his people, he started to end his *pitso* and *kgotla* meetings with the words: *Are shueleng fatsi la rona!* (Let us die for the land that is ours!) 'The first time he did it the whole assembly was electrified, but soon afterwards nothing else was heard, but the words, repeated a thousand times: Let us die for the land that is ours.'

When he heard that the son of Queen Victoria was to visit South

Africa in 1860, Moshoeshoe urgently requested to meet him. During an interview in Aliwal North, the old king gave a written request to the young prince, hoping that the son could at least speak to and for the mother:

> My trust had always been in the Queen from the first, and I am the oldest of Her Majesty's servants and subjects in this country ... and in spite of everything that has happened to me, and in the midst of many troubles, I have been faithful in my allegiance to Her Majesty. My prayer today is that I may be restored to the same position among the Queen's servants that I first held, for I am become as the least of them. Let whatever fault I may have committed be to-day forgiven. You are the Queen's own Son, give me peace in her name.

The letter elicited no response. Moshoeshoe sent another plea, with the same result. When President Brand took over the reins in the Free State Republic in 1864, Moshoeshoe pleaded once more with the British. The newly appointed Governor Wodehouse eventually decided to hold a conference with all interested parties near the Caledon River, and a determined Moshoeshoe set out in full force and great display. His soldiers and those of Letsie, dressed in civilian clothes, formed a line of honour for several kilometres along the banks of a raging Caledon River. The king arrived carrying a British flag, as a sign that he was an ally. As there was no boat, an old leaky barge was quickly fixed and Moshoeshoe was ferried across with a few of his sons.

One of the missionaries described the event: 'The Governor and Lady Wodehouse received Moshoeshoe with great kindness. The latter then went to greet the president of the Free State ... As always Moshoeshoe was the most remarkable of the members of this kind of little congress. It was obvious that he had donned his state dress for this interview. He wore a wide sleeved riding coat of sorts, not unlike an ample ladies' pelisse, all laced with gold; a magnificent garb which the natives must undoubtedly have greatly admired.'

The debate about the land began. Brand stood up and suggested that the land the Free Staters were occupying had been bought from a Bushman. Moshoeshoe, seated to the left of the Governor, became so agitated that he could hardly wait his turn. He jumped up and demanded to know the name of this Bushman. Brand withdrew the remark. Thereafter Moshoeshoe gave a constructive speech explaining the difference between providing hospitality and giving away land permanently after a *pitso* agreement.

But, again, despite a good speech and an amicable conversation, nothing happened to remove the Warden Line that ran close to the Caledon River. This river, called Mohokare (river of willows) in Sesotho, represented the nailbed of Basotho territory and it was seen as an unacceptable violation when it was crossed by the enemy. In a praise poem for the river by K.E. Ntsane, it is said that if Major Warden had never seen the river, the land all the way to Winburg would still belong to the Basotho. The river is celebrated in this long poem for its ability to twist white men out of their coats when it was in full flood and for carelessly cutting across the land claimed by the whites.

Asked to study all the documents, Joseph Orpen, who was married to one of the French missionaries' daughters, found evidence that the Basotho indeed occupied the land from Winburg all the way to Lady Grey, so that, although historians suggested in later years that Moshoeshoe was 'pushing out' the boundaries of 1830, he was in fact only confirming existing ones. In his appeals to the British to recognize the Napier boundaries, Orpen cited the presence of ruins and graves as proof of long ownership.

In vain. A month after the meeting at the Caledon River, Moshoeshoe received a letter from Governor Wodehouse, and another from President Brand, ordering him to remove his people from what they described as 'the Free State side of the line'. The missionaries reported that Moshoeshoe was deeply wounded by this order. Orpen observed the effect on the king's sons: 'I could see Moperi's lips quiver as he spoke about the narrow Lesuto that one could cross and recross in a day ... "What a destroyer without pity the white man is. Where are we to go?" ... And Molapo ... broke out into a bitter laugh as he said, "How am I to explain it to my people, that they are to leave their own villages where they were born?"'

Whatever the leaders were negotiating, the Basotho themselves never stopped raiding livestock from white farmers. Daring operations were carried out deep into the Free State where, during one set of raids, more than a hundred thousand sheep and thousands of cattle were seized.

But by the end of that month, Basotho people were streaming southwards towards Thaba-Bosiu with livestock, corn supplies and other properties. The British were impressed by this cooperation, but the Free Staters wanted revenge for their humiliation at Thaba-Bosiu. Knowing that he could not fight both the Boers and the Colony, Moshoeshoe again pleaded for assistance from England, 'for all persons know that my great sin is that I possess a good and fertile country'. His request was ignored.

In what became known as the Seqiti War, the Free State attacked the Basotho. Moshoeshoe remained on Thaba-Bosiu, ill and old, while his kingdom broke into chiefdoms, each of which fought the war on its own. Finally the Free State commando, under the command of Louw Wepener, attacked Thaba-Bosiu and twice tried to storm to the top of the mountain. On the second attempt, Wepener reached the summit before he was killed. The Basotho, some of them under the command of Masopha, the-Falcon-whose-teeth-open-against-the-void, were so enraged by his cheek and enamoured of his blind courage, that they charged down with great elation and attacked President Brand and his men. Brand joined the long succession of leaders whose men had failed to conquer the Mountain of the Night: Matiwane, Sekonyela, Mzilikazi, Cathcart and Boshof.

In an unbelievable twist of logic, the Boers only increased their demands: Moshoeshoe had to become an ordinary citizen of the Free State, evacuate Thaba-Bosiu and pay 40 000 cattle, 60 000 sheep and 5 000 horses as cross-border and war damage to the republic, while *all* his land had to become part of the Free State. Moshoeshoe repeated his pleas to the British. In the meantime his nephew raided prosperous farmers in Natal, killing and mutilating a group of trekkers. This was the excuse the Boers were waiting for, and President Pretorius and his commander Paul Kruger from the Transvaal declared war. Boer commandos systematically began to destroy Basotho villages, plundering the grain supplies and crops and capturing vast numbers of livestock. By March 1866 the Basotho, who had once produced all the grain used by themselves and the Free State, were facing starvation, and Moshoeshoe was forced to sign the humiliating Peace of Thaba-Bosiu (*Khotso ea Mabele*).

After what was left of the harvest had been gathered in mid-1867, the king, not intending to honour any of the terms of the latest peace accord, prepared for war. Brand got his army ready, while a diplomatic flurry ensued as Moshoeshoe tried desperately to get the British to act on his behalf.

Although everything had been thrown into the battle for survival against overwhelming forces, Moshoeshoe's set-up was vulnerable to the coarse competition and sweeping appropriation of colonialism. The society that he and his people had built through immense energy and charisma, intellect and skill, humaneness and visionary ambition, accommodating a variety of groups and cultures, found itself eroded and fragmenting. Uprooted, dislodged, bereft and sensing Moshoeshoe's end, the Basotho began to fight among themselves. According to Arbousset, lawlessness descended on Lesotho.

The surrounding powers took note. On 13 January 1866, Wodehouse suggested that Basotholand be annexed, but the colonial secretary refused. Meanwhile, the Free State bypassed Moshoeshoe and forced all the remaining chiefs under him to sign documents that resulted in their losing land and herds of livestock. To remove Western-educated supporters among the Basotho, all the Paris missionaries were expelled. New land was taken and divided into 3 000-acre farms. Moshoeshoe's son Molapo and his people, initially placed to consolidate the Napier boundary, became part of a 'reserve' and had to pay annual tax of ten shillings per hut, were liable for military service and had to carry passes. Several chiefs under Moshoeshoe broke out in acts of angry raiding, in reaction to which President Brand sent an ultimatum. Moshoeshoe's reply was strident: 'I beg to know what is the cause of this year's war. Last year it was through the wish to enlarge your country. This year it seems that it is caused by your wish to exterminate the Basutos.'

Infuriated, Brand sent out commandos to destroy what they could find. In a last-ditch attempt, Moshoeshoe approached the Natal government for protection, playing it off against the Cape. Then the seemingly impossible happened: a special deputation on behalf of the expelled Paris missionaries, led by none other than Eugène Casalis, reached London and urged the British government to intervene on behalf of the Basotho.

On 13 January 1868, Moshoeshoe was told that his request had been granted and that his people could become British subjects. On 26 January he responded: 'I have become old; therefore I am glad that my people should have been allowed to rest and to lie under the large folds of the flag of England before I am no more.' This announcement stopped the third attack of the Free State Republic in its tracks.

Moshoeshoe's joy was soon crushed by the miserly terms of the boundary settlement. Becoming a British subject didn't restore his kingdom, but rather gave him remnants of it. In one of his last letters Moshoeshoe said: 'I have been covered with shame, – and I feel great grief; for the hope I had has fallen to the ground and the affairs have been settled in quite a different way to that which we have been led to expect.'

In January 1870 Moshoeshoe performed his last official duty. He convened a meeting of chiefs and headmen on Thaba-Bosiu and stepped down as king, in favour of his eldest son Letsie. True to his nature, Moshoeshoe's act was reconciliatory. As there was already a destructive rivalry between Letsie and Molapo (the very two sons who had welcomed the missionaries on horseback when they had first set foot in Lesotho and who lived with them during those first years), Moshoeshoe suggested an elaborate plan to heal the division, but because his proposition was against custom, it was ignored by the Basotho.

Over the years, Moshoeshoe had sent requests, letters, petitions and documents via officials, politicians and even her son to the Queen of England without ever receiving any direct response from her. During his last days, sick and ailing, he sent her a leopard-skin kaross – described in several texts as absolutely 'magnificent' – as 'a token of my gratitude for the precious peace we enjoy since we have been proclaimed British subjects'. Ironically, or comically, it would be this item, this 'splendid trifle', that finally moved the forty-year-old Queen into action. In an immediate response she instructed Wodehouse to tell Moshoeshoe that she would 'always feel an interest in the welfare of himself and his Tribe under British protection'.

But by the time the message reached Thaba-Bosiu, the king was dead.

PART THREE

The Long Conversation:
Whose Context?

chapter seventeen

21 April 2008

Only three months left. And Berlin breaks out into a spring so verdant that even the sky seems the lightest of green. The branches are still covered in winter moss, but they sprout light-green fountains, tassels, threads or chic tails of leaves. It seems as if every tree tries to press as much green life as possible from its thinnest ends. The shrubs simply burst fully occupied into green. The air sizzles with bird sounds, small, clear chisel sounds, beautiful solo cadenzas by blackbirds, and from the grass shoot daffodil, narcissus and all the fairy flowers. The first full shroud was from the willows, followed by white and pink bursts of blossoms that swirl in wind patterns on the air.

Do I want to go back? Can I go back to Africa, rotten to the core as I have become? Not only is my skin whiter than it has ever been before, but my mind is white. A white mind? What is that? To enjoy a punctual bus, regular trains, safe surroundings, is that white? Not to be confronted by poverty, is that white? To listen to classical music and read European literature, is that white? To be moved as I have never been moved by anything in my life, bodily moved, by the poetry of Paul Celan, does that make me white?

I admire the Berliners for dealing with their guilt with such consistent, sober and extended gravity. I admire them for the way they have built up their devastated city (which had had the first tramline, the first electricity) after two World Wars, and for recently incorporating East Berlin with all its magnificent complexities and complicities. I admire the strong socialist debates in the newspapers, the way in which culture and not money remains the yardstick. Does that make me white?

In the eighteenth century the Swedish naturalist Carolus Linnaeus described European man (*Homo europaeus*) as the pinnacle of humanity, with his qualities of being versatile, shrewd and inventive (*Levis, argutus, inventor*). This is not what I am, nor what I necessarily want to be. I am trying to become others, plural, interconnected-towards-caringness.

I try to read as little as possible about South Africa. All the news is depressing, because it reflects crime, violence and astonishingly cruel behaviours and crass, unthinking racist articulations. Why do I want to go back?

Hasensprung stands in diverse clauses of green, in scriptures of light. It looks like a Gothic cathedral with green buttresses.

1 May 2008

If depression doesn't have an evolutionary function, why does it still exist? According to one of the colloquiums, depression assists humans to save energy, to avoid danger, to manipulate others, to reconsider strategies and to avoid attacks by the dominant. A low mood sees to it that you reconsider your activities and goals and lower your expectations. In other words, one becomes depressed when one's expectations have been too high. The depression compels you to recalibrate to lower and possibly more achievable expectations.

What made this colloquium interesting is how it made the difference visible between Anglo-American and European, especially German, thinking. 'You use the word depression but you never use the word *Melancholie*,' said a German philosopher. 'Aristotle already used the word melancholy to describe a particular kind of wistfulness. Melancholy, of which only a small subsection is depression, is the inability to act, an inertness, and lies at the heart of man's insight and lack of insight into death. Even more importantly, melancholy is the other side of creativity.'

From what I could gather, melancholy is accepted by most Germans as an integral part of being human. Things are different in America, where one is constantly fed with goals and desires. (Evidence of this is that only 10 per cent of the population suffers from depression in South Africa, Italy and Germany, and only 8 per cent in Nigeria, while 22 per cent of the American population is depressed.) Nobody can fulfil these desires instigated by consuming and money, so one is doomed to feel a failure. The European ethos, with its emphasis on culture, provides for a resigned sadness, because the world is beautiful, or filled with mortality, or empty.

'That is why we find the emphasis in America on so-called happiness, even contained in its constitution, completely inexplicable. The opposite of melancholy can never be happiness.'

(I sit with my laptop at Hagenplatz cake shop. Swirls of pink blossoms drift over me just as I saw in the children's books by Astrid Lindgren. My stomach is sick with horror. Zimbabweans appear on my screen, swollen, terrified, with raw, ripped backs and burnt bodies – done by us, by South Africans. The violence that whites always feared would turn towards them has now, once again, turned towards blacks. I cannot bear it.)

Liewe Ma
Today I saw:
- A woman in Bismarckallee in a mink coat, gloves and slippers sweeping the pavement outside her house. (How does it feel to put on a mink coat and then slip into a pair of worn-out slippers? How does a broom feel underneath expensive kid gloves?)
- A delivery truck in Erdener Strasse: '*Hier wirkt der Meister noch selbst.*' (Is he saying that mostly the Meisters do not work them-

selves any more? Or is he aware of the well-known Celan poem's most famous line, 'Death is ein Meister aus Deutschland / his eyes are blue', and that this is actually a signal to neo-Nazis?)
- Every tree in Berlin is numbered!
- A hair salon called *Lohengrin*.
- A trade union called *Verdi*!
- On a piece of paper at the bus stop a student advertised: Want garden work. Can come whenever. (Working on PhD and looking for breaks with real hard physical work.)

What can I say, except something unutterable like the ontology here is devouring the epistemology?
   Your *stumme* daughter.

14 May 2008

A visit to Istanbul starts at the airport in Berlin. There are more people seeing the passengers off than there are passengers. The Australian professor and I are travelling to Turkey to participate in a conference, 'Dealing with the Past', organized by a German foundation.

   With us in the queue are several short, broad-shouldered men with kofias and moustaches, and older women with unfashionable headscarfs, cinnamon-coloured coats and little round shoes. There are huge loads of luggage, all neatly wrapped in plastic and canvas bags. They don't understand German and the German officials don't speak Turkish. The elderly gentleman and his wife in front of me slow down the queue as they say their goodbyes to those who are staying behind in Berlin. They cry and embrace, shout messages, exchange pieces of paper with numbers.

   When at last they move forward, the security officer asks: '*Guten Tag, mein Herr und meine Dame, haben sie einen Laptop in ihrem Rückgepäck?*' The couple converse in order to work out what is being asked. From behind the glass partitions one sees the anxious faces of the staying-behind family members. Some of them make gestures of distress. At last one of the men hammers against the glass and shouts what sounds like: 'Nein, nein. Just say nein! Just say nein to everything!' The old oom says: 'Nein.' With relief on his face the security officer puts their luggage on the conveyor belt for the X-rays. Alarms. Pandemonium. Officials are called to the screen: in the enormous suitcase one can clearly see the outline of two copper lamps (the djinni kind) and a water-pipe smoking contraption.

Another bout of pleading rises in Turkish from the couple and in German from the family behind the screen. In the meantime the officials have opened the old woman's bag and found it stuffed with food: butter, yoghurt, rice, bottled vegetables, dried vegetables, bottles and bottles filled with what looks like rose water. There are also three sets of hair clippers.

The official points to the rubbish bin: everything, right in there. The oom grabs his chest as if anticipating a heart attack. The auntie throws her arms to the side and wails to the ceiling. One of the family members breaks through security and starts negotiating in German, with asides in Turkish. Some things are quickly put in a kitbag he has with him to be put through as hold luggage, but most of the food ends up in the rubbish bin while the auntie watches, her mouth covered by her hand. Needless to say, the flight was heavily delayed.

The professor and I are sitting together in the aeroplane and, as agreed beforehand, I explain the process that set me thinking about blackness and whiteness.

'Being with black people during the struggle years made me feel not white or black, but intensely human. We felt that we were one another's brothers and sisters. But since the Truth and Reconciliation Commission I have become aware (and when I wrote my book about the commission I was not yet registering this at all!) of a way of being human that I find to be more ... superior is too strong a word, but something like that. A way that, suddenly, made me *sense* the world, made me make sense *of* the world. Archbishop Desmond Tutu spoke of a moral universe – I don't necessarily know about that, but I felt in touch with something into which I could dissolve while simultaneously becoming more what I am.'

'As an individual?'

'I don't know. Being a child in a large family I obsessively cultivated my individualism. At one stage as a student I became immersed in Ayn Rand's virtue of selfishness, and on the Boere-campus where I was, I lived a life as cold and self-demanding as I could, despising everything selfless as weak. But then through politics I learnt from black people another way of being of which I realized immediately that I understood nothing. This was brought home to me very powerfully through three interviews about my work as a journalist reporting on the activities of the Truth Commission.

'The first interview was done by a film maker from Tel Aviv. Brimming with compliments for the Truth Commission process, he remarked in a throwaway phrase that, of course, such a process would never work in Israel. "Why not?" I asked. "Christians," he muttered. "Christianity is what makes forgiveness tick."

'Of course, how stupid of me, I thought at the time.

'In the same month, one of Ireland's top radio journalists interviewed me in a specially set-up studio in the Cape Grace Hotel. He had just returned from interviewing a woman who lived in a squatter camp in Hout Bay. His eyes were rolling with incredulity, his body language filled with exasperation. "This woman talked about forgiveness. We pointed to the big mansions of white people within walking distance of her shack, while she, after so many years, still had nothing. And what did she say? Was she angry? No, she said things cannot change overnight, and then she talked about forgiveness!"'

In the meantime a little Indian boy, seated with his family in front of us, starts to cry, loudly, while looking everywhere and particularly at us in the back. He has a pair of wonderful brown, long-lashed eyes that do not have a single tear in them, while his nose and mouth flood. And the sound! A continuous roar. Under his challenging gaze, I continue.

'During the interview, I had a feeling that the journalist's thoughts were still with this woman and that he was battling feelings of scorn.

After we had finished, I asked him about the possibilities of a similar process in Ireland. He vehemently shook his head. "It will never work in Ireland with the Protestants, never! Confession, contrition, these are Catholic things." Again I thought, of course, how stupid of me! Our Truth Commission had been based largely on the South American examples, with their Catholic ethos.

'The third interview was with an Australian law student, for her PhD thesis. After a laborious interview, with a sense of hostility that was difficult to source, she made no bones about her view: "The TRC is nothing but white people bulldozing black people into forgiveness and reconciliation. And this I find even more atrocious and unjust than apartheid ever was."

'As I walked back to my car, her words rang in my ears. Was this true? I had seen and heard hundreds and hundreds of black people come daily to the commission, listen with their headphones, or talk peacefully into the microphone, or confront perpetrators – was this merely a front controlled from behind by whites in an effort to get themselves off scot-free? Or was her suggestion one of the biggest insults to millions of people who had just overthrown apartheid? Surely I could not accept that people like Nelson Mandela, his first democratic cabinet, our vibrant civil society, Desmond Tutu, the church, the youth movements were in fact all stooges or at best puppets manipulated by whites to forgive them.

'Apart from anything else, it simply did not tie in with what I was experiencing in the Truth Commission process. It was in fact *whites* who were uncomfortable about this reconciliation and forgiveness business.'

By this time in our flight to Istanbul, the mother has given up and is crying herself, and so is the elder brother. The father walks up and down the aisle with the boy bellowing through his splayed mouth, spreading the torture through the cabin.

'Many white people assumed that the new ANC government would take revenge through property and economic extractions, and put various measures in place to protect themselves. It didn't happen.

When the Truth Commission was introduced, whites thought: Here it comes, the Great Revenge! But, again, despite the commission travelling across the country listening to two thousand horrific stories of human rights abuses, not only were there no revenge attacks, but some people were actually forgiven.

'I heard whites say: What is going on with these people? Why do they forgive? Some of them forgive even before forgiveness has been asked. What kind of people are these? "You see, they are not like us; they can't even hate properly." So their very humaneness was used to describe their inhumanity.

'White people were prepared for the worst at the hands of a black government. What they weren't prepared for was to be forgiven. It made and still makes whites deeply uncomfortable: we respect fury, we understand hatred and, at its deepest level, we admire revenge. So I am trying to understand what specifically underpinned the forgiveness by black South Africans.'

'Why must it be something specific? Why can't it be a mixture of Christianity, be it Catholic or Protestant, human rights and an African sense of restorative justice?'

'Because the usurpation of the TRC process by Christianity and human rights obscures how, as I see it, a radically new way, embedded in an indigenous view of the world, had been put on the table by black people at the end of the twentieth century. I am not saying it is a better way than the post–Second World War approach, but it is a *different* way of dealing with injustice so that it becomes possible for a country to break out of its cycles of violence.'

'But I still don't understand what difference it would make to say it was all these things plus political acumen etc. that played different roles.'

'By saying it is all these things or particular individuals like Nelson Mandela, the *credit* that something remarkable originated in *blackness* or a black world view is removed.'

The father with the crying son returns to his seat, and when we touch the runway the professor says: 'You've got to give the child credit; the flight didn't impede his volume intensity at all!'

Liewe Ma

How do birds die? I asked the ornithologist here, because despite all the bird sounds one does not see enough bird skeletons in the forest or on the street to understand anything about this. One cannot see that a bird is old, he told me. And an ordinary bird with its small body mass has to build up only one milligram of fat per day to survive the night. If it doesn't manage to do that, it will fall off its branch during the night. He also told me that a guard at Auschwitz carefully kept a record of the birds and their habits.

Liewe Ma

Did you know that Berlin has bunkers – all in working condition, with water, food, radiation-clearing machines and beds, even a screen on which you can see what is happening outside on the street? The bunker I visited is fitted out to protect more than two thousand people during a nuclear incident. It is so totally crazy! My heart bleeds for us, from another planet, who can't even manage to protect ourselves against robberies! Imagine actively protecting yourself against nuclear threats! It also suggests of course that hunger is solved, and housing, health, water. Ag tog! The guide says Austria is the only country in Europe that has enough bunker space for all its citizens. Germany can protect only a third of its people, but a bunker such as this one on Kurfürstendamm has to take anybody on the street who wants refuge during a nuclear threat. So the law stipulates that even you (the guide points at me), who are not a citizen, have to be taken in when you come down the steps to be protected. I am pleased. Not for the bunker space, but for recognizing that I am 'not from here'.

We are picked up at the airport and the first thing to take one's breath away is the outline of Istanbul. It is poor. The whole city consists of endless jagged rows of ten-storey flaking buildings, but here and there are exquisite, enormous mosques, pressed like saucer-shaped spaceships among the square buildings. I have never seen anything like it.

We decide to go and see the mosques before the conference begins. Unlike the mosques in West Africa, they are open to tourists, and the spaces inside are absolutely breathtaking, with an airiness and masterly control in sober decoration that creates an atmosphere of delicate lightness. At the Hagia Sophia, a basilica that became a mosque and is now a museum, the professor reminds me of a colloquium we had in which it was said that the very first account of eye movement in art history was about the Hagia Sophia. During the sixth century, a text described how one's eyes are captured immediately by the golden dome, but because the eyes do not discern any pillars holding the dome up, because nothing leads the eye to the dome, one has the impression that the dome drifts. Even the walls on which the dome rests are perforated with arches and pendentives which create the sensation that one is seeing something holy that floats. In the eighteenth century, art historians said that Italian eye movements always isolate objects and prefer mobility, while German eye movements tend to link objects and to observe calmly and steadily.

'Ethnic eye-movement differences?' I joke. The professor smiles lightly.

That afternoon I listen to his paper, titled 'Why Treaty? The Moral Case for Unfinished Business', about the Aborigine request for a treaty between the Australian government and themselves in order to begin relations on more 'just foundations'. I make notes:

'What is meant by justice? What would constitute a just settlement to the unfinished business of colonization?

'The Australian philosopher Richard Mulgan points out that by accepting the state and the constitution, Aborigines are accepting the injustice and dispossession in which the state came into being. Mulgan wants the colonized Aboriginal people to have an exclusive power to withhold their agreement to the moral legitimacy of a nation state built upon their dispossession.

'Reparation for past injustice is an accepted principle in law, but there is scope for disagreement about the *principles* that should govern such compensation. It is also difficult to calculate and distribute appropriate amounts for such compensation, but these things are not insuperable and do not justify the reluctance of the Australian government and courts to fully embrace the principle of reparative justice.

'The Canadian government paid two billion Canadian dollars to Native American former pupils of residential schools. It paid sixty million Canadian dollars for a truth and reconciliation commission to promote awareness of the abuse suffered by those caught up in this system. Why is the Australian government's response so inadequate?

'In his reply to Habermas, Rawls notes that all societies are more or less unjust and that the idea of a just society has the status of an ideal: it is something to be worked towards.

'Recently, white settler nations began to accommodate ethnic cultures, while post-colonial politicians found ways to include indigenous people in ways that would seem fair and appropriate. But these actions serve merely a legitimizing function for the settler state.

'The sorry-saying of the Australian government has opened up a space to outline an approach to reconciliation that would genuinely decolonize an internal colonial situation.

'The act of "recognition as reconciliation" has to start from the premise that the notion of *terra nullius* or empty land and its consequences were imposed on the Aboriginal people without their consent or regard for their laws and practices of government. Until this is acknowledged and rectified, Australia will remain a fundamentally colonial state with unfinished business.'

The next session is in Turkish and behind closed doors, and from everywhere people slip us cards that indicate organizations linked to the Armenians, to Cyprus – an area with much 'unfinished business' of its own.

We walk down the street towards a recommended place called Güllüoğlu, established many years ago and still using a recipe for baklava, so we are told, brought from Damascus.

'Why does it sound so wonderful, a recipe from Damascus?' I ask.

'The place of revelation, scales falling from Saul's eyes,' suggests the professor, as we pass a large demonstration taking place under massive police presence.

'It is such a relief that my country has said sorry,' he says. 'At last the discussions about reparation have begun.'

'It somehow seems to me that it is easier to say sorry when you are in power and in the majority. It is very confusing with us. Instead of whites being asked to pay back, they were asked to step back. Instead of being taxed, they're being blamed.'

The baklava is indeed an experience worth a thesis. Three small wedges arrive on a plate. After the first mouthful we fall into sublime silence – no talking, no academic thinking, only deep, intense, empirical abandon. Our tongues verify the menu: the syrup of Turkish baklava is made not from honey but from special sugar; the pistachios super-finely grated on top were handpicked in Barak; the butter in the pastry comes from Şanlıurfa. It is sheep's milk butter 'made clear' in the heat of the sun.

We sit enraptured. Speechless, we drink the Turkish coffee. The money we hand over seems immaterial. The professor goes to a bookshop and I rush back for my panel discussion with a Turkish journalist and a Greek journalist who uncovered mass graves and atrocities on Cyprus. Their governments don't like this debunking of 'official explanations', and the two journalists are being harassed in terrible ways. Both of them look anxious and stressed out.

My input starts with a quote by Cynthia Ngewu, one of the mothers of the Gugulethu Seven, which I used in my book about the Truth Commission:

This thing called reconciliation ... if I am understanding it correctly
... if it means this perpetrator, this man who has killed [my son]
Christopher Piet, if it means he becomes human again, this man, so
that I, so that all of us, get our humanity back ... then I agree, then I
support it all.

'Let me set out what this amazing formulation says: it says that
Mrs Ngewu understood that the killer of her child could, and did,
kill, because he had lost his humanity; he was no longer human.
Second, she understood that to forgive him would open up the
possibility for him to regain his humanity, to change profoundly.
Third, she understood also that the loss of her son affected her own
humanity; her humanity had been impaired. Fourth and most
important, she understood that if indeed the perpetrator felt driven
by her forgiveness to regain his humanity, then it would open up the
possibility of the restoration of her own full humanity.

'In the TRC final report, Mrs Ngewu's response on prison sentences
for the perpetrators reads as follows: "I think that all South Africans
should be committed to the idea of re-accepting these people back into
the community. We do not want to return the evil that perpetrators
committed to the nation. We want to demonstrate a humanness
[ubuntu] towards them, so that [it] in turn may restore their own
humanity."

'This was being said at the end of a century dominated by revenge:
that to punish would be to perpetuate inhumanity. Analysing the
sentences in TRC testimonies about forgiveness, one picks up how
both literate and illiterate black people formulated forgiveness in terms
of this interconnected humaneness.

'What I am trying to say is that Christianity (or human rights,
restorative justice, or, for that matter, the theology of Tutu and the
politics of Mandela) is not simply linked to, or an *add-on* to, a kind
of African interconnectedness, but is in fact *imbedded* therein.
Interconnectedness forms the interpretive foundation of southern
African Christianity, and it is this foundation that enabled people to

reinterpret tired and troubled Western concepts such as forgiveness, reconciliation, amnesty and justice in new and usable ways.

'In other words: these concepts moved across cultural borders and were infused and energized by a world view of interconnectedness-towards-wholeness to assist people to break out of their past and make a new future possible.

'So what would be the difference? Christian forgiveness says: I forgive you because Jesus has forgiven me. The reward will be in heaven. "African" forgiveness says: I forgive you so that you can change and I can begin to heal and all of us can become the selves that we were meant to be. The reward is here on earth.

'Forgiving is therefore never separate from reconciliation, but the first personal step. It demands a response from the forgiven one, to change, to become human, to share. Forgiveness is thus not an uninformed embrace of evil, it is not a miracle brought about by an individual, but an interconnected act that makes a changed relationship possible, a future, a new way of being.'

But I see the audience sitting in front of me: a fierce gleam of hurt, anger and bitterness in their eyes. The world will never learn anything from Africa, my friend Sandile Dikeni once said. We are just something cute, a mask to hang in a television lounge, but we will never be recognized for having contributed something worthwhile to the world.

30 April 2008
Liewe Ma
It is your birthday today: I think what I saw in Hasensprung this morning was a red robin.

Liewe Ma
Suddenly this morning an email: when do I want to go back to South Africa? Our last dinner is on 19 July. Outside, the trees burst into green, ranging from fluttering, breath-light greens to cool,

dark, moss-quiet greens. It is light until after nine in the evenings; people sit outside, drinking beer, talking 'sweet nothings'.

I returned late last night from a 'New South Africa' celebration where a shabby video was shown, with poor Mandela dragged out to ask people to invest in South Africa. Using him when he is so old makes him not an asset, but proof of our inability to produce any new leadership with integrity. I was so depressed after the function that I took a short cut through the woods next to Hasensprung, even though it was after eleven. I stopped at one stage simply to take notice of how fragrant, how beautiful and quietly safe it was in this midnight-blue darkness, when, suddenly, there it was. First two loose sounds, clear, unmistakable, then as if a velvet bundle was flipped open and little silver bones, or bells, began to roll out. I think I stopped breathing until the bird's tiny throat finally gave way to all the beauty in the world, silver liquid pouring onto the lake. A nightingale! It must be! The bird's singing came from the tree across the water, but glided so pure and swift and rinsed-through over the lake's surface that it hit me like an arrow. The wood and park were breathlessly quiet, waiting to be dazzled briefly into magnificence. I stood wounded with wonder. This is all I want to do with my life: marvel at the earth. How I will miss this.

The next day I learnt that there is a research group in Berlin that records the return of the nightingales every year, each one's territorial area and the variations of their singing. These experts can tell you exactly on which date the nightingales will start singing, where and at what time.

chapter eighteen

'You share a bedroom here with your mother and two remaining brothers. You sleep with your mother on the same bed. In Cape Town you have your own bedroom. What for you is the biggest difference between waking up here in Semonkong and in Cape Town?'

Bonnini and I are walking back to the lodge.

'Waking up in Cape Town is different. My first, first awareness there is always one of anxiety, as if it is cutting through me, but somehow, immediately, it is followed by something much stronger: I can make it; I'm okay. Waking up in Semonkong, all the years that I have woken up here, I am first, first aware of my mother, whether she is awake or not, her body heat, the breath of my brothers. But simultaneous with that is a feeling of …' I can see Bonnini searching for a word '… gosh, I don't know, exposure? Feeling exposed to everybody else's awareness of me. As I awake aware of them, they awake aware of me. But mostly I think, Wau! I could do with a shower now.'

'I see people waving at you and talking. As we walk here now, how much are you aware of, how much do you feel part of, this community? And compare it to Observatory in Cape Town, where I also have seen how well you are known.'

'I'm changed. I'm a different person than the one who left.'

'I know, but I'm trying to understand in what way. If I had to come and live here with your family, how would I have to change, *what* would I have to change to live here with the same ease with which you live in Obs? And I'm not talking material comfort.'

Bonnini laughs. 'You will die here! One learns one's self from very young. The first thing is that you would have to change your sense of parenthood completely.'

'Parenthood! You're not serious!'

'I am. I'm my mother's child, but every grown-up woman here in Semonkong is also my mother. I am surrounded by brothers and sisters, uncles and aunts, who are not really related to me, so I have lots and lots of roots into a wide community – even down to Maseru. When I moved to Cape Town I was immensely excited. I assumed that I would pull out all these various roots, go to Cape Town and replant them there into a much more empowered and widespread community. In other words, I would still have many mothers, fathers and sisters, but they would be so much more powerful than the Semonkong community, so I would be able to achieve anything; fulfil my wildest dreams; simply be loved and adored while at the same time still having the same kind of access to everybody's hearts and resources that I had in Semonkong. And that was my biggest shock. Actually, that was like an enormous and I think permanent scar. The realization that this was not so changed me for ever. Of course, the new community was not only very powerful, it was also immensely generous and accepting of me, but there was not that simple interconnected accessibility to any- and everybody that I grew up with in Semonkong. Remember also that I grew up without apartheid in Lesotho. So my sense of myself is within a community not so fiercely determined by white people as my friends in Cape Town.'

I remember a black student, who was studying in the US, telling me about a dream that had upset him. His grandmother had appeared in the dream, as she often did. But this time his dream had been in English, which his grandmother couldn't speak. He told me how it upset him that his grandmother, whom he loves, could no longer speak to him. 'But she was there, all the time in the dream, so maybe that is what counts.'

I also remember a discussion between two students about how many youngsters they knew who had become 'mad' because they studied too hard. It seemed that they all turned out fine, but that the successful continuation of their studies depended on a kind of emotional breakdown. Is that the 'permanent scar' Bonnini is talking about?

'You used the term roots,' I venture. 'Are you saying, if I understand you correctly, that you felt you arrived in Cape Town with these exposed, pulled-up roots, some long, some short, some so intertwined that you perhaps didn't really know which were yours? In Cape Town you thought you could replant them in more fertile and layered ground, becoming more empowered?'

'Something like that.'

I feel I'm standing on an edge. 'Bear with me Bonnini. There are two kinds of root systems: a taproot, with one dominant primary root going deep down, and a diffuse root, which is fibrous, which branches in all directions and anchors the plant. So if we swop places we will have to change our root systems?'

'I don't know; it feels more like I am in a nursery, having to accept the small black plastic container around my trunk, rearranging the lay of my roots and decreasing my dependence on them.'

'Or?'

'Or wander around with exposed roots, regarded as mad, as thankless, as incapable of coping in First World surroundings.'

'And now, when you are back here in Semonkong, can you allow these roots out of the container for a while?'

Bonnini shakes her head. 'You were at my house now. Nothing there belongs only to one person. Not even where you sleep. I had nothing that was solely my own; even my clothes belonged to or would go to somebody else.'

'Wait. You have lost me. Are you not describing the "normal" sentiments and developments of leaving one's struggling family? Are the poor in India or South America not also a collective? And do you not lose the richer black people in Maseru from this collective?'

'I wouldn't know. But why would somebody like Mandela, who grew up in a relatively affluent community, also have that sense?'

'So you are not talking about a sense of being a particular ethnic group, because that is what, say, Zulus, Afrikaners, Jews or Vendas also have. You are talking about a self that conceives of itself, that forms itself, mainly through the community around it – whether living or dead? – from birth and on a daily basis?'

'You're getting too complicated. I don't know. All I know is that in Cape Town I was well cared for, though never excessively, as in being spoilt. So when I went home the first time, people would come in and say: Hi Bonnini, this is a beautiful thing for one's hair, can I take it? Or, May I wear these shoes while you are here? And I felt my whole insides jump. And where I needed no privacy before, because there was no private person (I would bath in front of my brothers, without any of us being aware that it was a private act), I suddenly needed private space. So I think those roots, once confined, can never be released again. At the same time they are too … *whatever*, through their previous intense connectedness, to ever be able to function in the Cape Town surroundings without constantly recollecting what they once were.'

'Is your family aware of any of this? Your mother?'

'Since the day my studies were paid for, I was regarded as the one who "got away", who escaped Semonkong. And I somehow feel responsible to honour that impression: yes, I left, but – and it is an important but – I haven't changed; I am still the Bonnini who left.'

'Is that important enough for you to lead this double life?'

'It's not a double life. I value the fact that they respect the old Bonnini as being a real person. For you it is a double life, for me it is simply my life that had to become warped to adapt.'

'To modernity?'

'No! To survive what I am confronted with in Cape Town. If you say modernity you imply that I have a sense of self that is pre-modern, primitive. Maybe *your* single-rootedness is the thing that is primitive; your inability to imagine yourself consisting of others is a crude form of life.'

But it is that individuality that makes me survive anywhere, I wanted to say. In actual fact, I don't need to become more black, because for black to survive, it will have to become white. But Bonnini has already turned on her heel and is marching back across the bridge – her red coat and braided hair sweeping in the opposite direction to two exuberant young men racing each other down the embankment. As I walk to my cottage at the lodge, I suddenly remember research that proved that a kind of ant that existed as a nest of individuals came from an earlier, more 'primitive' time than ants that function as part of a cohesive whole.

chapter nineteen

One day Moshoeshoe took an egg and said: 'If it breaks when it falls, my form of government will collapse; if it does not break, it will remain firm.' The egg did not break.

During the last decade of his reign, many of Moshoeshoe's sons and chiefs openly ignored the border stipulations. Visiting the Free State side of the Warden Line, Governor Wodehouse came across Basotho living in the abandoned white homesteads on about sixty farms. There were discussions about a further two hundred farms that had been given to white farmers under British authority but were now held by Basotho. As if to confirm the slipping of power from the ageing king, quarrels broke out between Letsie, the heir apparent, and his Cape Town–educated brothers, who regarded him as illiterate.

Without Casalis, Moshoeshoe's written voice lost its authority. The consequences were dire. The records show that many more people were now writing letters to white authorities claiming to be on behalf of the king. The letters that *did* come from the king lost their firm yet strategic tone. In one, written by the missionary Théophile Jousse in 1863, the Landdrost of Winburg was told:

Sir, – I am requested by the Chief Moshesh to inform you that he has duly received your letter. As regards the meeting of the Land

Commission, he says the Basutos are very much busy in their gardens and they have no time to spare to do anything else at the moment. I remain, &c., Signed T. Jousse.

Not disputing that Moshoeshoe said these words, one can hardly imagine such a letter coming from the hand of Casalis. Jousse signals a clear distance between himself and what he had been told to write. Many of the letters written 'by' Moshoeshoe after Casalis' departure began to carry personal remarks indicating that the letter-writer was not on the king's side.

It was the year 1870. While Moshoeshoe's sons and advisors were frantically trying to avert a full-scale destruction of the Basotho by the Boers in what would become known as the Third Basotho War, visitors regularly noted the wasted condition of the king. His eyes were covered in cataracts; he started to doze off during important discussions; he sometimes babbled incoherently, sometimes burst into fits of anger. Many days he was too weak to walk, and had to be carried on a skin to lie in the sun. Moshoeshoe was reaching his last days on Thaba-Bosiu.

During the first years after their meeting, Casalis recorded a 'singular habit' of the king: 'that of going out of doors in the first gleams of the morning and crying, *Ah! dia ha!* "I have again seen the light;" after which he re-entered the house, went to bed again and slept generally to a somewhat late hour.' Moshoeshoe told Casalis that he began to utter this 'cry of joy' as a regular thanksgiving after a period in his life when he was so constantly surrounded by hostile forces that he feared every night that he would be massacred before the morning came. Now, in his old age, the king slept most of the day.

Moshoeshoe might have been weak and dying, but he was, perhaps more than ever before, a trophy for the missionary who succeeded in converting him. Surrounded by a number of mission stations, he was swamped by missionary zeal and, as he became weaker, they descended on him in what can only be described as unseemly greed.

Probably intrigued by the fierce competition among the religions as they opened their missions in Lesotho, Moshoeshoe advised his followers to investigate them all and decide for themselves where they felt at home. As the various denominations emphasized different icons and rituals, it became clear to the Basotho that the Protestants saw life as a moral journey of self-improvement based on the example and salvation of Jesus, while for the Catholics life could be changed by confession, atonement and absolution. Moshoeshoe was especially interested in the hierarchical structure of the Catholic Church and the practical worth of nuns during crisis times. He liked to participate in the Catholics' services, with their use of intriguing items such as incense and holy water and their diverse colourful clothing. They tried to convince him that the Protestant faith could not be the true faith of Christ, as it was established 1500 years after his death.

Moshoeshoe apparently said, 'Though I am still only a pagan, I am a Christian in my heart' – but who would succeed in bringing about the public manifestation of this heart? When Jousse, Casalis' successor at Thaba-Bosiu, arrived to visit the ailing king, to his great fury he found the Catholics busy praying for him. He then forbade the Catholics to see Moshoeshoe without the presence of somebody from the Evangelical Paris Missionary Society.

More than one narrative exists of these highly contested last days of the king's life. There is a Protestant rendition, coming mainly from Casalis' daughter, Adèle, who had been born and raised at the foot of Thaba-Bosiu and who was very much aware how often and fervently her father and mother had hoped and prayed for the conversion of the king. Although remembering that Moshoeshoe once said to her, 'beyond a certain age one can learn new things, but one does not re-make one's heart', she hoped to succeed where her parents had failed. During a visit in January 1870, she and her husband, Adolphe Mabille, a missionary at Morija, tried to convert the king, but they were unsuccessful. Through-out the service they held at his bedside, Moshoeshoe hid his face in his hands. When Adèle told him that God would have mercy on him as a sinner, he shouted aggressively: 'You bad child, who said I was a sinner? I too shall go to heaven.'

According to the Protestant version, Jousse made the first breakthrough by telling Moshoeshoe that a throne would be prepared for him in heaven on condition that he believed that Jesus was the Saviour of the world. Jousse received a messenger from the king that very night to ask him to convey to Casalis and Arbousset that he, Moshoeshoe, had become a believer. The next day, many missionaries visited Thaba-Bosiu and confirmed that the conversion was genuine. This is according to Jousse.

Casalis' acceptance of this version in his memoirs enhances its credibility. Casalis asserts that Moshoeshoe was converted on his deathbed:

> Let it be here said, that it was long after our arrival, in fact, only towards the approach of death, that Moshesh openly declared himself a Christian. He did it in a very touching way ... He died with this filial cry, 'Let me go to my Father, I am already very near to Him!'

Casalis goes on to explain Moshoeshoe's hesitation, as well as his concept of evil. Here his account loses much of the perceptive engagement that characterized his earlier writings. His accusing tone leaves little space for complexity and seems to be hiding more than it reveals.

> How are we to explain the tardiness of his avowal? The fact is, in spite of his intelligence and of his fine qualities, he was excessively attached to the usages of his fathers, and still more to his possessions, which he increased at times by means which were not defensible. The comparison which his followers and himself could not fail to make between his humanity and the harsh and arbitrary proceedings of other African chiefs lulled his conscience. In a word, as I have already said, a bitter experience of human perversity had rendered him a fatalist. To struggle with success against evil seemed to him almost an impossibility. To be converted was in his eyes a dream which certain white men entertained, and which he admired without being able to accept.

Casalis is, of course, writing about something he didn't see. One also senses that Moshoeshoe's affirmed conversion means little for him without a public baptism. How much of his thinking is informed by irritation at the failure of successive generations to bring home the golden trophy, and how much is about having written off Moshoeshoe as a moral character long before – perhaps after the death of 'Mamohato?

The king's last days are also described in terms of the worldly contestations common at the deathbed of a powerful man, namely inheritance. A month after Adèle's visit, Moshoeshoe called his sons together and told them that he was going to be baptized. Some of his sons, of whom at least three studied in Cape Town, were upset about the baptism because they learnt that the missionaries had the king signing forms in which his property would be distributed in a Christian, as opposed to a traditional, way. This meant that many of Moshoeshoe's wives would not be able to depend on royal household support after his death, as the church did not recognize them as legal spouses.

One source says that Moshoeshoe requested that all his cattle be brought to the palace. Such a herd represented not only an impressive livelihood, but also the archive of a long and intensely engaged life. One can imagine that among those cattle were the offspring of those he raided *shwe-shwe* in that name-giving expedition of his early days, those from the sons of Mohlomi who settled under him, those sent by Shaka or Moroka, those raided from white farmers or from Sekonyela, and those paid to him for his daughters, who had married into various clans and groups in southern Africa. Supported by his sons, Moshoeshoe walked for the last time among his cattle, setting aside a number to give to various people, some to the junior wives as *bohadi* for their children, before handing the herd to his eldest son, Letsie.

According to the Catholic version, on 26 January 1870 the king became deeply moved during a visit from Father Gérard. Gérard was, however, prevented by those looking after the king from speaking to him at a follow-up visit. As he was only allowed at Moshoeshoe's bedside with Jousse by his side, Father Gérard started to visit Thaba-Bosiu at night or during bad weather, when the Protestants would be in their houses. When the Protestants found out about these secret visits, they doubled their own. On 4 February, Moshoeshoe pleaded with Gérard not to put pressure on him, as he was too ill to make a decision: 'I have two eyes … the one looks at the BaRuti Fora [French missionaries], the other, the BaRoma (Roman Catholics).'

Perhaps the king was using metaphor in a last attempt to explain the false and unfair dichotomy the missionaries once again forced on him. He had two eyes, but they belonged in one body; how could he choose between his eyes? Behind the seemingly distinct and separate eyes was the unity of the single person accommodating and processing various fields of vision: to choose would not only be impossible, but silly.

Moshoeshoe, the Catholic story goes, asked Gérard to arrange a baptism ceremony in which both these faiths could be accommodated, but Gérard refused. He reported that the king expressed his preference for the Catholic faith but felt prohibited by the Protestants from following his desires.

Then there is another version. According to Seboni's oral witnesses, Moshoeshoe's words to Adèle Mabille were somewhat different than recorded. The Basotho who were looking after him heard him say: 'To me Jesus Christ is but one of the many ancestral spirits. One of your own ancestral spirits. He is by no means superior to the ancestral spirits of our tribe … the spirits of my fore-fathers have served me so well that I can see no good reason to forsake them so late in my life.'

Among the Basotho it was also known that, when he heard that a nearby king was to be baptized, Moshoeshoe sent him a gift of ten head of cattle, two horses and a gun, with the promise of more guns if he would *not* let himself be baptized.

Seboni concludes: 'It was obvious that Moshweshwe would not be converted.' He had reservations about Christianity. He allowed and encouraged his followers to be Christian, because he himself learnt a lot from them, but that did not affect his personal life and beliefs.

In such a contested terrain, the baptism of the king could not be an intimate occasion. The missionaries felt that it needed to be a public affair to prevent others from saying that they had manipulated him. In addition, why would the Protestants, seeing the growing popularity of the Catholic Church, not use the occasion as a mighty advertising event?

The royal family tried to postpone the baptism, and the first agreed date was Sunday 20 March 1870. But early that month Moshoeshoe went into a coma, so the date was urgently brought forward to the Sunday before, 13 March. Thousands of people streamed from all across southern Africa to attend the baptism. On the morning of Friday 11 March, Moshoeshoe apparently awoke and in a thin wheezy voice called his sons, Letsie and Tladi, who slept at his bedside. When they reached him, he slipped beyond reach. By nine o'clock that morning, Moshoeshoe had died.

With Moshoeshoe's death the Basotho had lost the man whom they called their foundation, the Great Binder-together.

Poet David Cranmer Theko Bereng described it as a day in which heaven and earth, nature and beast, the living and the dead, faltered:

> Everything turned into grief for us, the day that Moshoeshoe died. Outside, we saw bewildering things. We saw warriors streaming to the palace in great numbers; we saw them streaming their regiments full; they pegged themselves into the ground like spears and stood like that for a long time – on the day that Moshoeshoe died.
>
> On the day that Moshoeshoe died, the sun dawned green. It refused to set. It hit the peaks of the huts. On the day that Moshoeshoe died, the cattle refused to leave the kraal; the birds refused to fly; without singing they shuddered only short distances into the air – on the day that Moshoeshoe died.
>
> The thought about Moshoeshoe made my body shiver. I could not even open my mouth to talk about him, to talk about his deeds, to tell about his works, to do justice to Our Big One, our Warrior, our Beloved King.
>
> The day that Moshoeshoe died dawned green. The nation, in large numbers, attended the wake for the king. The nation sprinkled their tears over the body of the king; they sprinkled them over the royal corpse as it was being washed; the corpse of the king was being washed not with water, but with tears.
>
> On the day that Moshoeshoe died, we washed him. With the wailing of a nation in mourning, we washed him. With sorrow, we took

the body of the king. With grief, we bathed the body of the king. With shaking hands we touched his corpse. We washed it, we bathed it, the day that Moshoeshoe died.

The young women covered their faces with cloth, when we buried Moshoeshoe. The brooks stopped flowing, when we buried Moshoeshoe. The bushes stopped shivering in the wind, when we buried Moshoeshoe. The sun lost its power, when we buried Moshoaila. The earth became dusty, when we buried the king. The sky rumbled in a peculiar way, when we buried the king.

With both hands he had scooped out peace for us. We buried him, Thesele Matlama, the Great-Binder-Together, the king of the rich and the poor.

A hundred years later, the moment of Moshoeshoe's death was documented by one of his descendents: 'As he died the earth trembled. The pots in the houses started moving but did not break, and my grandmother (who told me this) was unable to go over to the crawly baby (which was my father). Immediately afterwards, messengers arrived announcing the death of Moshoeshoe.'

Instead of a baptism, the assembled crowd attended Moshoeshoe's funeral on top of Thaba-Bosiu, next to the graves of his father Mokhachane, who had died five years earlier, and his wife 'Mamohato. Around his grave stood his family, followers, about four thousand Basothos, the missionaries, neighbouring chiefs, traders, five indunas from King Mpande, and the British envoy sent by the Queen to thank Moshoeshoe personally for the leopard skin. One of the renditions says that the body of the beloved king was passed from Basotho hand to Basotho hand until it reached its grave.

The day of the burial was heavy with heat. Jousse conducted the service, while Ratsiu, Makwanyane, Letsie, Tladi and others used their oratory skills to praise Moshoeshoe. The day was filled with laments and crying until a 'cairn-like mound of rocks' was built over the grave during the afternoon. Historian Peter Becker describes the scene: 'Letsie placed a simple slab of stone, hewn from the hillside, at the head of the mound.

It bore a solitary name crudely carved into its chalky surface – the most honoured name in all the Lesotho – MOSHESH.'

Much has been written about the fact that Moshoeshoe died without being baptized. Some say that he died with one foot in the traditional world and the other in the Christian world; others say that, once again, he had slyly outmanoeuvred everybody.

But perhaps Moshoeshoe died as he had lived: to the end misunderstood and unadmired for his remarkably consistent striving to get people to live reconciled, accommodating lives in peace and prosperity. His unwillingness to convert was blamed on his arrogant refusal to acknowledge that he was a sinner; his desire to have both denominations baptize him was seen as an old inability to make up his mind; receiving sangomas as well as missionaries on Thaba-Bosiu was evidence that one could take the native out of the bush but never the bush out of the native; his manoeuvres to avoid wars were seen as cowardice; his insistence on living a life with and like his people showed that he was too weak to commit to the stern demands of a civilized Christian life; allowing his people to engage in cross-border raids was seen as part of the sly, dishonest nature of a thief; his refusal to reprimand his people when encroaching powers complained about their behaviour was regarded as part of his immoral nature that never stood up 'for any principle', as Arbousset remarked.

In fact, it seems that most of what Moshoeshoe had been saying was misunderstood within the framework of French missionary beliefs, British imperialism and Afrikaner land hunger. He was unable to convince any foreign power that the diversity he had accommodated in his nation was extended to them (at least initially) and that goodness could come into a society when its interconnected humaneness was prioritized. One also gets the impression that, faced constantly by this non-hearing and non-understanding, the Basotho as a whole became obstinate and flaunted those parts of their culture that most irritated the missionaries. Something like: these people seem incapable of understanding us, but we understand them all too well, so let us shock them with the last convulsions of an emaciated country.

The recognition of this kind of leadership only dawned when the most famous African leader ever, Nelson Mandela, appeared on the political stage. But, like Moshoeshoe, Mandela also had to experience being exceptionalized, extracted as an individual from his people. Although both leaders confirmed on public platforms that they were what they were because of their people (Mandela in his speech opening the first democratic parliament and Moshoeshoe in the idiom for which he is credited: a king is a king through his people), a culture based on individuality could not hear that: the exceptional leader was welcome, his people not.

Bereng, the poet of the laments on Moshoeshoe, emphasizes the characteristics that made the king great: an interrelationship with the physical and metaphysical world:

> The king lies in the earth of his country. The king of goodness that was never pretence; the king of truth and no partiality; the king on whom we leaned when we had nothing, our long stick of peace watching over us, our kierie to walk safely – he sleeps now, the Binder-together-of-those-who-suffered, the ruler of the Basotho, the giver of the gifts of kingship. He sleeps now.
>
> He distributed to everybody with a hand used to giving; his heart was the bearer of the weak. He who brought light in the darkness sleeps now, the power of the Kierie of the Basotho rests. Nobody surpassed him in royal command. Nobody surpassed him in being adored by his people. Nobody surpassed him in wisdom. Nobody loved us more. Are you saying Moshoeshoe is dead? Are you saying he has left his people? Left us and moved to another place?
>
> He wouldn't die while his people kept on living. What would they live for, if he had died? They have buried the bones, but the king lives, the house of Moshoeshoe lives, the king isn't dead; he sleeps. The king sleeps among his people. Listen carefully, his people will never forget him. Bushes, on the mountain, you can stop shivering! Dry grass, stop rustling. Plants, stop growing. Birds, stop singing. We buried His Majesty. He sleeps. He is us.

'Khotso!' we cried at the funeral of the King.
'Pula!' we pleaded at the funeral of the King.
'Nala!' we asked from our Ancestor.

chapter twenty

I'm writing this on the verandah of the Morija Lodge overlooking the valley chosen one and a half centuries ago by Eugène Casalis and Thomas Arbousset to establish their first mission station because of its proximity to a fountain and dense woods. The air is alive with frog and cricket sounds.

Years after he left Lesotho, Casalis described Morija lovingly: 'A small lake existed in a depression, in which waterfowl and herons played, and where otters and a good many water snakes were to be seen. The water which came down from the mountain was strong enough and its flow sufficiently continuous to collect at the bottom of the valley, where it fed a number of very clear pools and charming brooks. The certainty of finding duck, teal and snipe often drew us to the spot.'

Early this morning I noticed several small groups of people studying newspapers intensely. Soon the first ululation resounded through the village, followed by another, and yet another somewhere else. The newspaper carried the matric results.

It felt remarkable walking down into the village. Would Moshoeshoe, Casalis and Arbousset have taken pride today if they were walking with me and witnessing the houses ringed by luscious vegetable gardens, children swinging from heavily laden apricot trees, the sounds of singing from a prayer meeting somewhere, the celebrations of successful matriculants right through the morning, the quiet confidence in the body language of the horse riders as they take their cattle through these majestically formed mountains, as if saying: We live what is called a 'good life'.

Although it is said that England returned Lesotho to its people after a hundred years with only one doctor for every 27 000 people and a few kilometres of railway and tar road, the country, already then, had the highest literacy rate in Africa. Driving through Lesotho one sees a country largely at peace with itself. Although the people in the rural areas are poor, their lives seem intact and whole. In Semonkong or here in Morija, people go about their early-morning chores of cutting spinach, opening up irrigation furrows, making pap, sweeping the yard, exuding a peaceful sort of pride that seems both earned and sustained.

I had the same feeling driving through Maseru: it was a city formed in the way the majority wanted it to be, unlike the cities and towns in South Africa, which were built for minorities but which now belong to no one, and reflect the attempts of a people to adapt to spaces never designed for or by them.

My first stop was the famous Lesotho Book Depot at Morija. In sober, neat piles, books on Lesotho history, culture and geology, literature, and school and university textbooks were being sold at affordable prices.

One could live an informed life through these books. *An Outline of Physiology and Hygiene*, for schools, was printed here at Morija in 1948. It explains the working of the body; how to prepare food hygienically; how to treat illnesses and recognize body lice, head lice and fleas; how to build an incinerator, or a toilet; where to situate kraals, front doors and play areas; why aloes draw rats; how to process rubbish; and so on. Other books contain the praise poetry to the Basotho kings, all the folk-tales, songs and church material. And it felt wonderfully strange to be among books produced not in the hope that something glamorous would catch the eye of a listless buyer, but in the secure knowledge that what they contained was worthy of printing, simply produced to keep down the cost. It would sell because of itself. While I was there a big stack of one of the oldest newspapers in South Africa, *Leselinyana*, was delivered, printed on the oldest printing press outside Cape Town.

I worked away in the imaginatively presented Morija Museum, with its friendly staff and its wealth of documents, books and photo albums. In photographs I saw Morija covered in snow, a small wooden bridge crossing a stream, the consecration of the Morija church, a grasshopper infestation, white people in Victorian dress – some of their faces moist with self-righteousness – with groups of black pupils or theological students. In the backyard of the museum one could buy food to eat under the large pepper trees. After five I walked down to the church.

Within ten years of the arrival of Casalis and Arbousset at Morija in 1833, a small church was built. By 1842 it had twenty-eight members, five years later more than two hundred members. To provide for this growth, François Maeder, who joined Arbousset as artisan missionary, began building a larger church, which was to become the landmark of Morija.

The church, which took ten years to build, was extensively damaged by the Free State burghers in their clashes with the Basotho in 1858: two doors were broken off their hinges, the bell was stolen, the pulpit destroyed and the walls sprayed with bullets.

One of the attacks is described by missionary Louis Cochet from the nearby Hebron station:

> The Boers were already on the march and rapidly advancing ... [T]he Englishmen who trade in Morija had placed their families and the greater part of their belongings and merchandise in the vast church of the place, intending to remain neutral ... The missionaries thought likewise ...
>
> The farmers halted in front of the station and, after a volley of musketry, fired a few cannon shot. With the third discharge, a shell penetrated Mr. Arbousset's bedroom. The family fled in alarm to the mountain. His eldest daughter, an invalid, was carried thither by two people. Mrs. Arbousset, who is very weak, also had to be assisted ...
>
> While the Boers continued their work of destruction, the fugitives searched for a refuge in the mountain. We found them gathered together in a den under the shelter of a huge boulder. There were fifty-five women and children there, exposed to the bitter cold. The

poor Arboussets had only two woollen blankets, one of which had dropped in the flight and which an Englishman had turned back to retrieve at the hazard of his life. During the next two days, it snowed and it was impossible to go out; the natives who were hiding in the neighbourhood brought us a little food.

'Everything is white with snow,' Arbousset wrote. 'The sun is shining. Black objects appear at various points of the mountain; these are Boers.'

After the Boers sold off the contents of Arbousset's house, they burnt down the house itself. They were looking for him because they said that blood from a bullet wound was found in one of the beds of his house, indicating that he assisted Letsie during the battle. The missionary decided to flee to another mission station. He tied his eldest daughter to a horse, carried his youngest on his shoulders, and with a staff in hand walked with his family through the snow along mountain paths to Bethesda, where Constant Gosselin awaited them.

Arbousset lost his archive, and all his Sesotho books were burned – as if, he reflected, the Boers wanted to say, 'These black people will be ours; they don't need you, nor your teaching'.

I stretched my arms in the cool mountain breeze and noticed that the church door behind the pulpit was open. Inside were simple wooden benches, eye-catching wooden pillars, apparently made from salvaged ship masts, and the words: *Ke'na Tsela le Nete le Bophelo* (enter with a joyful heart) behind an unassuming pulpit.

Although one glimpsed parts of mountains, gathering clouds and trees through the rectangles of old, uneven glass, one was closed off in the church, really sealed off from whatever was outside. And as I sat down in the somewhat neglected and rickety gallery, I wondered why God made sense to me only within these kinds of surroundings? When the church selflessly cares, when it doesn't mind being poor, when it creates a sanctuary of tranquillity, when it tells its message simply, when it indefatigably serves the lives of the marginalized.

But it was when leaving the cool, dark church, opening the front door and stepping out, that one became transported, at once, by an immediate swirl of pure all-encompassing sunlight, because there it lay, stretching from the little step below one's feet, a valley breathing its pure blue beauty up the golden flanks of the mountains, pencilling pine and cypress into the silver lapping sounds of poplars. As the people around one moved among these majestic mountains with such unhurried ease, one became convinced that, yes, it was for them, the Basotho, that the mountain necks leaked streamlets of water, that the birds rowed in stately grace against the clouds, that the sandstone peaks invented late light, that the thunderstorm exploded in echoing layers, round and round from mountain cliff to mountain cave. One simply had to experience the world differently living among such natural splendour.

Eight of the nine Arbousset children were born here at Morija. Their only son, Jean-Thomas, died at the age of one. A year later his sister Mariette died at four and was buried next to him. Their neglected graves stand next to that of Casalis' wife, Sarah, under the large oak and poplar trees behind the Morija printing press.

One wonders about the pull of a grave, about Arbousset's heart's cry after he had left: 'My attachments, my inclinations, all of them are in Lesotho. That is what is making me feel tired, I am groaning about it every day.' One wonders about the last time Casalis stood here, next to his wife's grave, just before he left for Europe, because for him, the moment he lost her, his life in Lesotho ended. What are the quiet spaces a grave inhabits in one's psyche?

It is fascinating to note how many members of the Casalis family returned: Sarah Casalis' daughter Adèle came back as Mrs Mabille, obsessed with converting Moshoeshoe; Sarah's son, Eugène Casalis, returned as a medical doctor working with his uncle, Sarah's brother Hamilton Dyke; Casalis' son Alfred returned as director of the Morija Bible School, editor of the first black newspaper and reorganizer of the Book Depot – all these activities clustered close to this grave with its quiet solidness under the lightly rustling trees.

As the sun sets that evening in fragile pearl- and quince-coloured light, my thoughts go back to the possibility that Moshoeshoe was responsible for the death of 'Mamohato – her name has accreted such a sad heaviness since I started to think about her. If it's true, does it matter, I ask myself. Yes. And the silence around her matters. 'Mamohato disappears completely from Arbousset's and Casalis' published texts, with nothing to be found anywhere about how or when she died, her funeral, the king's reaction or that of her sons. The missionaries' complicity in a conspiracy of silence around her sends clear signals that there was something untoward about her death. On the other hand, from the sparse records of his speeches one becomes aware of how Moshoeshoe himself continued to invoke her name as a kind of lament, and the more he talked about her, the less the missionaries seem to have responded.

And, in a strange way, for me now, here where I sit with the voices of children and goats resounding in the valley, the spiral smoke of fires, this does not make Moshoeshoe less. He knew that he had it in him to kill easily. He also felt stirred by ambition beyond himself. But, unlike Shaka, the Basotho king spent a lifetime building his stature by being good to people. He strived, he cared, he bound his society together, he made terrible mistakes, but he never lost sight of the infinite broadness of the world, the necessity of kindness and his own internal failures.

It is dark when I go to my room. There is a compelling sense of lastingness here at Morija. An immanence.

CONVERSATION 6
XENOPHOBIA

'Okay, now for the obvious question. How then do you explain the xenophobic attacks that we saw on BBC last week?'

'I think there are two important factors. The first is that you have the influx of rural people from tight interconnected groups coming to the cities. Their daily connectedness with their community, with its spiritual presence of ancestors, nature, etc., is broken. Some of their family members have moved on and disappeared into the better suburbs in town. Other members have died of AIDS. Grandmothers look after orphaned grandchildren, often not their own; young and grown-up unemployed men have to beg pension-receiving grandmothers for money to buy soap and razors. In other words, those who live in the squatter camps live there with their interconnected roots lacerated, torn loose and exposed to a context in which there is nothing to replant them in, as it were. These 'organs' or roots, connecting them to others, guiding them via caring, are shrivelling away in the squatter camps where people fight for resources, which they can access through the municipality only as individuals, and are battling to work out now: who is the community, who is the 'stranger', how can I accommodate him or her? Into this already potently dysfunctional mix come people from other African countries, with their own anguished experiences of uprootment and loss.

'Despite being poor and struggling, most South Africans regularly see on television news desolate images of African cities; they see hungry skinny people streaming to South Africa because their own countries have failed. Africa to most South Africans spells failure. So here you live, you have nothing ethical, cultural or spiritual to connect with for guidance and nourishment, few of your rituals still make sense, you are very aware that some of your family members or neighbours or clan are 'making it' in the new South Africa, and suddenly you are surrounded by people whom you identify with failure. You want to wash these Africans away from you, get rid of them, so that they will not make you fail as well, hamper your only chance at succeeding in the new environment. In other words, it is not a case of ubuntu is dead, as I originally thought, killed by black people; it is the opposite: ubuntu is so very much alive that people do not survive these brutalizing-into-being-an-individual surroundings.'

'Cultural dislocation is deeply problematic. But I am not quite clear: are you saying that this interconnectedness is the origin of great men like Mandela and Tutu, but the origin also of despicable deeds like in Zimbabwe and the xenophobic attacks?'

'Yes.'

'So what goes wrong then?'

'Several things. First, people are often so hasty to proclaim themselves as equal to the West that they do not openly want to acknowledge interconnectedness as a value force. Maybe they feel that it would taint them as tribal and therefore primitive. Ignoring interconnectedness becomes a big problem when things like forgiveness, or attacks on others, or the behaviour of African leaders, are read divorced from this interconnected world view. Read within Western terms only, many deeds become irrational, illogical, nepotistic and evil – as the news on BBC or CNN, or human rights watchmen, keep on telling us. The second thing that goes wrong is its opposite: people can be so eager to proclaim themselves *different* from the West, that they conflate interconnectedness with race and never debate who and what this community is or should be that they are interconnected with (not a mistake that Mandela or Tutu made). So the community is black, and what is black is per se for the common good. So if Mugabe behaves atrociously, you do not criticize him, because that would be bad for black. A black leader who ridicules the West is good for black, and that far outweighs the fact that he is living in total disregard for his community, destroying it. Who Mugabe's community is, or should be, is never debated, not by Zimbabweans and not by us. In contrast, Mandela and Tutu have always used interconnectedness, even with strangers, to redefine their political and religious communities.'

'I want us to return to the xenophobic attacks. One can assume (and it is also the case in Australia) that the destruction of people's cultures makes it no longer possible to internalize the community voice as the voice of the self, because what made the internalizing possible were particular rituals, behaviours and forms of life. What sense do these things make when the life around one simply decontextualizes everything?'

'It is you from the West who are decontextualizing us. It is you who say Tutu veers "unhelpfully between the poles of justice and religion" while in actual fact Tutu acts from a centre-of-interconnectedness in which amnesty (law and justice) and forgiveness (religion) are not opposites but a variety of ways to restore interconnectedness. It is you who find Mrs Ngewu's words of forgiveness an embrace of evil while in truth, within interconnectedness, embracing the evil one is hopefully the beginning of a humanizing process in which compassion and change in the perpetrator brings justice.'

'I have to say something about John Rawls, the political philosopher.

He says that you don't have to assume a common moral framework in the multicultural and liberal world of today to have a stable political community. It is better to find a structure that can carry a variety of moral frameworks. He says, and listen carefully, it is almost impossible for such diverse groupings to find a common moral framework, but it is possible to design a framework that can survive the tension and renegotiations of different frameworks. One can agree through overlapping consensus, even if not for the same reasons.'

'Ja, but I have a feeling that the multicultural communities Rawls talks about live within a dominant Western framework. What I am trying to assert here is the possibility that on the African continent the dominant framework *is* not Western (as opposed to 'ought not to be Western') and that this framework should be more articulately discussed, refined and acknowledged with its own vocabulary. Africa always had a framework accommodating multiple world views, but this very capacity to accommodate becomes the terrible entry point for exploitation, plundering, racism, slavery, etc. by those who tolerate nothing else but their own. So I am not pleading that the West accommodate us; I am pleading that we understand ourselves, our triumphs and especially our failures, in terms of ourselves, and not look back at ourselves in an utter non-understanding imposed on us from elsewhere.'

'Whau. I notice the word *us*! But seriously, you're right: Rawls is talking about Western- and liberal-dominated political communities, but my question is different: is it possible to have a variety of Western liberal approaches to social justice alongside elements of traditional indigenous world views? Can we imagine the possibility of such a diversity of people finding common core principles of a just society?'

'No, because Western individualism feels to me like a virus – nothing survives uncontaminated, so it's never a real alongsidedness. It can be on the same table, but the one is a brooch and the other a gesture.'

'Yes, but the table accommodates them.'

'No, the gesture doesn't need a table, but now tries to be the kind of gesture that needs a table.'

'Homi Bhabha called for the right to tell one's story in order to bear witness to "the unequal and uneven forces of cultural representation" as everyone tries to have political and social authority within a moral world order.'

chapter twenty-one

Liewe Ma

To experience this year's only performance of Wagner's *Tristan und Isolde* under Daniel Barenboim is probably the most befitting conclusion to my time in Berlin. Through pure chance and determined charm the secretary of the *Kolleg* found me a ticket. The evening didn't fail my expectations.

One arrives on the big Bebelplatz in broad summer daylight. Tourists are still being led around and backpackers sit on their rucksacks, but, unmistakable in their evening gear, the opera lovers have already started to gather in front of the Staatsoper with its gigantic neoclassical columns and dramatic steps.

One quickly sees how the Germans in the queue underplay their wealth. The focus is never on glamour – in fact, when someone is flashing an ostentatious dress, heads simply turn away, slightly, as if smelling something disagreeable. The focus is on quality: subdued suit, with a subtle shine that says: pure wool; staid evening dress, but the buckle on the flat black shoe saying: personally designed. What is uncontained, however, is the white of the shirts. I have never seen so many glowing-white white shirts in my life.

Merely entering the Staatsoper metamorphoses one. You

feel ... despite the somewhat gaudy restoration by the communists after World War II, well, shall we say superbly placed. I go down to the basement restaurant to order in advance what I would like to drink and eat during the two intervals. At Table 7 a glass of red wine and a pretzel, and the second time a glass with berries, red wine and champagne, will await me.

I sit in the third row. While people find their seats amidst the reassuring cacophony of orchestra instruments pitching and warming up, I study the extensive and comprehensive programme on which musical cadences and shifts are indicated by notes and text, with famous quotes by former conductors and singers. On cue, the people at the doors close them, sealing us off from the world. Everybody is seated. A man appears on stage and announces that Isolde and King Mark of Cornwall will not be performed by the singers on the programme but by two others, whose names are loudly and wildly cheered. I ask the man next to me: 'Is it good or bad news?' 'The best news,' he says. 'The woman is the main soprano from Bayreuth and the man the best bass currently in Europe – something of a Finnish accent in his German, but a wonderful voice.'

Barenboim's entrance in the orchestra pit is applauded for several minutes. The audience is ready; they clearly adore him and they are craving the six-hour Wagnerian event.

The orchestra opens with the nine-minute-long Prelude, marked *Langsam und schmachtend* (slow and languorous). From the very first searing sound of the cellos my heart cuts loose and swirls into a spasm. Already at that moment, I have to prevent myself from making sounds that want to describe ecstasy. The curtains lift: right in front of us is an enormous angel bent forward, her face buried in her hands, her hips, part of her buttocks and back ascending from the floor. Her massive wings plunge away from her body in mighty curves. She turns slowly through the evening and is at times used as ship, mountain or castle. The performers have special shoes so that they don't slip from her back or neck. During the duets, they hold on to her head, which is hidden in her hands as if she is crying inconsolably.

The German text is displayed on a screen. Everyone around me knows the score by heart. In the next row somebody is conducting with fluttering hands and a body language that says, 'I'm dying to jump in', until his partner takes his hands and holds them forgivingly. Next to them a woman sways like a willow, throwing her head back as if in a trance. A man indicates to his partner the entry of each new leitmotiv. Behind me sits a couple with the thick score on their laps, but I think I hear only the first two pages being turned, before being swept away in a deluge of sound as the themes, flood upon flood, animate anxiety, despair, fury. The orchestra is as important as the voice, spilling the internal lives on stage into the ether.

After the first act, the man next to me looks at his watch and nods his head with satisfaction: 'Exactly one and a half hours!' The people applaud as if it is the end. (Or so I think!)

I collect my wine and pretzel and go out through the side doors onto Bebelplatz, bathed in the golden late-afternoon light where the audience mix with smoking orchestra members and a few last tourists. The air is light and warm and I cannot help thinking how different visions of humanity have shaped this very space where we are standing with the music still ringing in our ears.

It was the Prussian king, Frederick the Great, regarding himself as first and foremost 'a servant of the people', who decided to create, instead of fighting interminable wars, a space for the people. He built a boulevard where they could stroll to an opera house and a library, to which he added a palace, which later became the Humboldt University. Centuries later, here we are, benefiting from this foresight.

In contrast, in the middle of the square is a grave-like glass-covered hole, which becomes more visible at night, when a light emanates from the enclosed underground room. Peering down through the transparent cover one sees a small space walled with white empty bookshelves, reminding one that once, here, amidst all this heavenly culture, the Nazis burnt the books of 'decadents and traitors to the nation'.

On this tightrope, culture walks in Berlin.

The second act includes the famous love duet '*Oh, sink hernie- der, Nacht der Liebe*' (Oh, descend, night of love), Waldtraud Meier's voice soaring gloriously above the orchestra and Barenboim not holding back. Chord progressions dissolve into one another, except for one. It is kept back, it is delayed, the climax cannot come, the chord is withheld, fulfilling Schopenhauer's idea that bliss can be found only through the negation of desire; that the greatest and highest experience of humankind, namely passionate love, is thwarted by the demands of one's fellow humans. From where I sit I can hear Barenboim passionately egging on the orchestra: '*Komm! Komm!*' One feels oneself ascending from oneself as pure passionate sound.

In the last act, Tristan lies wounded against the shoulder blade of the angel before Isolde appears. In the meantime, every leit- motiv has accumulated layers of meaning that in themselves now become presences or characters. After six hours, the opera sur- renders to blissful annihilation. Isolde sings herself into euphoric oblivion with her famous *Liebestod*. And at last, as it has been wanting to do the whole evening, the previous harmonic suspen- sion finally finds its chord and the music explodes – the audience around me groans audibly, consumed by yearning and ultimate bliss. Both lovers are dead.

But not the audience. The applause breaks into a frenzy. People stand up and yell and call the singers back ten times, then they shout for Barenboim and do not stop until he has the whole orchestra moving from the pit onto the stage. The applause itself lasts for more than half an hour. As I look at Barenboim's impas- sive face staring into the audience roaring their unrestrained praise, I wonder what he is thinking. Does he hear a deeply rooted approval only, or does he detect some guilt – an audience that wants to 'make up' to him? Does he think he has 'shown' them that a Jew can capture the heart of Germanness better than they can? Or does he think that they think: See, we did terrible, terrible things, but we also brought forth this? Does he think that it is quite frightening, this tumultuous adoration for music bordering on megalomania? Does he ask himself questions about why this music speaks to him so? Indeed, the applause is for him and his production, but how does he explain to himself the evening's excesses of both music and response?

Probably he has stopped asking these questions, simply remembering the admonitions of Goethe and Schiller that both Germans and Jews used to take (and still take) refuge in a religion-like reverence for culture. That wherever the Germans and the Jews are, to adapt Goethe's words, they will not perish because they are individuals – and as individuals they are so estimable, and yet, oh God, so wretched as a whole.

But what does it matter! Barenboim dabs the sweat with a white handkerchief and I applaud until my hands swell. People keep on applauding before they spill out on the square.

Outside, people are taking taxis, laughing, waving programmes, throwing their arms in the air with gestures of dramatic abandon. Even on the train I see long dresses, capes, scarves and coats – everyone with the glow of pleasure on their faces. An evening like this one does not forget.

And I write this to you, liewe Ma, because it started with you, many years ago, buying the LP record of *Tristan and Isolde* from the Jewish-owned record shop in Kroonstad. As you listened to it, it rubbed off on me. Now I wonder whether you were aware how deeply racialized this simple act was, of selling music, claimed by the Nazis, to you, a supporter of apartheid.

12 May 2008

I arrive at the dinner table ecstatic about the opera. One of the scholars at the table listens bemused.

'What?' I say.

'You have fallen for the seduction of German culture, my dear. Nothing unique about that; we Germans have been seduced for centuries to regard culture as something higher than realpolitik. *We* had culture, other nations had civilization. It was said that the democratic spirit was totally alien to Germans. We were more interested in metaphysics, poetry and music than in voting rights or the proper procedures of the parliamentary system. We have always regarded Immanuel Kant's *Critique of Pure Reason* as a more radical act than the proclamation of the rights of man!'

'But this is okay. To regard art or philosophy as more moral than politics has always sounded right to me. I believe anyway that all good ground-shifting art is moral at its core, and, I mean, how wrong can you go when you follow artists rather than politicians?'

He nods and fills our glasses with water. I rearrange the napkin on my lap and think: This is the wonder of my stay in Berlin. Within a few minutes you can engage in this kind of conversation.

'That is exactly what Goethe said: that whoever occupies himself with philosophy and art belongs to his fatherland more intimately than others. But it is quite dangerous to accept culture as a substitute for politics, because then people easily concur with the absence of morality in the public sphere. It was also said that because the Germans could never love politics itself, the authoritarian state is the only proper system that becomes the German people.'

'That sounds *so* familiar to me. Afrikaner culture with its diva Mimi Coertse and its poets of international calibre like N.P. van Wyk Louw, its newspapers and universities linked to Germany and the Netherlands, felt so proud about the quality and the morality of their remarkable culture that the immorality within the political system became immaterial. When H.F. Verwoerd started questioning the morality of Van Wyk Louw, the poets and writers quickly pulled the carpet back to art. And to push this a bit further; maybe that was the problem with the release of Nelson Mandela and the establishment of a democratic country: art had to then suddenly function within a moral system – it battled somewhat but is slowly reclaiming lost ground. Maybe the seduction of art is also an African problem. While Africans are being allowed to produce ground-shifting artistic expressions in music and art, the corrupt morass of politics does not really matter.'

This doesn't sound quite right. I try to rephrase.

'Maybe it's the other way round. The corruption and greed of the ruling African elites and their Western back-ups is scorching art into mere consumerism in Africa.'

My companion sits deep in thought and then says, 'The danger arrives when politicians start to use moral culture to dress up their immoral ideals.'

'I don't know. We had two presidents who famously quoted poets in their important speeches. One of them mostly used Yeats, or Shakespeare, but I liked that – good poetry immediately complexifies things.'

'But that is what the politician bargains on: hiding, in our case, the simplicity of race-driven politics. They say that the Germans fell for Nazi propaganda because it seemed, at least initially, pure and carefully-constructed-by-Bayreuth theatre. People came from all over Europe to watch these rallies and left stunned by the *spectaculaire*, by the beautiful grandeur of scale, colour, tone, text and precision. Even today that era is adored by television and film – the visual aesthetics immediately wants to hide the ethical point.'

'That's interesting! I was wondering why there is a film on the Nazis and the war every single evening on German television, while the radio and newspapers are busier with the united and divided Germany.'

'Precisely. It's not for nothing that Hitler called America a land without an opera, or first visited the Opéra Garnier when he invaded Paris, or had an opera house designed for Munich three times bigger than the Paris one. When things started to go wrong in Germany, the

most used expression initially was that it felt like being part of a
third-rate opera. So it is quite possible for people centred upon moral
culture to go devastatingly wrong.'

'I'm reading Hannah Arendt at the moment. She discards precisely
the desire to monumentalize the Nazi crimes and says that it was the
way in which ordinary citizens abandoned decency that made those
crimes possible. This, however, implies that there is a common
agreement about what decency is.'

'Exactly! This is why the fall of the Berlin Wall is such a wondrous
thing and completely in sync with what we regard as citizen decency.
The fall was not led by political parties or workers' unions, or even
intellectuals (although they were asked to speak at some events), but
it was ordinary people with mixed motives who courageously took
to the streets.'

'The problem in South Africa is that we have no common
benchmark of what we regard as decency, and we do not carry the
emphasis you have here on individual moral responsibility.'

'Except! Except that mankind here, in the meantime, has become
the haves who want to become the have-mores. Our cultural and
military invitations to the Third World must compensate for economic
discrimination. It has become both an escape and a cheap excuse:
cultural benevolence covering up for political indolence.'

'So bring this back to *Tristan and Isolde*?'

'Hitler believed that a strong state would produce remarkable
culture, while Nietzsche warned that people usually rejuvenate their
culture on the political sickbed, when they have lost their spirit by
seeking and asserting political power. However one looks at it, one
should be concerned when political leaders *and* ordinary citizens
transfer their responsibility towards decency to a mere cultural search
for the moral masterpiece.'

We get up to fetch dessert and notice that most people have left the
dining room. We go to sit outside.

'That is why we have human rights,' he says. 'To force a kind of
moral behaviour onto the individual as well as the state.'

'I hear you, but something in me wants more. I don't want to live in a country that only (I know I know I know!) protects the human rights of its citizens; I want to live in a country where people care.'

He smiles kindly as he gets up, patting my arm.

chapter twenty-two

'Wait!' says the old Mosotho man. He walks with his arms hooked on a polished stick over his shoulders. It is already exceedingly hot as we, out of breath and sweating, walk up past the famous stone fissures of Khubelu Pass. I become aware of the fragrant, aerated shade of the grass hat I bought at the ticket office. The Mosotho man stops in front of a large heap of stones just where the pass flattens out onto the top of Thaba-Bosiu. He picks up a stone from the ground, holds it up in the air and cries out, '*Lihkomo tseo!*' and puts it lightly on top of the large *sefika*. His cry literally means 'Many cattle for you,' and, figuratively, 'I come not to harm you but to wish you prosperity.' We follow suit and I see Bonnini's hand resting a bit longer on her stone, neatly securing its position among the others.

'This mountain initially had another name, but it became the Mountain of the Night because Moshoeshoe asked herbal doctors to secure the mountain before he moved here. The old people say that these powers spanned ropes around the mountain, so that when people tried to steal up during the night they became trapped. From there the name: Thaba-Bosiu.'

By night the mountain might have been protected by ropes and spiritual powers, but by day the Basotho did their bit, as I read in the account by Free State soldier John Fraser about the second attack on Moshoeshoe during the Basotho wars in August 1865.

> All went well while we climbed up the mountain. Although the Basutos opened fire upon us, we reached the actual rock fissure, which gave access to the top of the mountain in the immediate vicinity of Moshesh's house, unharmed, but then sharp, close fighting with firearms, assegais, and rock fragments set in, and the Basutos made a strong defence, and had us at a great disadvantage. Across the top of the fissure … a strong stone barricade had been drawn, and from behind this the Basutos fought … General Wepener found his way up to the left of the fissure … and with his revolver endeavoured to clear the enemy out of the schans on that side, an extraordinarily brave attempt, which unfortunately cost him his life, as it left him uncovered to the fire of the enemy, and he was shot dead, close to the schans … The Basutos seemed to have provided themselves with rough boulders of sandstone rock, and as soon as we made a rush these were hurled promiscuously over the top, coming down upon us with considerable force … Unfortunately a large boulder struck me too, breaking the stock of my rifle clean through, and hitting my thigh with such force that I was thrown down.

In great pain and unable to fight any more, Fraser was sent down to tell his commander, General Fick, that the remaining men could not take the *schanse*. While Fraser was relating this to Fick, 'we heard a terrible noise like a thunderbolt, and shouting from the mountain, and had to realise that the burghers had forsaken the point and were coming down the mountain like an avalanche, a truly heart-breaking sight'.

Many other versions of this incident have sprung up. One of them says that Wepener's heart was cut out and eaten by the Basotho in order to absorb his magnificent bravery. Another says his actions had less to do with courage than with the amount of alcohol in his blood, which prevented him from even noticing that he had reached the fissures and was exposed.

We follow the Mosotho man on a footpath through a wood of young poplars and sisal plants to the place of the *pitso*, where large numbers of people – 'male and female,' says the guide – used to gather for a general meeting with the king. In the space for the *kgotla* next to it, where the king met only with his advisors and diplomats, an uprooted bluegum tree lies on its side.

'This tree, given by the missionary Casalis to Moshoeshoe to plant for shade in the *kgotla*, was uprooted during one of the big storms,' he says. Despite the exposed hundred-and-seventy-two-year-old roots sticking into the air, the leaves of the tree show no sign of withering. It provides no shade any more, but it is far from dead.

We move to the edge of the steep stone ledge at Ramaseli Pass, where our eyes feast on an impressive display of mountains, especially the small free-standing Qiloane, which is said to have inspired the Basotho grass hat.

'Is this the ledge that Moshoeshoe's son Mateleka stepped onto when his father rejected his request to marry his sister?' I ask, but the guide, who can speak English but prefers to speak Sesotho to Bonnini, motions us unceremoniously onwards with his stick.

I read that Mateleka insisted that the girl from one of the many wives of Moshoeshoe was born from a 'lilepe' (axes) arrangement, where the king gave some men the 'duty' to 'cut wood' in some of his houses, and she was therefore not his biological sister. Moshoeshoe forbade the liaison, so the son stepped onto a ledge from which he soon realized he couldn't get back. He sat on the ledge for three days, cutting the shape of his foot on the rock with his spear, before he finally leapt over the cliff. Casalis records how one of Moshoeshoe's own wives, after a miscarriage, and delirious from measles, also jumped off the cliff nearest to his kraal. The cliffs and fissures clearly influenced not only those trying to scale the mountain from below, but also those who lived unhappily on top.

Of Moshoeshoe's abodes, the only structures still standing are the four thick rock walls of the simple stone house built for him by a man sent by President Hoffman. One enters through an open doorway; there are two

251

window frames, and the remnants of the rafters still rest on the walls. The ashes of a large fire are visible in front of the house and there are burnt-out candle remnants everywhere inside. 'People come to pray here. When times are difficult; when times are good. A big religious ceremony was held here last weekend, with pilgrims from all over Lesotho.'

Just as nothing in particular identifies Thaba-Bosiu as special when one approaches it from below, so nothing on this mountain, neglected and overrun by weeds and alien shrubs, indicates any of the richness of the stories, events and lives that once were lived here. One can see far, yes; one has water and can keep livestock, yes; one can defend oneself, yes; but in comparison to the majesty of the other mountains, Thaba-Bosiu seems more like a hyena among lions – and not a space that automatically calls forth the greatness of the Basotho.

These are my thoughts as we walk towards Moshoeshoe's grave, but I soon realize my mistake. The royal burial ground stands on its own towards the middle of the mountain among a large stretch of soft grass. Around us the sublime mountains of the Maluti stand guard in blue.

The Mosotho man has taken off his hat and stands, lips silently moving, looking intently at the simple sandstone headstone on which is carved *Morena Moshoeshoe*. Below these words is a stain that looks like blood, but could be weathering. The grave itself is a square mount of larger boulders and rocks, impressive in its humble statement.

To the left of Moshoeshoe's grave are at least thirty similar but smaller graves, with several headstones indicating the kings who reigned after Moshoeshoe as well as some of the princes. Some distance away is a fancy fenced-in, six-pillared, black granite mausoleum over pink granite headstones and text-covered surfaces bearing a solid encrypted banner: *Moshoeshoe II*. The contrast between the two Moshoeshoe graves could not be starker.

I notice small mounds of stones marking two corners of the first Moshoeshoe's grave. I remember hearing that a king may not arrive alone on 'the other side', so some of his cattle, friends or family are killed the moment 'the missionaries leave the grave' to be buried with him.

I ask. Bonnini seems embarrassed by my question, but it is as if the

Mosotho guide sees me for the very first time. With an exasperated movement, he turns and faces me squarely with an extraordinary intensity, his black eyes flaming, addressing me directly in English: 'This' – his gesture includes all the graves, the horizon and the sky – 'is us. This is our inside. This is our outside. It breathes upon us. All is us.' He puts down his hat and stick on the ground, moves Bonnini and myself to stand on both sides of him, and then, slowly, he sinks to his knees – not humble as if in prayer, but as if kneeling before a king right in front of us, straight up, freed. We follow suit. Then, in the most resonantly praising yet intimate Sesotho tones, he starts talking to somebody or something that is near. Here. With us. I close my eyes in loss – to nothing can I talk like this.

Maybe it is the immense silence with its temperate heat and grass, maybe it is the exhaustion of being so 'bent upon' everything I experience here in Lesotho, but I suddenly feel myself moving back, away, up, until I see, from high above, these stone graves fingerprinting the mountains that bulge like an enormous navel in southern Africa. And beside these stone marks are the tiny colour dots of the three of us kneeling together in a vast infinity of various battles, some centuries old, of becoming. Although we are three different physical forms in terms of gender and skin, genetics and history, below us, or before we were us, or, more accurately, before we became us, we were part of that which originated us, determining our difference. Next to this old man, his scruffy hand for a moment on my arm, speaking a language I cannot understand, I bodily feel something melting into what over many years has become for me the unassuming heart of blackness. Without opening my eyes I know that Bonnini is crying and the old man is preparing for death.

chapter twenty-three

Five years after the trial, Reggie and Jantjie appear before the Truth and Reconciliation Commission to apply for amnesty. At this stage I am heading the radio team that reports daily on the commission's activities, and I'm faced with a dilemma: of course I would die to attend the hearing, but it would be unethical for me to report on it. Besides, I have put it all behind me. I wrote a booklet about it three years after the events. It is over. It is a story like other ordinary stories. Having sent two of the best journalists to cover the hearings for radio, I soon find myself in my office poring over all the reports coming in from Kroonstad.

The first one says: 'The amnesty hearings of the Truth Commission started three hours late this morning, because too many people turned up at the hall of the Mphohadi Teachers' Training College in Kroonstad. While the TRC staff were trying to find a bigger venue, a carnivalesque atmosphere reigned outside.' Hundreds of schoolchildren had apparently been given the day off to attend the hearings, and drum majorettes accompanied the amnesty applicants to the hall. Thousands of people gathered, and ANC representatives told the media that the amnesty applicants were regarded by the community as heroes, because they liberated the township from murders, rapes and attacks. This was confirmed with loud cheers as amnesty was demanded for these heroes.

In my mind's eye I can see the TRC staff scurrying through my hometown to find a bigger venue, and I can see how fiercely those in charge of these buildings are stonewalling any attempt to accommodate a gathering, chanting township crowd. The next report says that the hearings are to be continued at the teachers' college, where the doors will be kept open so that people outside can also hear and see on monitors what is happening.

The most important difference between appearing in court and applying for amnesty is this: in court you try to prove that you are *not* guilty, while before the Amnesty Committee you have to prove that you *are* guilty, but that you acted with a political motive and within a political framework. So this time around there is no attempt to shift the blame, but a lot of energy goes into presenting the politics.

The hearings open with a thorough academic political contextualization of the Three Million and other gangs like them. Late in the evenings when everybody has left, I pull all the reports coming in, also from SAPA and Reuters, and an astonishing story unfolds. It seems that while on the one hand F.W. de Klerk had unbanned the ANC and released Nelson Mandela, on the other hand a strategic decision had been made: the security forces should intensify the fighting on the ground in order to reduce the liberation movements to mere political parties before a democratic election took place. In other words, release, unban, and get the moral high ground, while drawing out negotiations to allow the security forces to wreak the kind of havoc that would turn the liberation movements into disgraced, corrupt and powerless political parties.

This explains a great deal, I think as I make a cup of coffee. That is why the police in Kroonstad could keep harassing all of us while F.W. de Klerk was negotiating with Mandela. It was not merely old ingrained racism, it was a secret official order. At the same time, while Mandela was talking peace with De Klerk, the self-defence units, the militant SDUs, were secretly busy at grassroots level. No wonder we ordinary people were all confused!

The evidence before the TRC says that one of the major security force strategies was to pitch black people against black people, because this kind of violence proved that apartheid had a point while at the same time seriously undermining support for black-majority rule from sympathetic countries. Political parties like Inkatha were used to rope in existing criminal gangs, which were then supported logistically and legally.

According to Mr Nelson Ngo, called as an expert, the Three Million Gang was created and supported by the Security Branch on instruction from the highest regional level, as part of its counter-insurgency strategy to neutralize and undermine UDF- and ANC-aligned activism in the mid-1980s. The Three Million Gang operated on a part-time basis in Brandfort, reinforcing the operations of other vigilante groups. Leaders of these groups would meet with members of the Security Branch at the Brandfort police station to discuss their strategies and to receive equipment, weapons and money from the police, as well as tobacco and alcohol.

The group's task was to confront political activists from the UDF or civic organizations where they congregated in shebeens and recreational facilities, start fights with them, and plant knives and firearms – mostly of Russian origin, to indicate ANC-trained guerrillas – on the bodies of people who were killed. This was meant to help in the cover-up of the Security Branch's own activities.

The strategy was supported right to the top. Justice officials, including magistrates and prosecutors, worked to undermine criminal prosecutions against these gang members.

An SABC report reads: 'Testifying before the Amnesty Committee, Mr P.M. Thulo, former commander of the ANC SDU in Kroonstad, alleged that a prosecutor in Kroonstad supported the Three Million Gang and helped them evade prosecution by guiding magistrates in particular directions. One particular magistrate would be called in, together with the prosecutor, to deal with cases involving gang members, with the result that charges were invariably dropped. According to Mr Thulo, a munici-pal office-bearer assisted the Three Million Gang by giving his minibuses to transport gang members to attacks as well as ferrying gang members to and from town for court appearances.'

So this was the taxi the wounded Wheetie was trying to reach!

'This evidence was corroborated before the Amnesty Committee by police detective J.J. de Ru who said that, on the recommendation of the prosecutor, gang leader Diwithi Ramasimong was often discharged from custody whilst being held on serious charges. According to De Ru, the Three Million Gang would collect rent and service monies for the council, while municipal office-bearers supplied gang members with ammunition and paid for their funerals.'

The TRC also heard that more South Africans were killed between 1990 and 1994 than in the twenty years of Total Onslaught before. Is this possible? I phone one of the TRC lawyers. 'It's true,' she says. 'Remember that the majority of amnesty applicants are black and many many of them formed part of these roped-in groups, especially through Inkatha.'

So while the release of Nelson Mandela and the unbanning of the ANC seemed to many people across the world to be vindication that the morally right will eventually triumph, for millions *in* South Africa, and for my comrades in Kroonstad, the level of amorality simply deepened into all levels of existence.

In his amnesty application Reggie is very clear about what he regards as right and wrong, and denies ever asking for the killing. 'I can't agree that anybody needed to be killed. I don't think anybody can condone murder.' He also refutes the claim that a decision was taken at a meeting of the ANC Youth League that Jantjie Petrus, a member of the local self-defence unit, should be asked to kill the Wheetie. 'The purpose of the SDUs was to protect the community from these attacks and not to become the attackers.'

On the other hand, Jantjie sticks to his defence that he was simply carrying out the will of the community. According to him, the community took a decision at a meeting that the Wheetie should be killed, and he, Jantjie, was then approached.

Reading the reports coming in over the week is like looking at the same object through different lenses. The various frameworks brought together by the amnesty hearing expose a profound moral confusion. Read within the framework of the law during the court case, Jantjie was guilty, because he broke the law. Read within the framework of amnesty,

Jantjie was guilty, but deserves amnesty because he killed with a political motive within a political context. Read within a traditional framework, Jantjie was not guilty, because he exercised the will of the community by getting rid of somebody who lived in disregard of the community. Read within the framework of a naive white activist, Jantjie was guilty, because he killed somebody, and even more guilty because it was a black person.

Even the Amnesty Committee finds the evidence confusing.

AMNESTY COMMITTEE: Now where did you get the firearm from, the one which you used in killing Diwiti?

JANTJIE: I got the firearm from Sergeant Jacobs. Sergeant Jacobs, I think he was stationed at Langlaagte Police Station. I obtained the firearm from him to complete my shooting lessons which (*Side A of tape 1 ends*) … training.

QUESTION: You had dealings with the police yourself?

JANTJIE: No. This person loaned me the firearm. At that stage I was struggling to get my firearm licence so the firearm is given to me so that I could complete my training in order to obtain the licence.

QUESTION: Is there any relationship between yourself and this policeman who gave you the firearm?

JANTJIE: No, no there was no relationship between the two of us. We just attended the same church at some stage and I know that he was a good person. At the stage when he gave me the firearm he did not know anything about the act which I was planning to commit with the firearm.

QUESTION: But you've testified Mr Petros that you had no confidence in the police because the police were assisting the Three Million Gang, how do you explain your getting a firearm from the very police you don't have confidence in?

JANTJIE: This person lives in Johannesburg and he was not aware of circumstances in Kroonstad at that stage.

At one point one of the judges asks: 'Now who is the criminal gang? I am confused, what is political, where is the politics – all seems criminal?'

~

J. is already in bed when I enter the bedroom. 'You realize,' I say, 'that this is what Reggie and the ANC Youth League were up against?' I am surprised at the accusing tone in my voice. I read to him the detail from the TRC amnesty transcript.

'Are you now going to tell me you made a mistake?'

'Yes, in fact I made a triple mistake: what I did was politically naive, legally uninformed and morally wrong. Although I myself typed all those names of people accusing the Three Million of terrorizing them, I refused to believe that the white government was behind it and would go to the trouble of actively putting structures up in a tiny town like Kroonstad in order for black people to kill each other.'

'You're again missing the point here: what exactly was offered to kill another black person? What would make you kill a person who's fighting for your own political freedom? What kind of person does that? This collaboration between the police and the gangs was so deeply cynical and degenerate that I would say thank God that we didn't have the capacity to imagine such a pact.'

'I want to make another point. I instinctively chose the safety of the Afrikaner government's police. In the most morally loaded moment of my life I chose Afrikaners *and* – and maybe that is the worst – we, you and I, masked it in moral and legal language.'

Outside the southeaster is howling. J. gets up to push yet another piece of folded paper between the window and its frame to stop the rattling. 'Listen here,' he says. 'I know this is important to you, so let me make another suggestion. You used the word *instinctively*. If you believe, as you always tell me, that Africanness is defined by the idea of being interconnected to one's community, then perhaps you've proved your instinctive Africanness by choosing your own people, however bad and corrupt they were. This is who you are interconnected with. You have proved your Africanness!'

'Nonsense!'

'Oh, come on! Don't think for one minute that the others operated differently. They used their extended clans in Kroonstad – they were all related, remember – to help them wage a war against each other that they deftly clad in the language of politics and liberation.'

'I am not comparing things. I am trying to live a grounded life on this continent and the Africanness I understand encompasses ...' and I try to find words, real words to sprout from the root of my tongue, '*alles*, seen and unseen, known and unknown, that is breathing upon me.'

J. gets up. 'Listen here, this is the twenty-first century. What is just and civilized has been globalized and is being patrolled by human rights watchers with money. I'm going to watch the golf on TV.'

~

It is busy in the harshly illuminated Nando's in Potchefstroom. I sit where I can watch the entrance for the person I'm waiting for. Suddenly the doors open and a stream of about fifteen overweight police in blue uniforms saunter in, with a fizz of squad cars and blue lights outside. Instinctively I grab my handbag and cellphone and look for an exit. But they are all just picking up their lunch orders, sprinkling peri-peri and tomato sauce, buying soft drinks.

An SMS flashes on my cell: '2 bzy @ Ndos plse wlk rnd blok.' The message is from the person I paid to track down Jantjie Petrus and arrange a meeting. I walk around the block. When I return to Nando's the rush is over. I find a table and wait again. When he walks in, I recognize him immediately: the man who pulled the trigger; whose hand stretched across mine in a café long ago. We shake hands the comrade way. It appears that he was also unsure whether he would recognize me. So he came an hour earlier, lurked around outside, then recognized me and watched me wait.

It is only when he sits down that I notice that his left arm, just below the elbow, is missing. The very same hand that stretched over the counter to take a cooldrink straw, the same part that was visible to the Wheetie's sister below the seamless red sleeve. His front teeth are missing. I sit opposite him, finally, the man of my nightmares, but within seconds all my questions and moral anxieties are gone. He is a master storyteller. To my opening question about why one would *choose* to live in Potch, he transforms the shack areas and the outskirts of this Dopper town into a gripping theatre of immense survival possibilities if one understands how to enter what he calls 'the networks'. If you walk down the street, you are being surveilled by several networks. One assesses what there is to steal, and lets the boss know that they can get hold of a good jacket, or a car, shoes, and so forth. At the same time a second network assesses the potential victim's route and how muggable he is. Somebody from an altogether new network assesses the begging opportunities; a fourth tries to determine any drug-selling opportunities. These networks then link up within minutes and prices and risks are exchanged and negoti-ated. The biggest risk is those who need money for drugs; they disregard any network and often mess up one's plans. But all this networking is now too dangerous for him at his age, says Jantjie. He works purely on the selling side. People tell him what they need, he puts the order in and he can usually provide. I cut up the chicken he has ordered so he can eat it with a fork.

'Ja, the hand, I pushed it through a window and that is now what glass can do, *iets niks soos glas.* So I have stopped drinking – I mean, it's only me; who else will look after this other hand?'

He comes from a family of six children. Fifteen of his family members were stabbed to death in the seventies and eighties, but 'today it is mos net *krrrr-krrrr*' – spontaneously he holds his arms and hand in the position of gun shooting, the exact way several witnesses showed in court – only his left hand is no longer there. We realize that at the same time. He looks embarrassed and for one unguarded moment his shoulders grow slack and he appears a lost, threatened figure, but maybe I just imagined that, because he has already flickered back.

Yes, he has four daughters who he now forces into a better life.

'Force?'

'Even with *geweld.* I am not ashamed to say that. But they *will* have a better life than me. I do not care. The boyfriends who come to them, *ek werk hulle sake.* I work them over and I can call on many to assist me. I am not afraid to be killed. I am also not afraid to kill others. I killed to get rid of the bad; why would I not now kill to get hold of the good? My eldest daughter wants to become an air hostess, so I fit myself out to make that possible. It is important, you know, that she *wants* to. That she wants something better out of herself. I told her, I said, "Baby, the two of us will get there."'

Of his fourteen-year jail sentence he served five and a half years. When he came out on amnesty, his wife had already left him. 'Yes, the women come and go, but my children, my children are mine.'

While he is talking I phrase and rephrase the question that I want to put to him, but from whichever angle it suddenly seems outrageous to ask him whether he thinks what he did was right and how he judges what I did. And, whichever way I look, I find no space to say that I am sorry about my own role in the event. In fact, I become aware of how superfluous my sentiments are in Jantjie's life of poverty, dislocation and brutalization – that the murder of the Wheetie was but one in a range of events he lived through with killing as the modus operandi for survival. Nothing that I say or do or am makes any sense in the world where he has to live his daily life.

'But I have a *lekke huis*; if you come up the hill, you see the house, a nice house, my house; the children like to be with me: all the comforts and *allerhande ou jokies*.'

But he can't stay long; these *vretende polieste* wasted our time and he must be off to another appointment. We say goodbye. I pay, and when I drive down Voortrekker Street later, I see him turning into a side street – haughty gait, cap cheekily backwards on the head, challenging body language – clearly still a very dangerous man. But the vulnerability of the left hand is somehow readable from his back. The way he turns his body to protect the absent part and the weariness on his face are signs of a man who has nothing but his wits to survive in a land where the foothold to survival is not lodged in care, but in self-interest.

~

In the meantime it has grown dark and I follow my contact person in his bakkie towards Johannesburg. We take several turns and the area becomes completely unfamiliar to me. On a flyover the bakkie loses speed and I see somebody running out of the dark towards him and getting into the passenger seat. We drive towards a shopping centre and I am suddenly aware of a million networks watching us make our way towards a Wimpy bar.

Dudu Mofokeng is clearly nervous. He wears a balaclava rolled down to just above his eyes and has the tattoo marks of the 26s on his hand and wrist. Although he is black, he speaks, as did Jantjie, a fluent and very idiomatic Afrikaans. His father was a Mosotho and his mother a coloured woman from Kroonstad. Coming from two different race groups, they were not allowed to live in the coloured area. His parents divorced and Dudu grew up with his grandmother, where he started with pickpocketing, shoplifting and later petty theft from cars. When caught, he was caned.

Eventually he found work with a building team that built schools for the Free State administration. He met his wife, they settled and he started to lead a life without crime, despite having to move from place to place to build the schools. The building team decided to strike for better working conditions and everybody got fired. He fell back on crime and was arrested.

When he was finally released from jail he found that as part of forced removals, his area, neighbours, friends and family had been broken up and dispersed. Dudu uses an old-fashioned word when he describes his feelings: '*Ek was diep verskeur. Alles wat vas om my gestaan het, was weg.*' (I was deeply torn. Everything that was steadfast around me was gone.) He immediately started doing big crime and fled to his grandmother's to escape the police.

Then he found a job at Premier Milling, good money, good working conditions, and his wife came to visit him. To be with her he didn't turn up for work for days, so he got fired. He found work at the Panorama sweets factory in Kroonstad. The pay was bad, so he and his wife opened a shebeen. This went so well that he sponsored a soccer team and on

Saturdays his place was overflowing with players and supporters. A crime-free life seemed possible at last.

Then the Wheetie sent the Three Million into his place. They turned up whenever they wanted, intimidated the clients, knives were pulled; they refused to pay, harassed the workers and caused such a bad atmosphere that Dudu lost all his clients. In the meantime, one family member after the other was being killed by the Three Million. Jantjie Petrus's father came to recruit him and Jantjie to kill the Wheetie. They would each receive R50 000. Both of them had guns and both of them were good shots. They tossed a coin and Jantjie 'won'.

As they were following the Wheetie, Reggie got more and more nervous and Denzil wanted to back out, so they decided they had to do it immediately if any of them wanted to lead a '*gewone lewe*' in the future.

We order a steak for Dudu and he spills his heart out about his terrible living conditions. He lives in a 'zôzô' and has four children, the eldest currently serving a jail sentence. Although he has a little job, he cannot live from it and needs to get '*aanvullings*' from elsewhere. Nothing came of the promises of money in return for the '*opruiming*' of the Wheetie. He only sees that the lives of 'certain people' are coasting downhill all the time, while his whole life is just uphill. He asks if he may order more bread rolls, and then wraps them carefully in serviettes and puts them in his bag. As we walk out, he scoops a handful of tomato sauce and mustard sachets and disappears into the dark.

It has started to rain. The bakkie drives in front until I am on the highway. My tracer hoots; I hoot back. At my hotel I transfer the last payment into his bank account. I go to bed with the full knowledge that I am a coward. I couldn't say sorry within these unequal power relations. What are you saying, I reprimand myself, tossing around in the strange hotel bed. To say sorry is to take the first step towards change, towards repair. But how do I ever repair those coming from these stories with their undercurrent of apartheid devastation? I need all whites, all of us so obliviously unbent between country and chasm. If we don't repair, we will be forced to live with the mashed-in distortions and wrath of an uprooted, wounded and devastated community. Don't we know that it is not possible to live a sealed-off life in Africa?

~

The next day a neatly uniformed guard stops me at the private entrance of a big shopping centre. 'I was told by Mr Saunders to tell you that I have an appointment with him at eleven o'clock,' I say. The black man smiles broadly and literally throws the boom open for me: a friend of Saunders is clearly also a friend of his.

In a modern reception with big paintings and chrome furniture, I ask for Saunders. After a minute or so he walks in. I hardly recognize him with his sophisticated appearance. Gone is the hairstyle and moustache that said, I am from the security police and I don't take kak from anybody; gone are the boring clothes and the face filled with deep suspicion. Saunders opens his hands genially to welcome me and takes me to his office. His job here at the centre is to oversee the security of the personnel and the building. He wears a lovely shirt, his hair is fashionably gelled, he is at home and confident and, judging from the response of the personnel, also well liked. He takes me to a coffee shop where they know him, and we are served immediately.

'What is it that you want to know?' he asks in a friendly tone.

'What do you think I need to know?'

He suddenly turns serious. 'I read your booklet on the murder some years ago and, yes, you were well informed.' A paternalistic tone has crept into his voice.

'Was it a political or a criminal case for you?'

'Like everything in Kroonstad it was a bit of everything,' he says neutrally.

'Did you support the Wheetie?'

'*Jong*, you know how things were. Some of us supported him, others didn't know about it, and so people worked, sometimes with and sometimes against one another.'

'Who killed Hankan Petrus?'

He gives me a fatherly smile. 'Let us put it this way; if you find out please come and tell me.'

Of course he will tell me nothing, I realize. He is an Afrikaner; he is as close to me as a population group in South Africa could be. But out of his distasteful past there is nothing that makes him feel that he could have a conversation with me about what happened in the town where we grew up. He has moved from an ethnic position to a class one: where he protected Afrikaner power and interest in the past, he now protects class and money.

CONVERSATION 7
FORMATION OF THE SELF

'Let me challenge you today: isn't this interconnectedness the very bedrock of the failure of Africa?'

'I would not necessarily disagree. Black people allowed whites to move in with them assuming that they would interconnect. But instead they found themselves living with a white impenetrable bunker, with people coming out at times, shooting, destroying, rubbishing, yet sharing nothing. So the whole expansive root system was blocked by this impervious construct in their midst.'

'But it is an interesting question: how does one form a moral self within such an interconnected community? Even more relevant: how can people's imaginings of what kind of society they want function when the rites, rituals and stories that sustained their belief systems no longer have a place?'

'When the interconnectedness moves towards wholeness, it would elicit actions like building, caring and helping. But if the interconnectedness is simply about solidarity, no matter the values, then it becomes a problem.'

'If Socrates says, Though I am one, I am two-in-one and ... if I do wrong, I am condemned to live together with a wrongdoer in unbearable intimacy, then he is saying that the moral self is formed when the I steps into conversation with the self.'

'Maybe it is precisely at this point that an African awareness might say: I form the moral self in another way. Of course there is an I. Of course there should be mind-changing internal conversation. But in African thought, the conversation that eventually creates the moral entity is not with the self but with the people around one, the 'stranger-accommodating-community'. More bluntly: the Western moral self is created in the self through conversations with the *self*; the African moral self is also created in the self, but through conversations with the *community*. The scary thought is that if the community is distraught or brutalized, or if the self is cut off or disconnected from its community, it degenerates.'

'I don't know. Forming the self is a psychological question, a genetic question, a moral question, all on different levels. Kant did say that the conversation with the self is the beginning of the moral self, but as always with Kant it is the higher self, the rational self, that is truly moral through its relation to the Divine. For Kant it is the power of reason linked to the Divine that sets human beings apart from other species. It is literally a voice within ourself; this voice is formed by reason representing the Divine, and everybody has the capacity and grows into this voice.'

'Ja, but what if the inner voice talking to you is the voice of the community, or perceived by you as being the voice of the community? You will have no moral compass without the community.'

'How are you going to present this, our discussion? Are you writing a novel?'

This unexpected question is put by the professor five minutes before our discussion time ends. I answer without thinking.

'No, I can't, I don't *want* to write novels.'

'Why not? With novels you can explore the inner psyche of characters; you can imagine, for example, being black. So what is it about non-fiction that you don't want to give up?'

'The strangeness. Whatever novelistic elements I may use in my non-fiction work, the strangeness is not invented. The strangeness is real, and the fact that I cannot ever really enter the psyche of somebody else, somebody black. The terror and loneliness of that inability is what I don't want to give up on.'

'But how will you live together in your country (or in mine) if you don't begin to imagine one another?'

'I want to suggest that at this stage imagination for me is overrated.'

'That's a terrible statement!'

'I know, so let me not generalize and stick to the pronoun "I": I simply don't know enough about blackness, or birdness, or mountainness, or even Englishness for that matter, to imagine it in terms other than my exact self or the exotic opposite of myself. A famous Afrikaans poet Eugène Marais visited some Bushmen researchers during the nineteenth century and said afterwards: The Bushmen could speak lion, they could speak blue crane, they could speak wind. I want to be this embedded in my world. I want to speak black.'

'Am I hearing a suggestion that literature has failed you?'

Oh boy, I am so deep into this that I simply have to swim. 'I think I am saying that in a country where we have come from different civilizations, then lived apart in unequal and distorted relationships that formed generations of us, our imagination is simply not capable of imagining a reality as – or with – the other.'

'So you have changed your position? During our first conversations you were concerned that not being able to imagine might mean a hidden racism?'

'Yes, I now think that to imagine black at this stage is to insult black. That is why I stay with non-fiction, listening, engaging, observing, translating, until one can hopefully begin to sense a thinning of skin, negotiate possible small openings at places where imaginings can begin to begin.'

'I know becoming is for ever, but do you have a sense of where to ...?'

'No. ... No.' But the professor's clear face makes space for an attempt. 'Except perhaps that the integrity of the world should be inviolable.' It is quiet in the room. 'And being woven into such wondrous immensity compels me to care ... in a way, you know, every bird that falls affects me, every star that breaks reaches me, every death damages me.'

'And blackness taught that?' His voice is calm.

'Blackness released me from my white capsule. It has liberated me from the rule of all laws; it has taught me how to become other than myself. And through the life of a remarkable king I have learnt that there where one feels one has failed morally and has hurt indiscriminately, also there grace and forgiveness from black people will be. The mere fact that we care, care actively, makes us an infinitesimal part of the blue breath of the world ... a state of non-personal power ...'

Both of us are quiet. This will be our last discussion. I will miss him, the unobtrusive, secure way he allowed me to take risks, to dare; the curious way in which European philosophy, Australian history and German culture could wash in his presence over the African narrative I was trying to construct.

Unexpectedly the professor smiles and holds out his hand. 'Over-rated ... I'll remember that.'

I kiss his hand. 'Good luck with your country,' I say, 'which at least has said sorry.'

He hugs me. 'And good luck with yours, which doesn't know how.'

Everybody is summoned to the building, and those who know the procedure fall into a queue. We fill in forms indicating whom we want to see: name, number, section. I have only a name, and gather that as he is not awaiting trial and not doing life, he would be in Section C at long term. Some of the guards *ghai* with the visitors and some visitors greet one another like old friends. We come from all classes and races. We move into security, where we and our parcels are scanned. I put a copy of the novel *Agaat* on the conveyor belt. Early this morning, when I left the old-age flat where my mother stays, I remembered that I did not even have a present to bring. We looked through my mother's extra soaps and towels, but then she came out of her bedroom with Marlene van Niekerk's *Agaat* in her hands. 'I have two copies, and know no one to whom I can give it, so take it.'

The conveyor belt stops. The security guard picks up the book and shakes it as if expecting banknotes to fall from the pages. 'Whose is this?' I put up my hand. 'Is it a present?' I nod. He calls somebody from the back. They carry the book like an incubator into a room. We wait.

After a while a new security person comes out. 'You want prisoner 851 to read this?'

'Yes,' I say, wondering whether he expected me to say, No, I want him to eat it, or kill somebody with it, or smoke it … They try to read the jacket cover, but the people behind me are becoming impatient, as the first bus has just arrived. I am waved through.

Bus C takes us to one of the gigantic buildings on the prison grounds. One by one we move through different phases of security until about forty of us wait in a fenced yard. I sit next to a dignified elderly couple.

'Who are you seeing?' I ask.

'Our son,' says the black woman, and after quite a while she adds, 'Burglaries. We warned, but …' she pulls up her shoulders. Her husband looks away, as if he hasn't heard her.

I see a granny with two boys approaching puberty, one absent-mindedly crushing pimples behind his ears, the other yawning until his eyes water. A very thin woman with a tight-fitting blouse, very high heels and a Cindy Crawford beauty spot applied with a heavy hand shows us the Springbok cap and scarf she brought.

We move through another wire gate into a large room with rows of backless benches. 'You've come to see a reader!' says a young man, suggestively raising his eyebrows several times towards the book on my lap. 'A teacher, actually,' I say, wondering whether it sounds like a contradiction.

The number and name of every prisoner is called as he appears through the double doors. I recognize him immediately. Denzil – my former deputy head and head of our school's Afrikaans department, my high-school colleague and also my fellow state witness in a murder case. Initially his eyes pass me over in the way the eyes of black and coloured people skip one when they've registered white, because white means will-anyway-not-be-for-me. I remember how, when I started teaching at a black training college, I began to stop students in the streets, forcing them to recognize me, as I became aware how they simply did not look at whites, knowing that they wouldn't know them – just as I previously walked the streets not looking at individual black faces.

Perhaps Denzil is searching for his wife or kids. I get up from the bench and see him freeze. He stares at me. Then he starts to laugh in the way I have seen him laugh so many times in my life, with pleasure and abundance, but suddenly all of this falls away from him and he bursts into tears. Thick in the throat, I hold his wiry body clothed in a prison overall. What has happened here, to him?

I remember another visit. One morning he was not at school and the staff were told that he had been hospitalized with TB in the isolation wing for contagious diseases of Boitumelo Hospital. His wife and children were suddenly avoided by the rest of the community. My visit to him then was less dramatic than now, but I found a melancholy man paging listlessly through a trashy magazine. 'A week ago I analysed a Hennie Aucamp short story in my class, but look what they bring me to read.'

I give him the book. He looks astounded. 'Can you believe it?' he says, his voice breaking like a teenager's. 'I've heard about this book! Can you believe this ...' He weighs it in one hand, instinctively looking around for somebody to show what he has just found, but, like my mother earlier that morning, knowing the futility of looking for kindred reading spirits.

'One can buy food at a stall in the yard ...' I say.

'Rather buy me a telephone card; it has more currency inside.'

Piece by piece he tells me the story. After our murder court case, nothing wanted to work out in his life. He felt threatened, rejected at school and 'perhaps I started to drink a little bit too much, you understand?' He resigned as a teacher, and with the payout of pension and other money he bought the bottle store opposite his house. The seller of the store was very clever, however. He handed the shop immediately to Denzil, who had to run it without any experience and without knowing how much debt was hidden in all the documentation. The seller was slow to sign the transfer deed. In the end, paying the outstanding accounts while he was not actually the owner of the shop, Denzil's money ran out. The owner simply moved back into the shop and sold it to somebody else.

Out of work and out of money, he still had his car and started a transport business taking people to nearby towns – his wife fortunately had her permanent job at the shoe shop. One day he was asked to take three men to Viljoenskroon. They asked him to wait for them and then take them back to Kroonstad. What he didn't know, he says, was that they were robbing a shop. Just outside Viljoenskroon, the police caught up with them and they were arrested. Because of certain court procedures, says Denzil, the men were released but he has to serve a twenty-year sentence.

'Heavens, Denzil, but it sounds very much like your previous story with the Wheetie!'

'*Nou sien jy*,' he says passionately. 'Here I sit now, nobody and with nothing.'

I see the Springbok cap falling to the ground as the woman with the beauty spot is passionately kissed by the man. The elderly couple sit and talk to their son as if they are sitting somewhere under a tree, checking out the landscape around them. They talk non-stop, not looking at one another, but laughing in intimate ways as if sharing wonderful memories. The granny is preaching to her son, but he is wolfing down the hamburger she bought; the children roll outside on the winter grass, bullying each other with a mixture of cowardice and spite. One sees how family members try to look unobtrusively at their watches. Denzil, who wrote literary reviews for the book page I ran in Cape Town, presses *Agaat* like a treasure or a shield to his chest when we say goodbye.

I drive into the Johannesburg smog to catch the Sunday-afternoon flight back to Cape Town.

chapter twenty-four

2 June 2008

Only six weeks left before I fly back to Cape Town. I begin to sleep badly and drink extraordinarily; I get hay fever and have to buy homeopathic medicine. On the hay-fever eye-drop box I read what is called the art of applying: 'Lie your head somewhat back, pull the lower eyelid lightly away from the eye and carefully drop one drop in the "*Bindehautsack*". Take good care that the top of the dripper does not touch the eye. Let go of the lower lid and press it from the "*Augenwinkel*" lightly against the nose. "*Blinzeln*" your eyes several times slowly to spread the drops carefully over the apple of the eye.'

I cannot imagine something similar in Afrikaans or English on a South African box: the care in the language, the imaginative vocabulary, as if you and your eyes and your language really matter.

9 June 2008

Crossing the blue wrought-iron bridge from the Villa Walther, there's a sudden fragrance. Subtle. Very delicate. I look up; the Lindenbaum is blooming. My heart leaps: so it is this then! The song my mother loves so much: '*Ich atmet einen linden Duft*' (I breathe a waft of lime-tree blossom in the room, from a twig picked by your dear hand). I remain standing under the tree, as text and life come together in my body, in my breath, in my outstretched hand touching the pale yellow blossoms. Once again, poetry has taught me how to live a lived life.

Crossing the lake, I wonder, why is there this release within me when the world and the very text that probably kept me a foreigner in Africa at last match? Am I simply longing for a coherence between the world and texts I read? What does it say that I, as I stand enfolding into a fragrance, know a Gustav Mahler *Lied* which perhaps even the German-speaking couple walking past me have never heard of? What does it make me? Enriched or a misfit? It makes me broad, I think, stretching my arms in the fragrance of blossoms, grass and sun; it makes me broad.

18 July 2008

Today is my last day in Berlin. My computer is disconnected, my accounts are paid, my clothes packed, and the flat is empty, except for my room. I don't want to say goodbye to anybody.

In the late afternoon I walk the route I have come to know as well as the palm of my hand. In Bismarckallee I stop at one of the four sphinxes guarding the bridge over the Herthasee. This figure from Africa has been named by the Greeks as 'sphinx', meaning 'strangler'.

My eyes trace the proud head of the sphinx in her heavy stone curls. Her nose is slightly eroded by a filigree of moss, her eyes staring down the street, their sad curves countered by the neutral, resolute mouth. From her strong neck, her stone breasts splay out of folds of cloth, available, sturdy, functional. Her shoulders, at ease in the upper arms, flow into the furred forearms, the enormous lion paws – resting, spread out, unapologetically majestic on the pedestal.

What is she, I wonder. Is she simply a hybrid, doomed to sit at all crossings, guarding all transits, for ever trapped between two stages? She knows the world and the secret world, but is of neither, and this has a price. She can nourish and protect, but with those large paws she cannot caress a child's mouth to latch to her nipple. Despite the hybridical aptness of her body and mind, her paws will always betray her into clumsiness when she wants to hold a body, pick up a ladybird, sculpt a face or wipe away tears. In the same way those paws are betrayed by the human head. Having caught prey, what incisors will rip the jugular? What head would bear it down to be 'strangled' in blood? What tongue would caress a cub? What nostrils would smell danger? What pupils would open up wide at night, piercing the dark?

But it is the paws I touch, the fur, the nails, and as I do so I see they begin to glisten, to gleam as they slowly start curving down the pedestal. And suddenly I know how at night her eyes take on a fierce yellow glow and how light-footedly she jumps from her pedestal to prowl the streets, acknowledging and protecting the world's magic spaces of becoming. She guards and she gives milk, her humanity backed by muscular thighs and a powerful broad-backed rump from which the tail, thick and vigorous, caresses the flanks.

For me, she is not a hybrid, or a product of rape. She is what she is. Not split, not guarding dichotomies, but presenting beingness as multiple intactnesses, not with the singular self, but with a bodily akin-ness to the vulnerability of being in and beyond this world.

~

It is early morning. I hoist my rucksack on my back, pull out the handle of my suitcase, stop at the door and look for the last time at how the various shades of green and shimmering water flicker through the peaceful flat. I lay the key down on the table and close the door behind me, softly.

glossary

aanvullings: supplements

AF: African Foundation

Afrikaanse Kinderensiklopedie:
    Afrikaans Children's Encyclopaedia

ag: oh

allerhande ou jokies: various
    little jokes

alles: everything, all

ANC: African National Congress

Augenwinkel: corner of one's eye

AWB: Afrikaner Weerstandsbeweging
    (Afrikaner Resistance Movement)

bakkie: pickup truck

bankie: small wooden bench

beskuit: rusks

biltong: salted and dried meat

Bindehautsack: conjunctival sac

blik: tin

blinzeln: blink

boerbeskuit: type of rusk

Boere: Afrikaners

bohadi: bride pride

braai, braaivleis: barbecue

braaiplek: braai place

Casspir: police riot-control and
    combat vehicle

COSAW: Congress of South African
    Writers

Die Myrthe still und hoch der
    Lorbeer steht: The myrtle stands
    quiet and the laurel high

Difaqane: *see* Lifaqane

Dinge gaan taai: Things are going
    tough

Dopper: member of the Reformed
    Church

Dr Oetkers Onken Joghurt mit
    Rhabarber-Vanille-Geschmack
    – Gutes aus Milch: a brand of
    yoghurt that tastes like rhubarb
    and vanilla – goodness
    from milk

dumela: hello, good day

Ek klap sommer iemand as hy appels
    in my ore eet: I'd just hit someone
    if he ate apples in my ear

ek werk hulle sake: I work their case

Es schwindelt mir, es brennt / Mein
Eingeweide. Nur wer die
Sehnsucht kennt, / weiß, was ich
leide!: It dazzles me, it burns /
My intestines. Only those who
suffer know longing, / know what
I endure!

etwas neu: something new

Fokken los ons uit, Bennie, ons party
hier: Fucking leave us alone,
Bennie, we're partying here

Fuchs, du hast die Gans gestohlen:
Jackal, you have stolen a goose

Gaan Ma tronk toe?: Is Mom going
to jail?

Gans mit Kastanien: goose with
chestnuts

geweld: violence

gewone lewe: ordinary life

ghai: make funny small talk

God is liefde: God is love

Gots vrou: God woman

Guten Tag, mein Herr und meine
Dame, haben sie einen Laptop in
ihrem Rückgepäck?: Good day,
sir and madam, do you have a
laptop in your luggage?

Haai meneer: Hey mister

Hankan Petrus is lank op sy been en
fris en hy is nie so lig van kleur
nie, u edele. Jantjie se
gelaatskleur is lig: Hankan Petrus
is tall on his legs and well built
and he is not so light of colour,
Your Honour. Jantjie's face-
colour is light

Here God, help ons: Dear God,
help us

Ich atmet einen linden Duft:
I breathe a lime-tree fragrance

iets niks soos glas: something so
nothing like glass

Im dunkeln Laub die Gold-Orangen
glühn: In dark foliage the golden
oranges glow

indunas: advisors

Inkatha: Zulu-nationalist political
organization

ja: yes

Jammer, meneer: Sorry, mister

Jirre, Dok, wat maak *jy* hier?: God,
Doc, what are *you* doing here?

Jirre, maar die Boere drink vir jou:
God, but the Afrikaners are
drinking

jong: friendly term for younger
person

juffrou: miss, schoolmistress

kaffir: derogatory term for black
person

kak: shit

Kartoffeln: potato (mashed)

Kartoffeln oder Rotkohl: potato
(mashed) or red cabbage

Kegel: cone, skittle pin

Kennst du das Land, wo die Zitronen
blühn: Do you know the country,
where the lemons blossom

kgotla: meeting

khotso: peace

knobkierie: stick with knobbed head

knyptang: pair of pincers

kofia: fez

Kolleg: college

komm: come

lekke huis: nice house

Lied, Lieder: song, songs

Liewe Ma: Dear Mom

Lifaqane: period of Zulu
  and Basotho migration and
  associated wars, in the early
  nineteenth century (called
  'Mfecane' in Zulu)

mächtiges Hochdruckgebiet über
  Norden Russlands: powerful
  high-pressure area over Northern
  Russia

mafisa: a system in which poor
  people are assisted through cattle

manne: guys

maroho: green indigenous plant

'Me: Mother

meneer: mister, sir

mevrou: madam

mevroutjie: madam as diminutive

mielie: maize

Mitteleuropa kalt trockenes Wetter
  mit Schneeflocken: Cold weather
  with snow over Central Europe

MK: Umkhonto we Sizwe (military
  wing of the ANC)

mme re tsamaya ka pelo tse ntle re
  hlwekileng: and we walk with
  beautiful and pure hearts

moer: hit, angry ('the moer in')

moruti: preacher, minister

mos: obviously

mos net: simply

Muss i' denn: Must I then

nala: prosperity

Nein. Fleisch: No. Meat

Nico en Hans-Werner se pa werk
  by die tronk: Nico and Hans-
  Werner's father works at the jail

Nou sien jy: Now you see

oom: uncle

opruiming: clearing up

pap: porridge

peho: to give cattle as a thank-you
  gesture

pitso: big meeting of whole nation

pula: rain

rooskleurig: rose-coloured

Rotkohl: red cabbage

saalsak: saddlebag

schans: cliff

sien jy?: do you see?

sjoe: exclamation, phew

sommer: just, for no reason

soos die van die kleurlings: like those
  of the coloureds

Staatsoper: State Opera House

Stolpersteine: stumbling stones

stumme: mute

suka: go away

Sy naam is soos wasem vir my:
  His name is like vapour to me

teeverdaging: tea break

tsotsis: gangsters

tuisnywerheid: shop that sells
  homemade products

ubuntu: a world view based on the
  idiom *umuntu ngumuntu
  ngabantu* – a person is a person
  through other persons

uitroeiers: exterminators

Umkhonto we Sizwe: *see* MK
unbestimmt: undetermined
verlorenheit: lostness
vetkoek: dough balls baked in fat
voertsek: go away
voorsinger: lead singer
vretende polieste: eating policemen

wat dit ookal mag wees: whatever
    that may be
Wit Wolwe: White Wolves
    (right-wing organization)
wragtiewaar: truly
Wurst: sausage
zôzô: shack

source notes

p. xi *'You,* all of you ...' Ndebele, *The Cry of Winnie Mandela,* p. 113

p. 18 'There is Moshesh ...' Casalis, *My Life in Basutoland,* p. 176

pp. 18–9 'He appeared to be ...' Casalis, *My Life in Basutoland,* p. 177

p. 19 'a deeper yearning ...' Arbousset, *Missionary Excursion,* p. 51

p. 22 'He entertained this notion ...' Seboni, *Moshweshwe's Diplomatic Relations,* p. 6

p. 23 'Ke'na Moshoeshoe Moshoashoaila ...' Seboni, *Moshweshwe's Diplomatic Relations,* p. 9

p. 23 'His anxiety for megalomania ...' Seboni, *Moshweshwe's Diplomatic Relations,* p. 10

p. 24 'If you drive people away ...' Mokhehle, in Du Preez, *Of Warriors, Lovers and Prophets,* p. 53

p. 24 'with a roar of approval ...' Becker, *Hill of Destiny,* p. 19

p. 25 'Moshoeshoe ... took charge ...' Arbousset, *Missionary Excursion,* p. 134

p. 25 'This mountain is my mother ...' Casalis, *The Basutos,* p. 78

p. 27 'a son of the Difaqane ...' Seboni, *Moshweshwe's Diplomatic Relations,* p. 26

p. 27 'thin, slender, pale, horrible man ...' Arbousset, *Missionary Excursion,* p. 68

p. 27 'boiling away in pots ...' Arbousset, *Missionary Excursion,* p. 69

p. 27 'sunk his teeth ...' Arbousset, *Missionary Excursion,* p. 72

pp. 28–9 'In my infancy ...' Thompson, *Survival in Two Worlds,* p. 95

p. 29 'ethical foundation ...' Seboni, *Moshweshwe's Diplomatic Relations,* p. 27

p. 51 'there began to show itself in me ...' Casalis, *My Life in Basutoland*, p. 17

p. 51 'from morning till night ...' Casalis, *My Life in Basutoland*, p. 44

p. 51 'I had not even finished ...' Casalis, *My Life in Basutoland*, p. 45

pp. 52–3 'The horses were brought ...' Casalis, *My Life in Basutoland*, p. 52

p. 53 'wafting me a kiss ...' Casalis, *My Life in Basutoland*, p. 53

p. 53 'the celestial regions ...' Casalis, *My Life in Basutoland*, p. 59

pp. 53–4 'One night when all were asleep ...' Machobane, 'Mohlomi', pp. 21–2

p. 55 'stern and savage grandeur ...' Casalis, *My Life in Basutoland*, p. 65

p. 56 'a little mist ...' Casalis, *My Life in Basutoland*, p. 130

p. 57 'Without knowing it ...' Casalis, *My Life in Basutoland*, p. 136

p. 57 'Almost everywhere were human bones ...' Casalis, *My Life in Basutoland*, p. 171

p. 57 'a very intelligent hunter' Casalis, *My Life in Basutoland*, p. 136

p. 58 'where Europeans were for the first time ...' Casalis, *My Life in Basutoland*, pp. 172–3

p. 58 'Foreigners of Moshesh' Casalis, *My Life in Basutoland*, p. 174

p. 58 'winding serpent-like round it ...' Casalis, *My Life in Basutoland*, p. 175

p. 59 '*Lumèla lekhoa* ...' Casalis, *My Life in Basutoland*, p. 177

p. 60 'O Casalis ...' Thompson, *Survival in Two Worlds*, p. 77

p. 60 'by his example and interference ...' Thompson, *Survival in Two Worlds*, p. 81

p. 61 'My heart is white with joy' Casalis, *My Life in Basutoland*, p. 183

pp. 61–2 '[Y]our words are great and good ...' Casalis, *My Life in Basutoland*, pp. 183–4

p. 62 'encouraged the bolder spirits ...' Casalis, *My Life in Basutoland*, p. 187

pp. 62–3 'After a prolonged search ...' Germond, *Chronicles of Basutoland*, p. 26

p. 63 'in a solitude almost absolute ...' Casalis, *My Life in Basutoland*, p. 191

p. 64 'People ran from all sides ...' Casalis, *My Life in Basutoland*, p. 211

p. 64 'philosophy of the subject' Thompson, *Survival in Two Worlds*, p. 81

p. 64 'with feelings bordering on extacy' Thompson, *Survival in Two Worlds*, p. 81

p. 64 'Very good ...' Casalis, *My Life in Basutoland*, pp. 184–5

p. 65 'for French stomachs' Casalis, *My Life in Basutoland*, p. 202

p. 65 'Family affection is no longer a benediction ...' Casalis, *My Life in Basutoland*, p. 209

p. 77 'They came at last ...' Casalis, *My Life in Basutoland*, p. 219

p. 77 'I do not believe ...' Casalis, *My Life in Basutoland*, p. 213

p. 78 'Now ... you will be indeed my missionaries ...' Casalis, *My Life in Basutoland*, p. 218

p. 78 'because the Basotho didn't have a book ...' Casalis, *My Life in Basutoland*, p. 222

p. 78 'written in all our hearts ...' Casalis, *My Life in Basutoland*, p. 222

p. 78 'he discovered, to his great surprise ...' Casalis, *My Life in Basutoland*, p. 220

p. 79 'Our conversation was in full flow ...' Casalis, *My Life in Basutoland*, p. 229

p. 79 'I cannot see the wind ...' Casalis, *The Basutos*, p. 239

p. 80 'You are white ...' Casalis, *My Life in Basutoland*, p. 221

p. 80 'He was not wanting ...' Casalis, *My Life in Basutoland*, pp. 224–5

p. 80 'At the same time ...' Casalis, *My Life in Basutoland*, p. 225

p. 81 '*Beha molamu, mor'a Mokhachane...*' Damane and Sanders, *Lithoko*, p. 210

p. 81 'Everywhere on the way ...' Thompson, *Survival in Two Worlds*, pp. 213–4

p. 81 'To do good ...' Casalis, *My Life in Basutoland*, p. 223

p. 82 'It was excusable ...' Casalis, *My Life in Basutoland*, p. 224

p. 82 'The heart is deeply corrupt ...' Casalis, *The Basutos*, pp. 302–4

p. 83 'It was really so ...' Casalis, *My Life in Basutoland*, p. 240

p. 84 'The man who had brought us ...' Casalis, *My Life in Basutoland*, p. 217

p. 85 'mulatto sons of Dr Read' Casalis, *My Life in Basutoland*, p. 269

p. 85 'second self' Casalis, *My Life in Basutoland*, p. 282

p. 86 'You are a man now ...' Casalis, *My Life in Basutoland*, p. 284

p. 86 'Ah! polygamy ...' Casalis, *My Life in Basutoland*, p. 227

p. 87 'in spite of a universal perversion ...' Casalis, *The Basutos*, p. 248

p. 105 '"If you do," said he ...' Casalis, *My Life in Basutoland*, p. 199

pp. 106–7 'When it was wanted ...' Casalis, *My Life in Basutoland*, p. 200

pp. 107–8 'I should be unfaithful to my Master ...' Casalis, *The Basutos*, pp. 90–1

p. 109 'heavy with the fetid reek ...' Becker, *Hill of Destiny*, p. 169

p. 109 'a smudge lost in the sky ...' Arbousset, *Missionary Excursion*, p. 63

pp. 109–10 'Shaking off his drowsiness ...' Arbousset, *Missionary Excursion*, p. 64

p. 111 'In any other country ...' Arbousset, *Missionary Excursion*, p. 112

p. 111 'I am ashamed of myself ...' Arbousset, *Missionary Excursion*, pp. 76–7

pp. 111–3 'A young woman ...' Thompson, *Survival in Two Worlds*, pp. 96–7

pp. 114–5 'amuse himself by pinching our noses ...' Casalis, *The Basutos*, p. 83

p. 115 'The children of Thaba Bosiu die ...' Thompson, *Survival in Two Worlds*, p. 103

pp. 116–7 'Today you are a man ...' Becker, *Hill of Destiny*, p. 209

p. 130 'You ask me to *cut the ground* ...' Casalis, *The Basutos*, p. 157

pp. 130–1 'Listen to a story ...' Casalis, *The Basutos*, p. 157

p. 132 'They seemed so humble ...' Casalis, *The Basutos*, p. 118

p. 135 'The trader who fancies ...' Thompson, *Survival in Two Worlds*, p. 200

p. 135 'When anyone is killed ...' Thompson, *Survival in Two Worlds*, p. 201

p. 135 'assented to by Letsie ...' Thompson, *Survival in Two Worlds*, p. 201

p. 136 'increasingly convinced that the existence ...' Keegan, *Colonial South Africa*, p. 249

p. 138 'This remarkable person ...' Thompson, *Survival in Two Worlds*, p. 215

p. 138 'Moshesh is like this ...' Thompson, *Survival in Two Worlds*, p. 142

p. 139 'without the consent of my people' Germond, *Chronicles of Basutoland*, p. 156

p. 139 'Yes, as when a dog ...' Thompson, *Survival in Two Worlds*, p. 147

p. 140 'the enemy would come ...' Casalis, *The Basutos*, p. 287

p. 140 'The assegai, the battle axe, and the rifle ...' Germond, *Chronicles of Basutoland*, p. 192

p. 141 'I would ... recommend ...' Becker, *Hill of Destiny*, pp. 182–3

p. 142 'I beg you will be satisfied ...' Lagden, *The Basutos*, p. 154

p. 142 'I have received your letter ...' Lagden, *The Basutos*, p. 156

p. 142 '"To what purpose ...' Germond, *Chronicles of Basutoland*, p. 217

pp. 143–4 'You shall abide ...' Germond, *Chronicles of Basutoland*, pp. 219–22

p. 144 'while the snow fell hard ...' Damane and Sanders, *Lithoko*, pp. 118–20

p. 144 'a most affecting scene ...' Germond, *Chronicles of Basutoland*, p. 224

p. 145 'I am proceeding to Bloemfontein ...' Germond, *Chronicles of Basutoland*, p. 224

p. 145 'Fear drink! Let the drunkard ...' Germond, *Chronicles of Basutoland*, p. 227

p. 146 '"Moshoeshoe is a Christian ...' Germond, *Chronicles of Basutoland*, p. 227

pp. 146–7 'my help-meet and joy' Casalis, *My Life in Basutoland*, p. 288

p. 147 'It may be felt …' Casalis, *My Life in Basutoland*, p. 289

p. 147 'After having thus transcribed …' Theal, *Basutoland Records*, p. 139

p. 147 'And then – what means this silence? …' Casalis, *The Basutos*, p. 110

p. 155 'the light of the mind …' Brown, in Comaroff and Comaroff, *Of Revelation, Volume 1*, p. 143

p. 179 '[T]he summit of the mountains …' Germond, *Chronicles of Basutoland*, p. 33

p. 188 'Suppose the treaties …' Thompson, *Survival in Two Worlds*, p. 270

p. 189 'Bullets came down the hill like rain' Becker, *Hill of Destiny*, p. 223

p. 189 'The children of Moshoeshoe …' Mangoaela, *Lithoko tsa Marena a Basotho*, p. 212

p. 190 'Yes! Sir George is the fifth great man …' Thompson, *Survival in Two Worlds*, p. 251

p. 190 'What I desire is this …' Lagden, *The Basutos*, p. 314

p. 190 'He has not the slightest confidence …' Thompson, *Survival in Two Worlds*, p. 253

p. 190 'He will never be anything …' Thompson, *Survival in Two Worlds*, p. 262

p. 191 'My trust had always been in the Queen …' Thompson, *Survival in Two Worlds*, p. 268

p. 191 'The Governor and Lady Wodehouse …' Germond, *Chronicles of Basutoland*, p. 264

pp. 192–3 'I could see Moperi's lips quiver …' Thompson, *Survival in Two Worlds*, p. 274

p. 193 'for all persons know …' Thompson, *Survival in Two Worlds*, p. 278

p. 195 'I beg to know …' Thompson, *Survival in Two Worlds*, p. 294

p. 195 'I have become old …' Thompson, *Survival in Two Worlds*, p. 300

p. 195 'I have been covered with shame …' Thompson, *Survival in Two Worlds*, p. 308

p. 196 'a token of my gratitude …' Thompson, *Survival in Two Worlds*, p. 310

p. 196 'splendid token' Comaroff and Comaroff, *Of Revelation, Volume 1*, p. 184

p. 196 'always feel an interest …' Thompson, *Survival in Two Worlds*, p. 310

p. 219 'If it breaks when it falls …' Thompson, *Survival in Two Worlds*, p. 323

pp. 219–20 'Sir, – I am requested …' Theal, *Basutoland Records*, p. 188

p. 220 'that of going out of doors ...' Casalis, *My Life in Basutoland*, p. 229

p. 221 'Though I am still only a pagan ...' Thompson, *Survival in Two Worlds*, p. 319

p. 221 'You bad child ...' Thompson, *Survival in Two Worlds*, p. 320

p. 222 'Let it be here said ...' Casalis, *My Life in Basutoland*, p. 232

p. 222 'How are we to explain ...' Casalis, *My Life in Basutoland*, p. 232

p. 224 'I have two eyes ...' Thompson, *Survival in Two Worlds*, p. 321

p. 224 'To me Jesus Christ ...' Seboni, *Moshweshwe's Diplomatic Relations*, pp. 52–3

p. 224 'It was obvious ...' Seboni, *Moshweshwe's Diplomatic Relations*, p. 53

p. 226 'As he died ...' Thompson, *Survival in Two Worlds*, p. 324

p. 226 'Letsie placed a simple slab ...' Becker, *Hill of Destiny*, p. 275

p. 230 'A small lake existed ...' Germond, *Chronicles of Basutoland*, p. 26

pp. 232–3 'The Boers were already on the march ...' Germond, *Chronicles of Basutoland*, p. 240

p. 233 'Everything is white with snow ...' Germond, *Chronicles of Basutoland*, p. 242

p. 233 'These black people ...' Arbousset, *Missionary Excursion*, p. 24

p. 234 'My attachments, my inclinations ...' Arbousset, *Missionary Excursion*, p. 24

p. 250 'All went well ...' Fraser and Briggs, *Sotho War Diaries*, pp. 68–9

p. 250 'we heard a terrible noise ...' Fraser and Briggs, *Sotho War Diaries*, p. 69

bibliography

Arbousset, Thomas. *Missionary Excursion into the Blue Mountains: being an account of King Moshoeshoe's Expedition from Thaba-Bosiu to the sources of the Malibamatšo River in the year 1840* (edited and translated by David Ambrose and Albert Brutsch). Morija: Morija Archives, 1991 (originally completed in French in 1840).

Becker, Peter. *Hill of Destiny: The Life and Times of Moshesh, Founder of the Basotho.* London: Longman, 1969.

Bell, Richard H. *Understanding African Philosophy: A Cross-Cultural Approach to Classical and Contemporary Issues.* New York and London: Routledge, 2002.

Bereng, D.C.T. *Dithothokiso tsa Moshoeshoe le tse ding.* Morija: Morija Sesuto Book Depot, 1931.

Bhabha, Homi K. 'How Newness Enters the World: Postmodern Space, Postcolonial Times, and the Trials of Cultural Translation', in *The Location of Culture.* London and New York: Routledge, 1994, pp. 212–34.

Brand, Gerrit. *Speaking of a Fabulous Ghost: In Search of Theological Criteria, With Special Reference to the Debate on Salvation in African Christian Theology.* Frankfurt: Peter Lang, 2002.

Brown, J. Tom. *Among the Bantu Nomads: A record of forty years spent among the Bechuana, a numerous & famous branch of the Central South African Bantu, with the first full description of their ancient customs, manners & beliefs.* London: Seeley, Service and Co., 1926.

287

Casalis, Eugène. *The Basutos, or Twenty-Three Years in South Africa*.
Cape Town: C. Struik, 1965 (original English publication 1861).
———. *My Life in Basutoland*. Cape Town: C. Struik, 1971 (original English
publication 1889).
Comaroff, Jean, and John Comaroff. *Of Revelation and Revolution, Volume 1:
Christianity, Colonialism, and Consciousness in South Africa*. Chicago and
London: University of Chicago Press, 1991.
———. *Ethnography and the Historical Imagination*. Boulder: Westview
Press, 1992.
———. *Of Revelation and Revolution, Volume 2: The Dialectics of Modernity
on a South African Frontier*. Chicago and London: University of Chicago
Press, 1997.
Comaroff, Jean. *Body of Power, Spirit of Resistance: The Culture and History of
a South African People*. Chicago: University of Chicago Press, 1985.
Conrad, Joseph. *Heart of Darkness*. Harmondsworth: Penguin, 1983 (originally
published 1899/1902).
Coplan, David B. *In the Time of Cannibals: The Word Music of South Africa's
Basotho Migrants*. Johannesburg: Witwatersrand University Press, 1994.
———. 'Unconquered Territory: Narrating the Caledon Valley', *Journal of
African Cultural Studies*, 13 (2), 2000, pp. 185–206.
Damane, M., and P.B. Sanders (eds). *Lithoko: Sotho Praise-Poems*. Oxford:
Clarendon Press, 1974.
Deleuze, Gilles, and Félix Guattari. *A Thousand Plateaus* (translated by
Brian Massumi). Minneapolis: University of Minnesota Press, 1987.
———. *What is Philosophy?* (translated by Hugh Tomlinson and Graham
Burchell). New York: Columbia University Press, 1994.
Derrida, Jacques. *On Cosmopolitanism and Forgiveness*. London and New York:
Routledge, 2001.
Du Preez, Max. *Of Warriors, Lovers and Prophets: Unusual Stories from
South Africa's Past*. Cape Town: Zebra Press, 2004.
Eldredge, Elizabeth A. *A South African Kingdom: The Pursuit of Security in
Nineteenth-Century Lesotho*. Cambridge: Cambridge University Press, 1993.
Ellenberger, D. Frédéric. *History of the Basuto, Ancient and Modern* (translated
by J.C. MacGregor). London: Caxton Publishing Company, 1912.
Eloff, C.C. *The So-Called Conquered Territory: Disputed Border Area between
the Orange Free State (Republic of South Africa) and Lesotho (Basutoland)*.
Pretoria: Human Sciences Research Council, 1979.

Fraser, J.G., and James Briggs. *Sotho War Diaries, 1864–1865* (ed. Karel Schoeman). Cape Town: Human & Rousseau, 1985.

Fritsche, Petra. *Die Villenkolonie Grunewald und ihre Bewohner: Historische und architektonische Betrachtungen 1889–1945.* Berlin: Studentenwerk Berlin, 2001.

Germond, Robert C. (ed. and trans.). *Chronicles of Basutoland.* Morija: Morija Sesuto Book Depot, 1967.

Gill, Stephen J. *A Short History of Lesotho: From the Late Stone Age Until the 1993 Elections.* Morija: Morija Museum and Archives, 1993.

Gobodo-Madikizela, Pumla. *A Human Being Died that Night: A South African Story of Forgiveness.* Cape Town: David Philip, 2003.

Gyekye, Kwame. *An Essay on African Philosophical Thought: The Akan Conceptual Scheme.* Cambridge: Cambridge University Press, 1987.

Hegel, G.W.F. *Phenomenology of Spirit* (translated by A.V. Miller). Oxford: Clarendon Press, 1977.

Hountondji, Paulin J. *African Philosophy: Myth and Reality* (translated by Henri Evans). London: Hutchinson, 1983.

Hulley, Leonard, Louise Kretzschmar and Luke Lungile Pato (eds). *Archbishop Tutu: Prophetic Witness in South Africa.* Cape Town: Human & Rousseau, 1996.

Imbo, Samuel Oluoch. *An Introduction to African Philosophy.* Lanham: Rowman & Littlefield, 1998.

Jacottet, E. *Litšomo tsa Basotho – Buka ea pele* (fifth edition). Morija: Morija Sesuto Book Depot, 1985.

Jaggar, Alison M., and Iris Marion Young (eds). *A Companion to Feminist Philosophy.* Maiden, Massachusetts: Blackwell, 1998.

Keegan, Timothy. *Colonial South Africa and the Origins of the Racial Order.* Cape Town and Johannesburg: David Philip, 1996.

Krog, Antjie. *Relaas van 'n Moord.* Cape Town: Human & Rousseau, 1995.

———. *Account of a Murder* (translated by Karen Press). Sandton: Heinemann, 1997.

Kunene, Daniel P. *Heroic Poetry of the Basotho.* Oxford: Clarendon Press, 1971.

Lagden, Godfrey. *The Basutos: The Mountaineers and Their Country, Being a Narrative of Events Relating to the Tribe from its Formation Early in the Nineteenth Century to the Present Day.* London: Hutchinson, 1909.

Leoatle, Edward Motsami. *Morena Moshoeshoe: Mor'a Mokhachane.* Morija: Morija Sesuto Book Depot, 1952.

Lepenies, Wolf. *The Seduction of Culture in German History.* Princeton: Princeton University Press, 2006.

Machobane, L.B.J. 'Mohlomi: Doctor, Traveller and Sage', *Mohlomi: Journal of Southern African Historical Studies,* 2, 1976.

Mamdani, Mahmood. 'Reconciliation without Justice', *Southern Review,* 10 (6), 1997.

Mangoaela, Z.D. *Lithoko tsa Marena a Basotho.* Morija: Morija Sesuto Book Depot, 1931

Ndebele, Njabulo S. *The Cry of Winnie Mandela: A Novel.* Claremont: David Philip, 2003.

———. 'Leadership Challenges: Truth and Integrity in an Act of Salesman-ship', in *Fine Lines from the Box: Further Thoughts about our Country.* Cape Town: Umuzi, 2007, pp. 233–44.

Pasternak, Boris. *Second Nature* (translated by Andrei Navrozov). London and Chester Springs: Peter Owen, 2003.

Patton, P. 'Deleuze and Democracy', *Contemporary Political Theory,* 4 (4), 2005, pp. 400–13.

———. 'Becoming-Animal and Pure Life in Coetzee's *Disgrace*', *ARIEL: A Review of International English Literature,* 35 (1–2), 2006, pp. 101–19.

———. 'Deleuze and Democratic Politics', in Lars Tønder and Lasse Thomassen (eds), *Radical democracy: Politics between abundance and lack.* Manchester and New York: Manchester University Press, 2006.

Prawer, S.S. (ed. and trans.). *The Penguin Book of Lieder.* Baltimore: Penguin, 1964.

Rathete, Matome Bethuel. *The Reality and Relevance of Seriti in the Past and Present: Its Essence and Manifestation in an African Religion Perspective with Special Reference to the Northern Sotho.* PhD thesis, University of South Africa, 2007.

Rilke, Rainer Maria. *The Selected Poetry of Rainier Maria Rilke* (translated by Stephen Mitchell). London: Picador, 1987.

Rushdie, Salman. *The Satanic Verses.* London: Viking, 1988.

Sanders, Mark. *Complicities: The Intellectual and Apartheid.* Durham and London: Duke University Press, 2002.

Sanders, Peter. *Moshoeshoe: Chief of the Sotho.* London: Heinemann, 1975.

Schoeman, Karel (ed.). *The Bloemfontein Diary of Lieut. W.J. St John 1852–1853.* Cape Town: Human & Rousseau, 1988.

Seboni, Peter. *Moshweshwe's Diplomatic Relations with the Indigenous Chiefs of Southern Africa, 1822–1870*. PhD thesis, University of the Orange Free State, 1994.

Serequeberhan, T. *The Hermeneutics of African Philosophy: Horizon and Discourse*. New York and London: Routledge, 1994.

Setiloane, Gabriel M. *The Image of God among the Sotho-Tswana*. Rotterdam: A.A. Balkema, 1976.

———. *How the Traditional World-View Persists in the Christianity of the Sotho-Tswana*. Unpublished, no date.

Stifter, Adalbert. *Die Mappe meines Urgroßvaters*. Peter Suhrkamp Insel, 1864.

Thompson, Leonard. *Survival in Two Worlds: Moshoeshoe of Lesotho, 1786–1870*. Oxford: Oxford University Press, 1975.

Theal, George McCall. *Basutoland Records, 1833–1868*. Cape Town, 1883.

Tylden, G. *The Rise of the Basuto*. Cape Town: Juta, 1950.